THE COMPLETE HOSTESS

Also by Nell Heaton

SHELL FISH

COOKING DICTIONARY

THE COMPLETE COOK

The Complete Hostess

by

NELL HEATON

CRESTA BOOKS

Originally published by Cassell & Co. Ltd.

as

"HOSPITALITY"

Published in Great Britain by
Murray's Book Sales (King's Cross) Ltd.
157-167 Pentonville Road, London, N.1

FOREWORD

The main object of this book is to provide you with a variety of workable menus and the recipes to go with them. Basic cookery methods and other useful information will be found in my *Cooking Dictionary*. So often it is hard to plan well-balanced menus that fit in with your family's food habits. It is well to remember that at the main-meal-time no worries or troubles—whatever they may be —should be allowed to spoil the peaceful atmosphere of the family circle. The security, happiness and harmony at this time will long remain nostalgic memories when the family is scattered, and the strong bond forged between parents and children will never be broken.

The business of home-making is one which engages the attention of most of us, and with a proper knowledge of the underlying problems of marketing and of the preparation, cooking and serving of food, the home-maker will feed her family and entertain royally, and find much leisure time for living.

I hope you will enjoy using *The Complete Hostess* as much as I have enjoyed compiling it.

NELL HEATON

CONTENTS

Hospitality

There is an emancipation from the heart in genuine hospitality which cannot be described, but is immediately felt, and puts the stranger at once at his ease.

WASHINGTON IRVING

Pleasantest
Of all ties is the tie of host and guest.
AESCHYLUS

Since the earliest times the dining-table, like the fire-place in the living-room, has been a focal point of hospitality. It is the centre of the social life of the household and deserves very special attention.

To-day, although leisure is almost unknown to those who are responsible for catering or feeding their family or themselves, we can boast of many improvements in our culinary equipment and utensils; and although traditional menus of ten courses are not frequently planned, nevertheless we still try to enshrine our culinary traditions with care and thought.

Cooking is an art in which the garnishing and serving of meals play an important part, since sauces and garnishes give added zest and nutrition besides improving the appearance of foods. *Good cooking* does not need a large income. It means a thorough understanding of basic cooking methods and terms. It also means care in choosing the menu, the quantities and in costing. If you are a beginner it means trying the simplest recipes first, before going on to the more complicated dishes.

Whenever a special meal is arranged—the organization will differ from the daily routine.

The menu and other details must be specially planned.

The quality, quantity and cost of food to be purchased must be considered.

Both the preparation and the service of the food must be thoroughly planned beforehand and will need extra care in supervision. It is wise to have a small book to jot down details of dates, menu, costing, etc., which can be referred to when necessary; this also helps to keep the festivity within the housekeeping budget or the sum allotted for each occasion.

For special parties make out a list for the service of the food, also a list of linen, silver, glass, etc., which will be needed. Have these all assembled together the day before they are required for use.

When planning meals, concentrate on making foods both appetizing and nutritious, remembering that malnutrition is found not only amongst those who are short of food, but also among people who eat the wrong foods.

HINTS TO HOSTESSES AND GUESTS

Invitations may be friendly, informal or formal.

Sometimes they can appear very confusing by the wording on the card—but if carefully written they will never confuse.

Written invitations are so much more charming than telephoned ones, unless, of course, you are trying to fix a last-minute gathering of friends.

Sometimes you are asked to come at around 7.30; this may—or may not—mean that you are asked to dinner. It is best to suggest tactfully that you will be leaving about a certain time in order to have your evening meal—your hostess will then immediately tell you if you are asked to stay to a meal.

When you are invited for dinner it means that, unless you are asked to stay longer, you should leave between 10.30 and 11.00. Never outstay your welcome! Leave gracefully and always remember to thank your hostess. If you dine frequently with the same friends, sometimes take flowers with you.

When you give a friendly party and you are inviting a single girl friend, sometimes it is a kind gesture to ask her to bring a male friend along with her. Naturally, if she is engaged, her fiancé will automatically be invited. Do remember that it is extremely bad manners to take an uninvited guest to someone else's house.

Your Arrival

Should you be delayed, a telephone call or a telegram is always appreciated by your hostess.

When arriving at a party, the first thing to do is to greet your hostess.

Your 'Thank You'

After a dinner party a thank-you note, sometimes known as a 'bread-and-butter letter', should be sent within a day or two. This also applies to week-ends spent with either friends or relations.

If you have received hospitality from people, send some flowers as a token of appreciation. This is your 'thank you' for a specially good party.

A WEEK-END PARTY

When you arrive at someone else's house for the week-end, be considerate and ask your hostess what time she would like you to get up and ask her tactfully if she has any plans for your stay. If you are going for longer than a week-end, take a present with you. Some tasty delicacy is always appreciated, as are flowers, cyclamen, a bowl of bulbs, or a green-leafed indoor plant.

Never complain in other people's houses!

Pay for your telephone calls. Most hostesses, unless they have a full domestic staff, appreciate it if their guests offer to help with the domestic chores.

Never get into heated discussions about politics or religion in other people's homes! It puts your hostess in a very awkward position.

THE HOSTESS

A good hostess always tells her guests the meal-times and all about the domestic arrangements of the house generally. She also knows when her guests would like to be left alone. She takes care to see that the bedside light is working, ensures that there are ashtrays, a waste-paper basket, coat-hangers, a drinking glass, and sees that the gas fire or electric heater is not forgotten if the weather is chilly. She also appreciates it when guests refrain from reading the newspaper or personal letters at breakfast, and above all she likes guests who know when to leave!

The really successful hostess manages her entertainment according to the likes and dislikes of her guest. Make a gesture of thanks to your hostess. She will appreciate it when a guest offers to take her out for a meal.

INTRODUCTIONS

Remember always to stand up if someone older than yourself enters the room, and when you introduce people do speak names clearly. If two women are introduced—always introduce in order of standing and importance—the elder woman is always introduced first. A man should always be introduced to a woman. It is not necessary to remove gloves on shaking hands.

Never call people by their Christian names until you know them quite well—and never refer to them by their Christian names if you are talking to their subordinates.

INVITATIONS

Friendly invitations are often made verbally or by telephone, and they are answered in the same way. Should you by any chance find yourself unable to be present, you should write and apologize to your hostess immediately. Telephone conversations often begin "Are you doing anything on Sunday?" which is a little unfair to the person being invited. It is more correct to say at once what you want the person to do, where you are going, and the time you suggest for meeting. Then it is easy for a decision to be made. When it is impossible to accept any kind of invitation, there is no need to give an explanation.

For *family and informal dinners* it is quite in order to send the invitation a day or two in advance.

A *formal invitation* to dinner is issued in the name of the host and hostess. The initials R.S.V.P. are French in origin, they stand for the words "*Répondez, s'il vous plaît*"—or in plain English: Please send a reply. These formal invitations are usually issued two or three weeks beforehand and they should be answered at once. When accepted, the engagement should on no account be broken.

The usual hour for dinner is 7.30 to 8.30 p.m.

The following are suggestions for a formal invitation to dinner and a corresponding reply:

Mr. and Mrs. England
Request the pleasure of
Mr. and Mrs. Blank's
company at dinner on Friday
May 10 at 8 o'clock.

Greystone   April 28
                             R.S.V.P.

.   .   .

Mr. and Mrs. Blank accept with pleasure
Mr. and Mrs. England's kind invitation
to dinner on May 10.

Blaverthorp   April 30

Sometimes, for a very *informal party*, the hostess can send a visiting-card simply inscribed with the date and the time that she hopes to see her friends, and the words: Cocktails, Bridge, Canasta, Dancing, Music, as the case may be.

For an evening party, a ball, or an at-home, the invitations are issued in the name of the hostess only, as is shown by the following examples:

<blockquote>

Mrs. England

at Home

Thursday June 10.

Cocktails 6 o'clock

Greystone   R.S.V.P.

</blockquote>

. . .

<blockquote>

Mrs. England requests the pleasure of

Mr. and Mrs. Blank's

company on the evening of

January 10.

Dancing 10 o'clock

Greystone   R.S.V.P.

</blockquote>

A suitable reply would be:

<blockquote>

Mr. and Mrs. Blank have much pleasure

in accepting Mrs. England's kind invita-

tion for the evening of January 10.

Blaverthorp   January 4

</blockquote>

B

For a wedding this is the form of invitation sent by the parents of a bride.

Mr. and Mrs. England

Request the pleasure of the company

of

Mrs. Blank

on the occasion of the Marriage

of their daughter Mary

with

Mr. John Temple

Ceremony on Thursday June 12th 1953

at   Church

at 2 o'clock. Afterwards at the reception.

Greystone   R.S.V.P.

In reply to such an invitation it would be correct to answer simply:

Mrs. Blank has great pleasure in accepting the invitation of Mr. and Mrs. England to the marriage of their daughter Mary—and would be delighted to join them afterwards at the reception.

May 30th 1953

When a guest is invited to a wedding reception only, the invitation should be worded as follows:

Mr. and Mrs. England
Request the pleasure of the company
of
Mr. and Mrs. Forth
at 3 p.m. on 12th June at the reception
after the marriage of their daughter
Marie Lisa
and
Robert John Swann

Greystone   R.S.V.P.

The reply would be:

Mr. and Mrs. Forth have great pleasure in accepting the invitation to the reception to be held on June 12th.

For a garden party, here are two forms of invitation, and replies to them:

Mr. and Mrs. John Temple
Mrs. Blank
at Home
the Tuesdays in May
from 4 to 7 o'clock

Edenlodge   Lawn Tennis
                                       R.S.V.P.

Mr. and Mrs. John Temple have much pleasure in accepting Mrs. Blank's kind invitation for Tuesday May 10th.

Mr. and Mrs. Blank
Request the pleasure of
Mr. and Mrs. Gray's
company at a Garden Party
on Friday June 10th at 4 o'clock
Dancing after 8

Edenlodge   R.S.V.P.

.   .   .

Mr. and Mrs. Gray have great pleasure
in accepting Mr. and Mrs. Blank's invi-
tation to a Garden Party on June 10th.

May 10th 1953

For a formal afternoon tea party it is usual to send out invitations at least two weeks in advance.

It is usual for the hostess and her specially honoured guest to be near the entrance of the living-room so that they may receive. It is best to have a maid or someone in attendance at the door, and the guests are shown into another room, where they may leave their heavy coats. They are then received by the hostess.

Arrange the dining-table as a buffet table, and provide a variety of sandwiches (see page 99) and cakes (see page 101).

Let's set the Table

Spread the Table and contention will cease

JOHN RAY, 1678

O ! what's a table richly spread,
Without a woman at its head?
THOMAS WARTON,
The Progress of Discontent

Let us begin with the trimmings for table setting. They can be so much more intriguing than the essentials. An attractive decoration should be provided for the centre of the table. It *must be low* to allow an unobstructed view across the table. The decorations will be chosen to be in keeping with either an elaborate and formal meal, or just a 'home' dinner.

Flowers, of course, are an outstanding feature of these—the simplest table may be made or marred by its floral decoration.

When planning your centre decoration you should always remember that the flowers, like table glass and china, express degrees of formality. They should be selected with a view to their appropriateness, according to the type of meal to be served. While a simple bowl of buds is ideal for a breakfast table, it would be quite out of place at a formal dinner.

The centre piece should never conceal the guests from each other, nor should it act as a barrier from one side of the table to the other. An exception to this rule is when on a long table a few long-stemmed flowers, e.g., carnations, roses, irises, lilac, are sparsely grouped so that you can look between the stems. These blooms are placed in crystal vases, or urn-shaped silver or Sheffield Plate bowls, which raise the flowers above eye-level.

Let us now consider the appropriate selection for the season. Roses and carnations are with us the whole year round. Massed in bowls, or banked high, they are favourites for formal dinners.

For the spring, acacia, anemones, carnations, daffodils, gardenias, lilies of the valley, narcissi, pussy-willow, violets, all appear. For Easter, lilies are also available, but when cut to an appropriate length for the dining-table they lose their charm. The graceful clusters of lilac bend and nod, and so lend themselves to any desired height. Pansies, freesias, mignonette, hyacinths, Darwin tulips and irises are also spring flowers, while syringa (mock orange blossom) with bloom only and leaves removed, makes a delightfully graceful centre piece.

For the summer months, among the garden flowers we find ageratum, candy tuft, fuchsias, forget-me-nots, geraniums, love-in-a-mist, marigolds, nasturtiums, old-fashioned pinks, sweet peas, sweet-williams, spirea, zinnias—all of which can give sparkling high lights to your floral arrangements.

For small sectional centre pieces use moistened sand to make the flowers 'stay put'. There are many effective settings to be planned —according to the colour of cloth, mats, table wood, china and glass.

Clematis, gardenias, pansies, geraniums, roses and water lilies without their stems can be used floating in shallow bowls filled with water.

Nasturtiums make a colourful decoration when mixed with their own crisp leaves, or when used alternated in small vases with forget-me-nots and mignonette. With green table-cloth or mats, they cheer up the dullest days.

Pheasant-eye narcissi, massed in a bowl (when the stems are shortened), make a fragrant table decoration—while a 'spring bowl' of daffodils, tulips and pheasant-eyes is a delight.

For a simple decoration a glass bowl filled with lilies of the valley and their leaves makes irresistible green and white on either green or white linen.

Anemones in a pewter mug, wallflowers and French marigolds in a brown pottery bowl also make distinctive and simple decorations using deep gold or rust-coloured mats.

From the wild-flower group, buttercups, cowslips, forget-me-nots, mallows, wild violets, wild roses, all make the table look charming.

Both in July and in August the 'nicotine' flowers lend such grace and fragrance, while in September dahlias, with red leaves and berries, are effective. In winter, if flowers are scarce, mixed fruits— carefully combined so as to get the best colour scheme—can be used. Take, for instance, luscious grapes, in great clusters of green and black. They are so pliable that they can be draped over the sides of the bowl and combined with a little grape foliage, with its fascinating little tendrils, or with pears, peaches, apples and bananas. There is no cause at any season not to have a delightful centre piece.

The shining pansy, trimmed with golden lace;
The tall-topped lark-heads, feathered thick with flowers;
The woodbine, climbing o'er the door in bowers;
The London tufts of many a mottled hue;
The pale pink pea, and the monk's-hood darkly blue;
The white and purple gilly flowers, that stay
Lingering in blossom; summer half away;
The single blood-walls, of a luscious smell,
Old-fashioned flowers which housewives love so well;

JOHN CLARE

SCALE, BALANCE AND COLOUR IN TABLE SETTING

Remember that an over-loaded table, a small room, or a skimped table would be the ruination of any party. If your table is small, never use too large a centre piece; or if it is large, it is silly to use a small one. The wide open spaces can always be built up with candle-sticks and small vases of flowers. There must be balance, too, in the table setting. If the table is to be set for three, some people lay an extra place or restore the balance by having the centre decoration somewhat larger than they would normally have. It can stand more over to the empty side of the table, or you can have a bowl of fruit as well as the flowers.

Never clutter up a table. The most beautifully arranged table is spoilt if too full.

Candles, when used, should be the sole source of light, and they must be placed symmetrically upon the table—the flame *should not be at eye-level.* Choose white candles for formal occasions as they make a very attractive decoration with a low luscious bowl of fruit, or some very choicely arranged flat floral decoration. If coloured candles are chosen, match linen and room colour-schemes. Always use low candlesticks with tall candles. See that the candles do not drip. If they are really cool, dripping will be prevented. They can be placed in a refrigerator for some hours before use to harden them. (Never place candles in a draught when lit, because they will become very untidy with the dripping wax.)

" Yes," I answered you last night;
"No," this morning, sir, I say.
Colours seen by candle-light
Will not look the same by day.

E. B. BROWNING,
The Lady's " Yes"

You may, if you prefer, keep strictly to one colour: it is safe but rather uninteresting, for a colour can be used to more advantage with a contrasting colour. Decide your general colour-scheme: Remember that colours have definite effects upon us—sometimes subconsciously. Blue is soothing (but can be chilly in winter); red, stimulating—so don't emphasize reds and pinks too much on a hot summer's day. Yellow is cheery; orange, stimulating; violet, rather mysterious; while green is restful.

With white, spotless, creaseless linen, lace, net or filet lace, beautiful old glass or clear modern crystal goes well; but with hand-blocked or hand-woven linen, special pottery and modern casseroles of clear or coloured oven glass look attractive. Both fruit bowls and floral decorations can show the food off if they are chosen with care. The whole appearance of the table tells of the care with which a meal was thought out.

TABLE LINEN

Provide either mats or a silence cloth under the linen. This helps to deaden the noise, protects the table and also improves the appearance of a cloth or mat.

When laying a cloth, always unfold it very carefully on the table so as to avoid creases, and see that the centre fold comes exactly in the middle of the table, that the four corners are an equal distance from the floor, and that the cloth extends over both the ends of the table at least 9 inches.

A table-cloth should be ironed with one lengthwise fold running down the centre when the cloth is opened up, and each side should be folded to the centre crease (this makes three lengthwise creases). Should it be a very long table it may be necessary to have a crosswise crease to facilitate storage and handling.

The table linen, whether it be a cloth, mats, lace or gay seersucker, must be spotless. When using square or round mats a rubber or heat-proof mat should be placed underneath. Should there be a monogram or design on the linen, it should harmonize with the linen in both size and design and should be in the same place, when set, in each mat.

Embroidered linen cloths, lace covers or mats, sometimes with centre pieces and small doilies, are used for breakfast and luncheon, while more elaborate mats are used for dinner.

When collecting your table linen, the first item to invest in is a really good damask cloth (3 yards in length) so that you may accommodate more than six when necessary. Double damask table-cloths are shiny and patterned on both sides. Have one or two $2\frac{1}{2}$-yard cloths (these could be in pastel-coloured linen, or rayon mixture); three dozen gaily-coloured napkins and two or three sets of table mats; one dozen finger bowl doilies and six trolley or tray cloths.

THE CARE OF LINEN

The care of linen is well repaid. A damask cloth must never be starched very stiffly as it is apt to crack. This also happens if it is bleached or left in severe weather to dry.

Boiling helps to retain the whiteness of fabric, and two good rinsings before blueing are also a great help.

For coloured linens—which cannot be boiled—it is essential that they should be washed before they become badly soiled, and they should be moved about in quick water and dried in a shady place.

When fabrics show a tendency to run it is wise to rinse them in changes of water until the water shows no sign of colour. Colour can be 'set' by soaking in salt and water or vinegar.

These handy hints to *remove stains* from your linen may be useful:

Blood. Soak in cold water, changing when it becomes coloured. Never launder until stain is out, as hot water sets it in; when this has happened try using a little ammonia or peroxide— leave in a short time and then rinse well.

Candle-grease. Pick off when dry, or if well soaked in the material, wipe with benzine.

Fruit Juice. Stretch the material taut and pour boiling water over it from a height. If this does not remove it, cover with glycerine and then repeat. Ammonia and peroxide can be used alternately; then rinse well in diluted acetic acid and finally water.

Iron Rust. Apply vinegar or acetic acid, salt and lemon or oxalic acid.

Ink. Oxalic acid neutralized by ammonia may remove.

Mildew. Wash well with a strong soap and dry in the sun. Sour milk or ammonia may be applied after washing.

Scorching. Do not wet—keep quite dry—bleach in the sun.

Tea Stains. Remove as fruit juice.

Wine Stains. Cover at once with salt, then wash thoroughly afterwards. If the stains are old, cover with strong yellow soap—coat with powdered starch and bleach in the sun. Repeat until stain disappears.

These hints are for use with white materials only.

TABLE NAPKINS (Fr. *Serviette*)

These were introduced towards the middle of the fifteenth century —the table-cloth having hitherto been used for wiping the fingers at table. At one time it was the fashion to tie the napkin round the neck to protect the full ruffs that were worn, and from this practice arose the saying, "To make both ends meet"—a free translation of the French proverb, *Nouer les deux bouts de sa serviette*—being a playful allusion to the struggle of stout men with short arms to tie their napkins.

Table-cloths and mats must be spotlessly clean and creaseless. Generally they each have their own matching napkin. As napkins are rarely square they can be made so by turning in one side as much as will be necessary to form a square. This will give extra stiffness which is an advantage. They must be well starched or they will not remain in folds or stand up—they fold better when they are not quite dry.

Napkin corners must always meet when the napkin is folded oblong style.

When napkins are folded triangularly, if there is a monogram it must appear in the centre.

Table napkins should be folded according to type and setting.

1. If formal, many varieties of folding may be used.
2. If informal, simple foldings are used.

SOME WAYS TO FOLD

Arrowhead

Fold the napkin in three, lengthwise; double each end over towards the middle as shown in Fig. 1. Fold back *A* on either side to produce Fig. 2. Keep the two sides flat on the table whilst you draw them towards the middle, causing the dotted line in the centre to stand up; turn the napkin with top point towards you—fold this top point well over by the dotted line shown in Fig. 3, so that the centre portion again stands up, and cross the points *AA* underneath to produce the complete design.

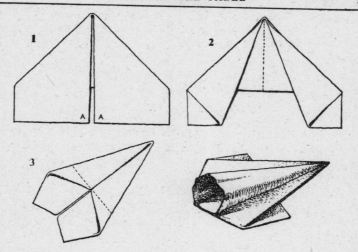

Bat

Fold the napkin in three so that a single fold comes on the top with the selvedge towards you, and turn back the two end points, leaving a space in the middle as in Fig 4. The dotted line in the diagram indicates where the lower edge is to be folded over once. Then proceed to kilt up the napkin like a fan from *A* to *B*, being careful to pleat the upright points evenly. When the lower part is placed in a wine glass the design will appear as in Fig. 5.

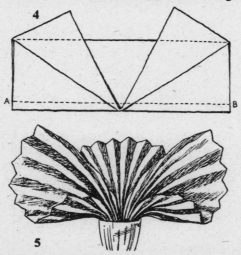

Bird

This is really the reverse side of the bat design; but after the kilting has been done, overturn the napkin and hold it firmly in the left hand whilst the inner fold of each of the pleats is turned down with the right hand. This is more easily managed if the napkin is grasped round the middle of the kilts, Fig. 6.

6

Everyday

Fold the napkin into three, crease the centre and turn down each side of the top edge towards the middle to meet at the crease as in Fig. 7. Fold two or three times, or roll the ends (*A* and *B*) till even with the lower edge. Turn the napkin over and bring the folds to meet in the centre. The bread is placed between or underneath the folds.

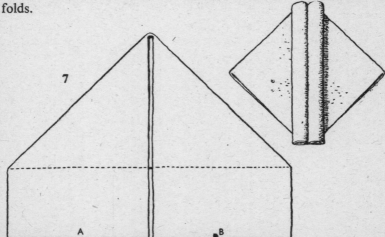

7

A   B

Fan

Fold the napkin into three, lengthwise, and then pleat half of it as evenly as possible in the centre. Pleat from the other side also into the centre, so that the pleats face each other. Press them down firmly and holding the napkin tightly together insert it into a large wine or claret glass. Spread it out at the top, Fig. 8.

8

Swiss

Fold the table napkin like a half handkerchief; turn the bottom over to within rather less than a third of the point. Turn this back again to meet the lower edge as in Fig. 9. Kilt it in small pleats all one way but only from a triangle *AA* leaving the two ends plain. Hold the napkin at the back in the left hand and with the right separate carefully the back pleats from the front ones; when putting the napkin into the glass insert the rim of the glass between the pleats and roll the ends away neatly at the back.

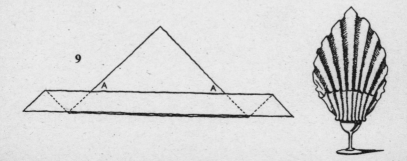

9

CHINA

Them that has china plates themsels is the maist careful no to break the china plates of others.

J. M. BARRIE

The word 'china' may be applied as a generic term to porcelain, china and earthenware alike. The four main groupings are ceramics and china, earthenware, porcelain and stoneware, and these groups are sub-divided.

Stoneware is exceedingly hard with a pitted surface requiring no extra glaze. *Earthenware* or *faience* is pottery made out of properly proportioned clay which before firing is satisfactorily mixed. *Soft porcelain* is not very plastic, and is difficult to shape. *Hard porcelain*, the natural hard porcelain, is so hard it does not scratch. *Bone china* comes midway between the two last-mentioned types. It is a special combination of china clay, china stone and bone ash, and is the English term for porcelain. *Biscuit* is the term denoting earthenware and porcelain after the first firing; this is before decoration and second firing. *Slip* denotes the thick semi-solid fluid composed of clay and water used as crude under-glaze decoration. *Under-glaze* is the decoration applied to the article before coating with liquid glaze. *Over-glaze*—the decorations or printing which are painted or printed on to the china after the glaze has been applied. *Salt glaze*—this finish is obtained by throwing salt into the kiln, causing fine layers of glaze to be deposited on the objects which are undergoing the firing process.

China can be obtained in sets, especially made up into early-morning tea sets, breakfast, luncheon, dinner, tea, coffee and dessert sets. Sometimes it is preferred to have all sets of china matching throughout so that they are interchangeable. The varied colour and designs allow for individual choice and menu planning, so that no food colour or character of food need clash.

Careful washing in clean hot water and thorough drying enhances the beauty of all china, and the proper storage of china to avoid cracks and nicked edges is essential.

TABLE GLASS

The word 'crystal' was derived from a Greek word meaning clear ice and rock crystal, which was applied originally to a mineral deposit which was formed from water.

The glass or glasses used for table setting are placed at the tip of, or slightly to the right of, the knife. Many people prefer goblets to tumblers for luncheon and they are always used for formal dinners.

To-day the setting of table glass is easy compared to that required for the formal, eleven-course dinners of the Victorian days, which took at least three hours to finish, when eleven or twelve glasses were set, and, in the nineties, cut-glass bowls, bon-bon and other dishes were set at intervals from one end of the table to the other.

The less ceremonious habits of to-day have simplified our table setting, but, even so, except at banquets and very formal dinners, four glasses are usually set for each cover. A sherry glass, a glass for red or white wine, a champagne glass and a goblet for water. For very informal dinners or luncheons only three are set; these are: a sherry glass, a claret or Sauterne glass and a water goblet. The glasses can be arranged in a triangle, or with the small glasses in front and the taller behind. At other times they will be found graded according to height from left to right. The water goblet—the tallest—is set at the left, and then they range right down to the liqueur glass on the extreme right.

Fingerbowls may be in a set, each fingerbowl with a matching crystal plate, or the bowl may be served on a doily-covered china dessert plate.

Other glasses used:

Beer may be served in mugs; lager is served in tall glasses, and for long drinks use sixteen-ounce-size glasses which take ice and sliced orange or lemon; while for *highballs* a wide range of decorated glasses is available. For ginger ale, iced tea, etc., either twelve or fourteen-ounce-sized glasses are sufficiently large. The number of glasses required is regulated by the habits, tastes and economic conditions prevailing.

Shell-fish cocktails are served in flat, bowl-topped glasses, some of which have hollow stems. There are also the glasses which are used for tomato juice, orange juice and other non-alcoholic cocktails, and the glass which is used to serve grapefruit for breakfast or other meals.

Sherbet glasses are often dual purpose, being used for both sherbets and champagne.

Punch bowls and glasses. The large glass bowl and matching cup-like handled glasses look most attractive when filled with punch, ice and sliced fruit. This is especially so with a light punch which resembles white wine.

THE COVER

No one thinks of table cloths
When love and laughter's there.

CHARLES DIVINE

Correct table setting is a complicated procedure because it reflects the habits of the household, and no matter how plain and unassuming it is—it must enhance the food through its sparkling spotlessness and blended colouring, through its floral decorations, its linen, china and glass. It is stimulating to change the daily décor, keeping, of course, your basic silver and china which should be of not too pronounced a colour. Vary your accessories, from cloths to mats, exchange your matching dishes, sometimes use soup bowls instead of plates, serve the vegetables in casseroles.

The cover is the name used for the glass, plate, silver and napkin to be used by each person. Twenty inches is considered the smallest space for each cover—25 to 30 inches is best when space allows. Covers must be arranged symmetrically, and the glass, silver and dishes required for the cover are placed all together as close as possible without crowding. All covers are best when compactly laid.

The silver must be shining and glistening and should be placed about one inch from, and at right angles to, the edge of the table; when the table is round it is only the outside pieces which can be so arranged.

The knives, forks and spoons are always placed in the order of their use. Those to be used first on the outside, the exception being the dinner knife and fork which may be placed immediately to the right and left of the plate, so marking the position. Sometimes the salad or dessert fork is placed next to the plate—this is dependent upon the chosen menu. Knives are always placed with the cutting edge turned inwards. If the menu needs no knife, omit it from the cover.

Always place the spoons bowls up, at the right of the knives. The forks are placed tines up, always at the left of the plate. The exceptions to this rule, should they be required, are oyster or cocktail forks. They are placed on the extreme right of the cover at the side of the spoons. When no knife is needed for luncheon, put the fork on the right side of the plate with the spoon beside it, if one is used (e.g. for *moules marinières*). Should more than one spoon be required it is best, then, to put the fork on the left side of the plate. When two forks and a spoon are needed, put them in the usual position with the spoon on the right side. When a small butter knife is used, put this across the upper right-hand side of the bread-and-butter plate with the cutting edge turned toward the centre of the plate, or, if preferred, it may be placed across the top of the plate putting the handle at a convenient angle. Sometimes the butter spreader is placed with the other knives, at the right side of the plate beyond the spoon.

Dessert silver is not placed on the table when the cover is laid, unless the silver required for the whole meal is small. More than six pieces of silver are never laid (this includes three forks); when a dinner is so elaborate as to require more than this, that needed for later courses is placed on the covers just before the course is served. When extra silver is brought in during a meal, it *must* be brought in on a serving tray, unless it is brought in with the course.

Salt, Pepper and Mustard

When possible, place individual salt, pepper and mustard directly in front of each cover, parallel with the edge of the table, and in line with the glasses. When there are more covers set, allow, when possible, one set between two cover settings. This saves the necessity of passing them.

Dishes for Bon Bons and Nuts

These dishes may be either silver or glass, and are placed individually in front of each cover; or, if large, symmetrically upon the table allowing one large one for six guests.

Service Plates

A service plate is used only with a formal service. It is usually a handsome 10-inch plate and is placed at each cover when the table is laid. It is always placed one inch from the edge of the table. The plates on which the early courses of the meal—such as oysters, fruit or soup—are served are placed on this service plate. Food is *never* placed directly upon it, and the service plate is not removed until it is changed for a well-heated plate on which the first hot course after the soup is to be served. The custom of a service plate originated because it was not thought good form to leave the guest without a plate before him until clearing the table for dessert.

THE TABLE NAPKIN

This is placed at the left of the forks or the right of the spoons, or, if preferred, on the service plate, or between the knife and fork. When no service plate is to be used, should the napkin be embroidered or monogrammed, this must be placed where it can be seen.

YOUR NEEDS FOR TABLE SETTING

An attractive table enhances a meal, and your choice of china may mean that it is not possible to get the whole service at once. Buy what you can and add to it at leisure. What you will need depends, of course, on the entertaining which you plan to do. It is possible to purchase just as many settings as you need. Eight is a convenient number to plan for, so that means eight each of the following (unless otherwise specified):

> Dinner plates (10 in. in diameter)
> Pudding plates (7 in. in diameter)
> Bread and butter plates (6 in. in diameter)
> Soup plates or cream-soup cups and saucers
> 2 vegetable dishes
> 1 large meat dish
> 1 small meat dish
> Salad plates
> Coffee cups and saucers
> Teacups and saucers
> 2 sauce boats and stands
> 6 cereal (or fruit) bowls

For everyday needs you will also require eight of each of the following:

> Goblets
> Tumblers
> Fruit-juice glasses
> Fingerbowls (which can be used for fruit salads)

For entertaining you need wine glasses: cocktail glasses, roughly a dozen, and then eight each of claret, sherry and port glasses. Or a dozen all-purposes glasses might do to begin with.

SILVER AND CUTLERY

Oyster fork, lobster pick.
Ice cream fork—used for fruit and desserts.

Pickle fork—used for pickles and relishes.
Carving set—fork, knife, steel, used for carving meat.
Poultry set—as above, used for carving poultry and game.
Table knives—small size, used for breakfast, lunch.
                    large size, used for dinner.
Teaspoons—used for tea or coffee.
Fruit spoons—(pointed), for orange, grapefruit.
Egg spoons—(pointed), for boiled eggs.
Coffee spoons—when coffee is served in small cups.
Dessert spoons.
Dessert knives and forks.
Table spoons—sometimes used for soup—primarily for serving.
Soup spoons.
Iced-beverage spoon—for iced coffee or tea.
Sugar tongs.
Sifter spoon, jam spoon.
Table fork—small, for breakfast, lunch and with dessert spoon
                  large, for dinner, entrées.
Fish knives $\Big\}$ silver and plated knife.
Fish forks
Individual salad fork—used for salads.
Cake fork—used for gâteaux and pastries.
Tea knife—used for afternoon tea and spreading jam, etc.
Butter knife—for serving butter.
Cheese scoop—for digging out Stilton cheese.
Ladles—used for gravies and sauces. Punch ladle.
Salad set—fork and spoon for serving.
Grape scissors, nut crackers, serrated fruit knives.

THE CARE OF SILVER

When silver is washed after each meal in hot soapy water and dried thoroughly—never left to drain, or stand soiled overnight—it is easily kept bright. Always clean off any egg or other stains on it. Keep your spare silver wrapped in flannel, as it is apt to tarnish.

KNIVES

It is best to hold the handles of the knives in the hands when washing them and never let them lie in the water.

Table Service

A faithful and good servant is a real godsend, but truly 'tis a rare bird in the land.

LUTHER, *Table Talk*

*If you would have good servants
see that you be good masters.*
RICHARD BAXTER

When a special party is being held it is always wise to give final instructions to those serving and waiting, about 15 to 30 minutes before the time set for serving.

STACKING DISHES

Stacking is the rule for each service. Put the plates in piles of a dozen within convenient reach of the foods. Put a pile of table napkins near them or stack them with a napkin between each two plates in a sandwich fashion. (This is, of course, for the first set of plates used.) Arrange the silver neatly by the plates; put the forks, spoons and knives in separate groups near to one another.

DISHING UP (Fr. *Dressage*)

The French term exactly expresses what happens in dishing-up—for much more is implied than the mere setting of the joint upon a dish. It signifies the art of the cook in decorating and garnishing to render meats convenient for serving and pleasing to the sight. It is essential that all the foods cooked shall be ready for dishing up at the same time, that joints shall not be kept back for vegetables, nor entrées kept waiting for sauces. The plan of service must be perfectly schemed so that there is no hurrying or scurrying. There must be no confusion in the kitchen, or delays will result between the courses.

TABLE SERVICE

FOR SMALL DINNERS

The first course may be placed on the table before announcing dinner.

FOR LARGE BANQUETS

It is best to wait until all the guests are in their seats; hot canapés and soups are always served after the guests are seated.

When no bread-and-butter plate is used, the salad can be placed on the table before the guests arrive.

Butter is always placed on the left side of the bread-and-butter plate.

Water may be poured out just before the meal is announced.

When the guests are seated, it is best to have two persons working together, one carrying the tray while the other places the food. Cocktail glasses, soup bowls or plates and canapé plates are always placed on the service plate (which is already on the table). The guest of honour is usually served first, and it is always best for the host to be seated farthest away from the kitchen, as he is served last. When the guests finish the last course, follow the same order in removing the plates.

For dinner-plate service—if salad is to be served too—the dinner plate is taken in the left hand, and the salad plate in the right hand, at the serving table. The service must be orderly and as quick as possible. When two tables are to be served, always finish one table first.

The plate with the fish, meat or poultry on it must be placed one inch from the edge of the table, with the fish, meat or poultry nearest to the guest. The salad is placed to the right of the spoons when no beverage is served with the main course. When a beverage is served, the salad is placed on the left, just above the napkin.

When a table has been served with dinner plates, salad, etc., then ice, cheese and rolls, and coffee follow on immediately.

At a large formal dinner or banquet, when serving an ice with the main course, carry the ices on trays and place each one directly above the plate.

Serve rolls twice; offer them at the left side, at a convenient distance and height.

The coffee is always placed at the right of the spoons, with the handle of the cups out towards the right. If desired, coffee may be served from trays. When two persons are waiting, one carries the tray, while the other sets the filled cups on the saucers and places them on the table.

Remember to see that the water-glasses are filled if necessary, and also to see that the service of the wine is faultless. At the end of a course always remove all dishes belonging to that course.

When serving dessert, remove all cutlery and dishes of previous courses, and leave only the wineglasses and salt-cellars. See that any crumbs are brushed off with a brush and crumb-tray. Then serve the dessert. Place the dessert plates, with finger-bowls (with a little water in them) and a silver knife and fork, in front of each guest. Put the fruit and nuts on the table.

Be emphatic that the coffee must be piping hot when served.

THE TEMPORARY HELP

A point worth making concerns the 'temporary'. Your temporary help may be a professional butler, or a maid who only goes out to assist at entertainments—in which case, no doubt he or she is likely to be thoroughly experienced. But this does not prevent the employer from going over the work and showing the ways of that particular household. On the other hand, you may get a student who enjoys this type of work, which helps to supplement her income.

Try always to see that your help's appearance is neat and trim and inconspicuous. No perfume, no nail varnish, and not plastered with jewellery.

A DINNER PARTY WITHOUT HELP

Do make out your menu in good time, so that it can be prepared a day before or during the morning of the day.

One can scarcely ever give an entire day to party preparation—there seem to be so very many other things to be done. Set your table in good time during the afternoon for either a sit-down or buffet meal; see that your dessert dishes and silver are ready, that your coffee tray, cocktail tray and salted nuts, olives and other cocktail 'titbits' are arranged. Measure your coffee, so that there is only the water to set boiling when the dessert goes in. Wash and drain your greens; pat them dry in a clean cloth. Soak a lettuce in ice-water, remove the root, drain only, then keep in a covered dish. The lettuce will stay fresh for quite a long time. Prepare the celery; keep the watercress, which you will need for garnishing, and the parsley in a covered jar after washing. Mix your salad, but do not dress it till just before serving, or the leaves will wilt. Keep a jar of French dressing in your refrigerator or cool larder (don't forget to add a clove of garlic to this). It is then ready for use, after being well shaken.

Have all your vegetables prepared during odd moments. See that your main dish is ready to bake or re-heat. Be sure to remember to freshen the rolls in the oven for a few minutes, or make some crisp, dry toast.

Then check that everything is in order. This is most important for your own peace of mind. And you must have an uncluttered-up kitchen. No pans or dishes to wash! Clear up as you go along. And if you are serving wine, see that it is at the correct temperature and that your glasses are ready. Now relax—then put on your party-dress and enjoy your party.

When you are having guests to dinner, delegate one of them to help you, and let your husband remain chatting to the other guests. It causes much less flurry and fuss, and your helper will feel very flattered at being chosen to help. He can carry the plates and silver to the kitchen, scrape and stack, so that later you'll not have such a hard job washing up. Get the dessert ready to be carried in, then join your guests and bring the coffee tray at the same time.

Finally when the last drop of coffee is sipped, find some comfortable chairs—men are apt to become restless if you leave them in the same chair for too long a time. If you prefer it, serve the coffee in another room.

The Guests
and Table Etiquette

Tis not good manners as soon as you sit down at table to bawl out, I eat none of this, I eat none of that; I care for no rabbit; I love nothing that tastes of pepper, nutmeg, onions etc. If you happen to burn your mouth you must endure it if possible, if not, you must convey what you have in your mouth privately upon your plate and give it away to the footman: for though civility obliges you to be neat, there is no necessity you should burn your guts.

RULES OF CIVILITY, 1685

In proceeding to the dining-room the gentleman gives one arm to the lady he escorts—it is unusual to offer both.

LEWIS CARROLL

THE GUESTS

GOING IN TO DINNER

At a dinner party the host tells each gentleman the name of the lady he is to take in to dinner. If they are strangers, he introduces his friend to the lady.

When dinner is announced, he then offers his arm to the lady who is to be escorted by him. This should be either the oldest lady or the lady of highest rank, or the greatest stranger. If a bride is present, then she is always escorted by the host; the other guests follow; the hostess closes the procession with the gentleman who is oldest, the highest in rank or the most distinguished.

LEAVING THE TABLE

To-day men and women ordinarily leave the table together; the hostess, of course, making the first move. At more formal dinners, it is usual for the women to leave the dining-room and drink their coffee in the drawing-room, while the men remain to drink coffee and port.

THE SEATING OF GUESTS

It is usually a mistake to invite talkers together. Brilliant men and women who love to talk want hearers not rivals, or at least voluble talkers. Silly people should never be put anywhere near learned ones, unless the dull one is a young and pretty woman with a talent for listening, and the clever man with admiration for beauty and a love of talking. . . . The endeavour of a hostess, when seating her table, is to put those together who are likely to be of interest to each other.

LILLIAN EICHLER

The seating of guests depends upon the degree of formality of the meal. When the dinner is a very formal one always put the guest of honour, if a lady, at the right of the host. If a man, he is seated at the right of the hostess. Those next in rank are seated in order away from them. At banquets and public dinners the woman guest always sits on the right of her partner. At 'Hen Parties', the guest of honour sits at the right of the hostess.

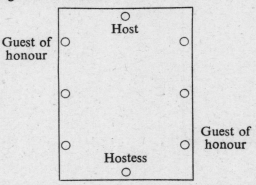

The good hostess places guests cleverly, so that their personalities provide a foil, one with another. She sprinkles the good conversationalists evenly round the table, in between the quieter guests.

The chairs should be comfortable though upright, and placed evenly round the table so that the chair need not be moved when the guests are seated.

For conventional seating, the host and hostess are placed at the two ends of the table, with the guests along the side.

PLACE-CARDS

To-day place-cards are much less used than formerly. But they are helpful at a very large dinner; otherwise they are really unnecessary, though at a special party such as a twenty-first, bridesmaid's lunch, etc., they can add charm and gaiety to the table.

For the formal dinner, cards should be perfectly plain. They should be placed above the napkin or above the food service plate. If menu cards are used, they should be placed where they can be easily read.

PRECEDENCE IN SERVING

In olden days it was the custom—dating back to medieval times—to serve the hostess first. This ensured that the guests were not poisoned. Service should begin with the guest on the host's right and continue around the table regardless of whether men or women are being served.

The procedure may be varied so that the same guest will not always be last. When there are two people serving, one begins on the right of the host and the other on the right of the hostess.

TABLE ETIQUETTE

> *The frightful manner of feeding with their knives, till the whole blade seemed to enter into the mouth; and the still more frightful manner of cleaning the teeth afterwards with a pocket knife.*
>
> FRANCES TROLLOPE

We sometimes encounter a question of etiquette, or some practice of entertaining which may either puzzle us or set us thinking about our customs, and could even cause a very awkward moment, and make us wonder, "Are we up-to-date?" "Do we know all about social living?" Not being entirely sure of one's ground has been known sometimes quite to spoil a party! There are some questions of table etiquette and table setting that need special emphasis, though to-day the rule is that one begins with one's outside 'implements' first and works inwards.

Query	Answer
Do you wait for everyone to be served before you begin to eat?	Yes, when it is a *small party*. Should one start immediately it is apt to appear as if one is greedy! At a *large party* the food does sometimes become cold, so there is a difference of opinion. But if possible—wait, or the timing is upset. Remember to try not to eat too fast—or too slowly!
Do you refuse food you don't like or that you think is indigestible?	Take just a little and 'nibble' at it. It would cause great embarrassment to your hostess if she thought the dish which she had provided was unwelcome.

D

Query	Answer
What do you do when you don't want to take wine?	Never turn your glass down, nor allow it to be filled and leave it. Just politely say 'No, thank you' when it is offered to you.
What do you do to remove something from the mouth?	If it is a fish bone or fruit stone, etc., drop it unobtrusively into a spoon or fork held to your lips. If you choke or find it difficult to remove—leave the table, and explain on your return.
What do you do when you burn your mouth?	Sip cold water—or put a little salt quickly to your mouth.
Do you use a tooth-pick in public?	NEVER!
What do you do if you drop food on to the tablecloth—leave it or remove it?	Try to lift it with the tip of the knife. *Do not* try to remove and rub with water.
What happens if you spill wine?	Put a little salt on to the stain.
Is dunking allowed?	In your own family's presence, but nowhere else. If you want to sop up a little gravy, put a small piece of bread on to a fork—but don't wipe the plate clean with it.
What do you do with your knife and fork when you stop eating?	If the pause is only for a moment, lay both parallel with the handles on the right edge of the plate, the cutting edge of the knife towards the centre of the plate with the tines of the fork up, with the food in the centre of the plate and both implements about two-thirds towards the centre of the plate. When you finish a course leave them the same way—but in the centre of the plate.
Are you permitted to use your fingers instead of a fork with chip or game potatoes?	Yes! But use a fork where possible. It is wiser to 'appear' to be finicky than careless.

Query	Answer
Do you drink the juice at the bottom of a fish or fruit cocktail glass?	No! Use your spoon.
Do you always have bread-and-butter plates?	Not at a formal dinner. At dinners at home the hostess usually decides this problem according to taste. Butter is not generally served unless specially requested.
When do you change a fork to the right hand?	In England the fork is kept in the left hand and used with tines down. In America it is customary to cut the meat with the knife in the right hand and fork in the left—then to change the fork to the right hand and use it tines up—so you both change the fork over from the left hand to the right hand and use it.
What do you do with a soup spoon when in use and afterwards?	Leave it in the soup plate or, if a soup cup is used, in the saucer.
Where do you leave the oyster fork?	For oyster cocktails, on the small plate beneath container—or the oyster plate.
What do you do with teaspoons?	Never leave them standing in the cup but always put them in the saucer.
Are you allowed to wipe off spots on silver?	Yes, if it is a distasteful stain. Remove the spoon or fork tactfully and deal with it under the cover of the table.
Do you bring a soup plate in without a plate or is it brought in on another plate?	Without a plate under it, but when the soup plate is removed the service plate is lifted with it, and at once replaced by a hot plate for the next course, whether it is fish, roast, etc. Soup cups are always brought in on a saucer and set on the service plate, and they are removed with it.
What is a cream soup cup?	It is a two-handled bowl and saucer.

Query	Answer
Are crescent-shaped salad plates essential?	They are used according to the taste of the hostess, but they are not essential.
What size is a service plate?	10 in. Set before each place when the table is set. It is used as a base for food but never used for food.
Do service plates, cover plates and place plates differ?	No, they are the same plate.
What is a grapefruit glass?	A stemmed glass with a large bowl.
Can you tell me the size of the different plates?	Bread-and-butter plates: 5 in., 5½ in., 6 in.
	Tea plate, salad plate: 7 in.
	Soup plate: 7 in. or 8 in. (the smaller size usually used at a formal dinner).
	Dessert plate: 8 in.
	Breakfast or lunch: 8½ in.
	Dinner: 10 in.
	Place or service plate: 10 in.
What is a sea-food cocktail glass?	A stemmed glass used for sea-food and sauce.
Should one cut a bread roll?	No, crumble it.
Should chicken bones be picked up in the fingers?	No, never.
Does one turn fish in a scallop out on to a plate?	No, never.
Does one smoke between courses?	Not generally. But it depends on your hostess.
Which is best to take before a meal—sherry or a cocktail?	Both are correct.
Which is the correct way to tilt your soup plate?	Tilt it away from you and gently scoop the soup into the bowl of the spoon.
Does one break bread into the soup?	No—leave it on the plate provided.
How does one shell prawns served with a first cocktail?	Hold them lightly between finger and thumb of both hands and pull the shell carefully away. After placing in cocktail sauce, use a finger bowl at once.

Query	Answer
If salad is served on a side plate, does one turn it on to the main plate?	No—leave it there and eat it with the same fork that is provided for the main dish—use your knife too, if necessary.
When melon is served, does one use a spoon or knife?	Melon should be cut as near the base of the skin as possible—then chop it into small pieces and place into the mouth with the fork. If the melon is soft and very ripe—use your spoon.
How does one eat an orange when served for dessert?	Slit with the knife into four quarters then pull the first into its natural section, peel with the fingers—leave peel on the plate—and use a finger bowl which is provided afterwards.
Do you use a spoon or fork to eat stewed or fresh soft fruits?	Use both spoon and fork.
What size is a table-napkin?	18 × 18 in.
What is a lapkin?	A large napkin, which usually measures 12 × 22 in.—but there is a smaller one, 10½ × 17 in.
What is the 'over-hang' on a table-cloth?	The amount of cloth which hangs from table to ground. It is between 12 and 15 in.
What is a silence cloth used for?	A heavy felt or padded cloth used under the linen cloth to protect the table, and dull any clatter or noise.
What is a brandy snifter?	The large curved glass used for brandy. It holds 9 oz.
What is a brandy inhaler?	The same as a brandy snifter.

The great secret is not having bad manners or good manners or any other particular sort of manners, but having the same manners for all human souls.

G. BERNARD SHAW,
Pygmalion, Act V

The Menu

You must reflect carefully beforehand with whom you are to eat and drink, rather than what you are to eat and drink. For a dinner of meats without the company of a friend is like the life of a lion or a wolf.

EPICURUS, *Fragments*

I do loathe explanations.
J. M. BARRIE,
My Lady Nicotine

Most people possess many books from which they can find the special recipes which lack of space makes it impossible to include in this book. But the section of menu terms has been included to help you when dining out to know your 'menus', and to be able when necessary, through the knowledge of small variations and menu terms, to plan different menus or to adapt your favourite menus by including a different hors d'œuvres or soup or entrée—or whatever you wish—according to the season.

MENU CARDS (how to write them)
Speak in French if you don't remember the English for it.
LEWIS CARROLL

When writing menu cards always use capital letters for the words, with the exception of conjunctions, articles and prepositions. Write your menu all in French, which is the culinary language, or else all in English. Never write in both languages.

Arrange in order of service. Write the main dish of each course across the centre of the card. Write any accompaniments as follows:

The first on the right hand or in the centre. If two—one is written on the right side and the second is written at the left side on the line below.

Write the beverage or wine at the bottom of the menu or with the course with which it is to be served.

Never write 'cream' or 'sugar' or such accompaniments on the menu.

Plan the main dish first and then plan the accompanying vegetables. Be sure to serve a salad. See that the bread is fresh, or hot, or toasted. Plan the first course, if one is to be served. Plan the pudding or dessert. Plan beverage or wine. Plan cereals, if they are to be used, and don't forget a good supply of fresh fruit.

Always see that hot foods are served *really hot* and that the plates are well pre-heated.

MENU TERMS

à la	*Fr.* To the, with, in the mode or fashion of, in. In this sense, the feminine singular is always used as it refers to the mode, which is feminine.
à la Bordelaise	*Fr.* The name of a French sauce (brown) in which claret (Bordeaux wine) is an ingredient.
à la Blanquette	*Fr.* With a white sauce, enriched with cream and eggs.
à la Broche	*Fr.* Roasted in front of the fire on a spit or skewer.
à la Carte	*Fr.* From the bill-of-fare.
à la Crème	*Fr.* With cream.
à la Diable	*Fr.* Devilled, seasoned with hot or pungent condiments or spices.
à la Ficelle	*Fr.* Tied with string.
à la Financière	*Fr.* With truffles, and cock's combs, used as a garnish for entrées.
à la Flamande	*Fr.* Flemish style.
à la Française	*Fr.* This is generally applied to a number of dishes of French origin.
à la King	*Fr.* Served in rich cream sauce, containing green pepper and pimento and mushrooms.
à la Mode	*Fr.* Denoting the style or fashion of a dish. (In U.S.A. when applied to desserts means 'with ice-cream'.)
à la Moutarde	*Fr.* In mustard.
à la Newburgh	*Fr.* Newburgh fashion.
à l'Huile	*Fr.* Done in oil or served with oil, vinaigrette, etc.
Allemande	*Fr.* German. *Sauce Allemande* is a smooth yellow sauce with the addition of butter, egg-yolk, catsup, etc.
Aneth	*Fr.* Dill.
Anglaise	*Fr.* English. *À l'Anglaise*—in English style. Usually signifies something roast or plain.
Antipasti	*Ital.* Appetizers. A course consisting of relishes, assorted appetizers of fish, cold cuts or vegetables.
Appetizer	A small portion of beverage or food served before or as first course of the meal.
Arête	*Fr.* Fish bone.
Aroma	Aromatic quality.

Aromates	*Fr.* Vegetable herbs used for flavouring, such as bay leaf, chervil, tarragon, etc.
Aspic	Jelly made from meat stock that has been boiled down so that when it is cold it becomes firm. Also fish, fruit, vegetable or tomato-juice stock.
au	*Fr.* To the, with.
au Bain Marie	*Fr.* To keep warm sauce and other foods in a hot-water bath.
au Beurre	*Fr.* With butter or done in butter, tossed or sautéed. *Au beurre noir*—with black or nut-brown butter.
au Blanc	*Fr.* Cooked white; white sauce.
au Bleu	*Fr.* Culinary term applied to fish boiled in salted water, seasoned with vegetables, herbs and white wine or vinegar.
au Brun	*Fr.* Done in brown sauce.
au Cari	*Fr.* Curried.
au Four	*Fr.* Baked or done in the oven.
au Gras	*Fr.* Term for meat cooked and dressed with a very rich gravy or sauce.
au Gratin	*Fr.* A term applied to certain dishes prepared with sauce, garnish and breadcrumbs, and baked brown in the oven or under a grill; served in the dish in which baked.
au Jus	*Fr.* A term for dishes of meat dressed with their juice or gravy.
au Lait	*Fr.* With milk, or cooked in milk.
au Maigre	*Fr.* An expression used for dishes prepared without meat.
au Naturel	*Fr.* Applied to food cooked plainly and in very simple fashion.
au Riz	*Fr.* With rice.
Aurore	*Fr.* A yellow colour; a culinary expression for food dished up with a garnish consisting of stuffed eggs, quartered bread *croûtons* and aurore sauce.
Aurore Sauce	Consists of Allemande or Béchamel and tomato sauce flavoured with chilli, vinegar and diced mushrooms.
au Rouge	*Fr.* Served with or in red sauce.
au Vert	*Fr.* Served with or in green sauce.

aux   *Fr.* With.

aux Champi-   *Fr.* With mushrooms.
gnons

aux fines Herbes   *Fr.* With a combination of finely chopped fresh herbs.

Avi (à l')   Burnt.

Ayoli   Compounded of *aye* and *oli*, garlic and oil, probably derived from the Spanish *ajo* garlic. This is the name given to 'butter à garlic' which is much used for culinary purposes in Provence and the South of France, and wherever garlic is held in esteem. It is especially coveted as a sauce for codfish, whether served hot or cold.

Baissière   *Fr.* Wine sediment.

Banquet   *Fr.* A sumptuous feast, an entertainment of eating and drinking.

Banqueter   *Fr.* To banquet, to feast, to treat oneself to a good feast.

Bardé   *Fr.* Larded, covered with slices of bacon or salt pork.

Barigoule (à la)   *Fr.* A way of dressing artichokes with olive oil and minced meat.

Bariolé   *Fr.* Speckled.

Basil   (Fr. *Basilic*.) An aromatic pot herb.

Basse-Pâte   *Fr.* Under-crust.

Bavarian   A gelatine dish into which whipped cream is folded as it begins to stiffen.

Bavarois   *Fr.* Bavarian.

Bay Leaf   (Fr. *Laurier*.) The leaf of a species of laurel-tree known as cherry laurel.

Béarnaise   *Fr.* A white sauce, with yolk of egg thickening; comes from the town Béarn, birthplace of Henry IV who was a great gourmand.

Béchamel   *Fr.* Refers to a cream sauce made of chicken stock, cream or milk and usually seasoned with onion. This term is sometimes used for all sauces having a white sauce foundation.

Beef   (Fr. *Bœuf*.) Boiled beef—*bœuf bouilli*; roast beef—*bœuf rôti*, braised beef—*bœuf braisé*.

Beef à la Mode   *Fr.* A well larded piece of beef cooked slowly in water, similar to braised beef.

Beignets	*Fr.* Fritters—anything dropped in batter or thin paste and fried in deep fat.
Beignets d'Huîtres	*Fr.* Oyster fritters.
Beignets de Pêche	*Fr.* Peach fritters.
Beignets de Ris de Veau	*Fr.* Sweetbread fritters.
Bénédictine	*Fr.* A religious sect. A liqueur made principally at the Abbey at Fécamp in France.
Berlinois	*Fr.* A kind of light yeast cake in the shape of balls, similar to doughnuts.
Beurre	*Fr.* Butter.
Beurré	*Fr.* Buttered.
Bill of Fare	(Fr. *Menu.*) Literally minute details in a culinary sense. A list of dishes intended for a meal.
Biscotte	*Fr.* Rusk, biscuit.
Bisque	*Fr.* A thick soup usually made from shell-fish.
Blanquette	*Fr.* A meat stew with white sauce.
Bleu	*Fr.* Blue; used with reference to fresh-water fish—*au bleu*—plain boiled.
Bœuf	*Fr.* Beef.
Bœuf à la Jardinière	*Fr.* Beef braised with vegetables.
Bœuf-rôti	*Fr.* Roast beef.
Bombe	*Fr.* A frozen dessert made of a combination of two or more frozen mixtures packed in a round or melon-shaped mould.
Bonne Femme	*Fr.* Good wife; in a simple home style. Applied to soups and stews etc.
Bordelaise	*Fr.* Bordeaux, *Sauce Bordelaise*—a sauce with a Bordeaux-wine foundation, with various seasonings added.
Borsh	(Russ. *Borshch.*) A Russian or Polish soup with beets. Often sour cream is added.
Bouillabaisse	*Fr.* A national soup of France. The word is derived from *bouillir*—to boil, and *abaisser*—to go down. A highly seasoned fish soup made especially at Marseilles. It is served in plates with dry toast.

Bourgeoise	*Fr.* Citizen style, served with simplicity.
Breakfast	(*Fr. Déjeuner.*) The first meal of the day.
Brioche	*Fr.* A slightly sweetened rich bread of French origin.
Broche	*Fr.* Skewer. A spit for roasting.
Café	*Fr.* Coffee. Coffee house, restaurant.
Café au lait	*Fr.* Coffee with hot milk.
Café noir	*Fr.* Black coffee, after-dinner coffee.
Carte	*Fr.* Card; bill of fare. *À la carte*—according to the bill of fare. *Carte du jour*—bill of fare, a menu for the day.
Chantilly	*Fr.* The name given to savoy cakes, scooped out, filled with preserved fruit and garnished with whipped cream.
Chantilly cream	Sweetened, flavoured whipped cream.
Chaud	*Fr.* Hot.
Chemise	*Fr.* Shirt. *En chemise*—with their skins on, generally applied to potatoes.
Chiffonade	*Fr.* Rags. Minced or shredded vegetables or meats used on soups or salads.
Cloche	*Fr.* Bell. *Sous cloche*—under a dish cover.
Confit	*Fr.* Also called *confiture.* Preserve or jam made from fruit.
Consommé	*Fr.* A clear soup generally made from two or three kinds of meat, fowl, veal and vegetables and usually highly seasoned.
Entremets	*Fr.* From the verb 'to place in between'. A side dish, a light made-dish which is served after the roast before the dessert. In French cooking it may be either a sweet or vegetable course.
Entremets de Douceur	*Fr.* A sweet dish.
Entremets de Légumes	*Fr.* Vegetable course.
Espagnole	*Fr.* Spanish brown sauce.
Farci	*Fr.* Stuffed.
Fermière	*Fr.* Plain, country style, farmer's-wife style.
Fines Herbes	*Fr.* Fine herbs.

Foie	*Fr.* Liver, *Foie gras*—fat liver. This applies especially to the liver of fat geese. *Foie gras au naturel*—plain cooked whole *foie gras*. *Pâté de foie gras*—the most popular form of *foie gras*. The cooked livers are seasoned with truffles, wine and aromatics. *Foie gras* was first used in Strasbourg towards the end of the 18th century by the chef to the Governor of Alsace.
Fondu	*Fr.* Blended or melted butter.
Franchotte	*Fr.* A small pie or tart with meringue.
Gratin	*Fr.* Crumbs. *Au gratin*, the French term for 'scalloped'. Cheese is very frequently used in *au gratin* dishes, and to many this term implies its use.
Gumbo	A thick Creole soup containing okra.
Haché	*Fr.* Minced, chopped.
Hors d'œuvres	*Fr.* Beyond the works. The small side-dishes served at the beginning of the meal—among these are: canapés, olives, pickles, fish, sausages, radishes.
Italienne	*Fr.* Italian.
Jardinière	*Fr.* The gardener's wife. A dish of mixed vegetables.
Julienne	*Fr.* Vegetables cut into fine strips or shreds. Also the name of a soup.
Jus	*Fr.* Juice or gravy. *Au jus*—served in the natural juice or gravy.
Kuchen	*Ger.* Cake, but not necessarily sweet.
Lait	*Fr.* Milk.
Laitue	*Fr.* Lettuce.
Lebkuchen	*Ger.* A famous group of German cakes. Also known as sweet or honey cake.
Lunch	(*Fr. Déjeuner à la fourchette.*)
Lyonnaise	*Fr.* From Lyons. Seasoned with onions and parsley, as in Lyonnaise potatoes.
Macédoine	*Fr.* A mixture or medley. This term is usually applied to fruit or vegetables.
Maître d'Hôtel	*Fr.* Steward. In the culinary sense implies the use of minced parsley. *Maître d'hôtel Sauce*, or Parsley Butter—a well-seasoned mixture of creamed butter, chopped parsley and lemon juice—served on grilled meats, grilled or boiled fish and on some vegetables, e.g. potatoes.

Milanaise   *Fr.* From Milan. Implies the use of macaroni, parmesan cheese, and Béchamel or other sauce.

Minestrone   *Ital.* A thick Italian vegetable soup.

Mulligatawny   A highly seasoned thick soup characterized chiefly by curry powder, meats, vegetables, mango chutney, coconut flesh, rice, cayenne, etc., according to taste.

Neapolitan   Also called Harlequin and Panachée. This term is applied to a moulded dessert of from two to four kinds of ice cream or water ice, arranged lengthwise in layers. The mixture is always sliced across for serving. The name is also applied to a gelatine dish which is arranged in layers of different colours.

Nesselrode   Containing chestnuts. A frozen dessert with a custard foundation, to which chestnut purée, fruit and cream have been added. It has been described as the most perfect of frozen puddings.

Newburgh   A form of creamed dish with egg yolks added. Originally flavoured with lime or sherry. Most often applied to lobster, but may be used with other foods if desired.

Nivernaise   *Fr.* A garnish of Julienne vegetables which are added to Allemande sauce.

Noir   *Fr.* Black.

Noisette   *Fr.* Literally 'hazel-nut'; nut-brown colour. May imply nut-shaped. A small piece of lean meat. Generally a chop which is minus the bone (fillet). *Potatoes Noisette*—potatoes which have been cut into the shape and size of hazel-nuts and then browned in fat.

Normande   *Fr.* From Normandy. *À la Normande*—a delicate smooth mixture which frequently contains whipped cream.

O'Brien   Cubed potatoes cooked in a small amount of fat with chopped onions and pimento.

Parfait   *Fr.* Perfect. A mixture which contains egg and syrup, but frozen without stirring; may be moulded but is more frequently served in parfait glasses.

Parmentière   *Fr.* Potato. Named after Baron Parmentier who introduced potatoes into France and who also originated many methods of preparing them. *À la Parmentière*—with, or of, potatoes.

Pâte   *Fr.* Paste, dough.

Pâté   *Fr.* Patty, pie, pastry. Also a meat preparation packed in earthenware jars and small tins, prepared largely in Germany and France, but also of domestic manufacture. The name comes from the fact that it was originally sold in pies.
Pâté de foie gras—paste of fat livers.

Persillade   *Fr.* Served with or containing parsley.

Petit   *Fr.* Small. *Petits pois*—new peas, little peas, a fine grade of small canned peas with delicate flavour but of low food value.

Petits Fours   *Fr.* Small fancy cakes.

Piquant   *Fr.* Sharp, highly seasoned. This term is also applied to sauces. *Sauce piquante*—a highly seasoned brown sauce containing capers, pickles, lemon juice, vinegar, etc.

Plat   *Fr.* Dish. *Plat du jour*—(as used on menu cards) the food of the day.

Pois   *Fr.* Peas. *Petits pois*—green peas.

Polenta   *Ital.* An Italian dish originally of chestnut meal, but now frequently made of semolina, to which cheese is added before serving.

Polonaise   *Fr.* Polish style, with beets and cabbage.

Pomme   *Fr.* Apple. *Pomme de terre*—'apple of earth' or potato: *Pomme d'amour*—'love apple' or tomato: *Pommes de terre à la Lyonnaise*—Lyonnaise potatoes.

Ragoût   *Fr.* Stew. Originally meant something to restore the taste and tempt the appetite. Usually a thick, well-seasoned stew which contains meat.

Ramekin   A small economical baking dish, a pastry shell. Also the name of a cheese cake.

Ravigote (Froide)   *Fr.* A mayonnaise sauce seasoned with tarragon vinegar, chives, shallots, etc., tinted with spinach greens.

E

Ravioli	*Ital.* Small square shapes of Italian noodle-paste which are filled with minced meat or vegetables and moistened with sauce. They are then poached in stock.
Rémoulade	*Fr.* A pungent sauce, made with hard-boiled eggs, mustard-oil, vinegar and seasonings. Served with cold dishes.
Rissoler	*Fr.* To roast until the food is golden brown, to brown. *Rissolé*—browned.
Rouelle	*Fr.* A round slice or fillet.
Roulade	*Fr.* Rolled, applied to rolled meat.
Roux	*Fr.* The term is often applied to the browned flour and fat used for thickening sauces, stews, etc.
Sorbet	*Fr.* A sherbet made of several kinds of fruit.
Soubise	*Fr.* A white sauce, containing onion and sometimes parsley.
Terrine	*Fr.* An earthenware pot resembling a casserole.
Torte	*Ger.* A rich cake made of crumbs, eggs, nuts, etc.
Tournedos	*Fr.* Small round fillets of beef.
Velouté	*Fr.* A smooth, white, velvety sauce.
Volaille	*Fr.* Poultry.
Vol-au-Vent	*Fr.* Flying at the mercy of the wind. Large patties of puff pastry made without a mould and filled with meat, preserves, etc.

THE COURSES

THE FIRST COURSE

(HORS D'ŒUVRES, CANAPÉS, FISH COCKTAILS, FRUIT)

HORS D'ŒUVRES

Hors d'œuvres may be served on individual plates, placed on the table before the guests are shown in to dinner, or they may be served in very small dishes: oblong, or oval, or circular ones, according to the number of different kinds of hors d'œuvres which are served. This is a useful course. It helps to dull appetite, and also it helps both to build a meal, or make a meal go further if you have unexpected guests; it is easy to get an hors d'œuvre together quickly from the odd tins you have in your store-cupboard, and from eggs and the pickles and chutney in daily use. The traditional ways of serving hors d'œuvres vary. In France, as in England, they are served on the dining-room table as a first course. In Sweden, where they are known as 'Smörgåsbord', people help themselves—and there is usually such a varied assortment that they frequently forget there is other food to follow and they make a meal of their first course.

It is never really necessary to provide more than four kinds of hors d'œuvres, though some people consider the greater the variety, the better the hors d'œuvres. Choose any from these lists which follow. Vary your garnish according to the season—watercress, mustard and cress, heart of lettuce leaves, freshly chopped chives, parsley, mint. Remember that the blending of colours in hors d'œuvres is most important. And that sometimes chicken and fish scraps can be used up as salads, in mayonnaise, as fillings in vol-au-vent.

For a large dinner, serve any of the following:

Anchovies

Small fillets of anchovies marinated in oil and vinegar, then rolled and served on slices of hard-boiled egg, garnished with finely shredded lettuce or mustard and cress.

Fillets of anchovies served garnished with capers and anchovy butter, or devilled anchovies served on strips of toast.

Caviare

Caviare served in its jar with lemon quarters and toast.

Caviare spread on buttered *croûtes*.

Eggs

Stuffed hard-boiled eggs.

Sliced hard-boiled eggs, dressed with mayonnaise.

Fruit

Melon sliced fruit cocktail, or grapefruit.

Olives

Ripe, green or stuffed olives.

Oysters

Oysters served in their half shells (after removing beards), with lemon quarters, and a plate of sliced brown bread and butter.

Salmon

Smoked salmon, cut into tissue paper thin slices, accompanied by quarters of lemon, and a plate of brown bread and butter.

Shrimp or Prawn Cocktail

For a smaller dinner, the hors d'œuvres may be served on a trolley so that the guests may help themselves, or if preferred, set on the table—arranged always with an eye to colour, because the finely chopped parsley or dust of paprika, or a chopping of chives makes an attractive-looking dish.

Almonds. Salted.

Artichoke leaves. With shrimps on each, and garnished.

Asparagus tips. In vinaigrette dressing.

Beans. French, sliced and dressed with chilli sauce.

Beans. Haricot, dressed with tomato sauce.

Beetroot. Cooked and grated; or diced, with French dressing, garnished with parsley; or diced with a little grated onion, dressed with cream or mayonnaise; or raw, grated, with mayonnaise or French dressing.

Cabbage. The white heart, finely shredded, dressed with French dressing.

Cabbage, red. Pickled, and served finely chopped.

Celery. Stuff the grooves with Roquefort cheese and butter, cut into neat pieces; or diced with mayonnaise or French dressing.

Celery and apple. Dressed with cream, garnished with paprika.

Cheese. Cubed, and sprinkled with celery salt.

Cod's roe. Smoked, sliced.

Corn. Sweet corn, creamed.

Cream cheese. Rolled into small balls and sprinkled with finely chopped nuts.

Cucumber. Diced, with vinaigrette dressing.

Egg, hard-boiled. Sliced, and dressed with mayonnaise.

Egg, scrambled. Garnished with chopped chives or parsley.

Fish. Any cooked flaked fish, dressed with mayonnaise and tomato sauce.

Goose liver. Served in pâté, accompanied by hot toast.

Haddock. Smoked finnan haddock, served with cream sauce.

Herrings. Soused or pickled.

Kipper. Flaked or served in fillets.

Macaroni. Plain, seasoned with salt and pepper, or dressed with oil and vinegar.

Mushrooms. Creamed.

Noodles. Plain, or seasoned with salt and pepper and garnished with grated cheese.

Olives. Ripe or stuffed.

Onions. Pickled silver onions.

Onions. Spanish, finely sliced and put in layers with orange, dressed with French dressing.

Orange. Peeled, sliced, dressed with French dressing.

Potato. Salad.

Prawns. Curried; or shelled and served garnished with finely chopped parsley.

Rice. Boiled, plain or in a curry sauce.

Salami. Slices.

Sardines. Served whole, or in boned fillets.

Sauerkraut. Served plain, or with a sour cream dressing.

Sausage. Bologna or liver sausage, sliced.

Shrimps. Shelled or potted.

Vegetables. Raw, grated; or cooked, diced and served in mayonnaise.

Walnuts. Pickled.

Watercress. Sprigs dressed with French dressing.

CANAPÉS

Anchovy and egg. Butter small, thin, round pieces of toast, then spread lightly with anchovy butter. On this place a poached or steamed egg. Garnish with parsley.

Caviare and egg. Cut slices of hard-boiled eggs, remove yolk, fill its place with caviare. Serve on very thin slices of buttered brown bread, arranging the sliced yolks as a border.

Caviare and potato chips. Chill 3 oz. caviare, season with lemon juice, spread on the chips, garnish with a little sprinkling of paprika.

Cheese and chutney. Toast rounds of brown or white bread on one side. Cover the other side with chutney. Sprinkle with grated cheese. Place under the grill to brown, and serve immediately.

Cheese and tomato. Cut white bread into small rounds with a biscuit cutter. Toast on one side. Butter the untoasted side, cut slices of firm tomatoes about ¼ in. thick. Place on buttered side and flavour with salt and a little grated onion. Pile on grated cheese and place under the grill to brown.

Crab, egg and parsley. Toast rounds of brown or white bread. Cover on one side with butter, add scrambled eggs mixed with flaked crab meat, and garnish well with parsley.

Crab or lobster. Spread rounds of toasted bread with finely chopped crab or lobster meat. Add sprinkle of salt, cayenne, paprika and a few drops of lemon juice. Moisten with a little mayonnaise or thick white sauce. Sprinkle with cheese and brown in a hot oven.

Liver. Toast slices of bread. Butter on one side. Add, piled high, thinly shredded liver fried in butter, garnish with parsley.

Mushroom. Toast slices of bread, cut into small rounds. Butter on one side and add a fried mushroom or two. Season with salt and pepper and serve immediately.

Salmon, smoked. Spread toasted bread with butter. Place thin round of smoked salmon on top. Garnish with chopped parsley.

Sardine. Mix together equal parts of hard-boiled egg yolk and sardine. Add a squeeze of lemon juice. Spread on toast and serve garnished with the sliced white of egg.

Shrimp. Toast small rounds of bread and butter on one side. Pile potted shrimps on to each, add a grating of nutmeg and a small knob of butter. Place under a hot grill for two or three minutes. Serve very hot.

FISH COCKTAILS

Use this cocktail sauce:

6 *tbsp. tomato catsup*	2 *tbsp. wine*
1½ *tbsp. Tarragon vinegar*	*Juice of half a lemon*
½ *tsp. Worcester sauce*	*Cayenne and salt to taste*

Shake well. Serve over any cooked flaked fish or shell fish.

Crabmeat Cocktail. Shred the crabmeat and combine with the sauce.

Kipper Cocktail. Take cooked flaked kipper and combine with the sauce.

Lobster Cocktail. Use flaked lobster and combine with the sauce.

Oyster Cocktail. Put five or six small oysters in a glass, cover with cocktail sauce, chill well and serve.

Prawn Cocktail. Shelled prawns, combined with the sauce.

Sardine Cocktail. Boned and skinned sardines, combined with the sauce.

Shrimp Cocktail. Shelled shrimps, combined with the sauce.

FRUIT

Any fruit juices, plain or combined, may be served, well chilled. Or sliced melon, accompanied by sugar and ground ginger. Or a halved sliced grapefruit may be served.

Fruit Cocktails. Serve in glasses with a stem.

Use either of these dressings:

(a) ¼ *lb. sugar;* ⅛ *pt. sherry;* 2 *tbsp. lemon juice.* Chill and serve over any fruit.

(b) Mix together lemon or orange juice, and sweeten with sugar.

    i Cube apples, pears, peaches, and garnish with cherries.

    ii Grapefruit sections, or halved grapefruit, garnished with a cherry.

    iii Avocado and pineapple.

    iv Fresh strawberries, grapes and orange slices.

    v Watermelon cut into balls.

A little sherry or white wine may be added to enhance the flavour, if desired.

THE SECOND COURSE—SOUP

Some people can never enjoy their meal unless they begin it with soup. Other people use soup as a main course for either lunch or supper. This is very easily done by serving a good thick soup with diced vegetables, macaroni, spaghetti or rice. Sometimes, at a large dinner, two soups are served, one clear and one thick. These two classes are divided as follows:

(1) **Clear Soups** (*Consommés*). These clear transparent soups which have a floating garnish, take their name from this. The garnish can be any of the following:

Vegetables—Diced or cut into strips, e.g. leeks, onions, lettuce, carrots.

Carrots or turnips, scooped out into small balls.

Peas, beans, whole vegetables.

Asparagus, globe artichoke bottoms, heads of vegetables.

Quenelles—Little quenelles of ham, cheese, chicken or spinach.

Rice—Rice grains, cooked separately and added before serving.

Macaroni, Spaghetti or Noodles.

Custard—Cut into squares, or passed through a colander making it into threads.

Eggs—Poached, or hard-boiled and diced.

(*Bouillon*). Unclarified beef broth which may be served with rice or poached egg to garnish.

(2) **Thick Soups** (*Crèmes purées*). Cream soups are passed through a sieve and they are smooth in consistency. Sometimes, owing to the ingredients used to make the soup it is necessary to add a little colouring to make the soup look more appetising.

(*Potage lié*). Vegetables diced, rice, macaroni or spaghetti are added.

To enhance the flavour, sherry is added just before serving, and cream is added to cream soups. *Croûtons*, sippets, melba toast or grated cheese are also served with soups.

THE FISH COURSE

Fish may be served either plainly cooked or, when dressed, as an entrée. Most people prefer fish when it is cooked in the simplest way, and accompanied by a succulent sauce.

Should two fish be served at a dinner, the boiled or whole fish, i.e. the solid fish, should be served before the fried, braised or stewed fish.

There are many different fish dishes (*plats de poisson*) to choose from and it is essential to take into consideration the rest of the menu when choosing whether the fish is to be plainly cooked, e.g. grilled, baked or fried, or whether it is to be stewed with wine, mushrooms and other vegetables.

The succulence of the sauce served with the fish course can make or mar this course.

ENTRÉES

Dishes which follow fish or precede the remove, when such is served, are called entrées—which when translated into English means "entrances". These dishes are considered by the epicure as the first of the essential dishes of the dinner—because a dinner may be without hors d'œuvres or even without soup, remove or relevé, but there is no properly served dinner without an entrée course. Dressed or made-up elaborate dishes are always composed of more than one ingredient. When two entrées are served the first should always be the lighter of the two. They are generally made into fancy style so as to avoid carving, or served from the side table. The sauce must be rich, and plays an important part in this dish. Some light entrées are also suitable for supper dishes, buffets, etc., and can be served cold.

Beignets. Fritters.

Boudins or **Boudinades.** Small oblong, cylindrical or border shapes which may be made of fish, meat, poultry or game—a soufflé-like mixture which is served with a good sauce. They can be poached or steamed in the oven.

Bouchées. These puff-paste cases are filled with savoury preparations of meat, fish or game.

Cannelons. Small rolls of puff paste which are filled with savoury mince, game, poultry, meat, etc., then egged and baked in crushed breadcrumbs or vermicelli and fried in clarified butter.

Coquilles. Scallop shells filled with coarsely minced meats, then baked or placed under the grill to brown the surface.

Crépinettes and **Ándouillettes.** Small square-shaped meat mixtures, which are wrapped in pig's caul, egged, crumbed, then fried in clarified butter (or dripping). *Andouillettes* are made similarly to *Crépinettes*, but instead of being crumbed and fried they are braised in butter and then served in paper cases.

Cromesquis (sometimes spelt **Kromeskis**). Small rolls of savoury preparations which are called *Salpicon*. These are rolled in thin slices of bacon, dipped in frying batter and fried in hot fat; they are always served garnished with parsley.

Croquettes. This name is given to oval or round shapes of minced fish, game, poultry. They are egged, crumbed, and fried in clarified butter.

Croustades or **Cassolettes.** Oval or spherical shapes of baked or fried paste, bread, rice or potato crusts, which are filled with ragout or game or meat.

Friandines. Puff paste rolled out very thinly, then cut with a 2 in. fluted cutter; a small portion of prepared mince of game, meat or poultry is placed in the centre of each. This is covered with paste, egged, dipped in crushed vermicelli, then fried in clarified butter or dripping.

Petites Caisses. Small round or oval-shaped paper or pastry crust cases, which are filled with savoury mixture.

Petits Pains or **Darioles.** Are made with certain kinds of forcemeat, which is placed in suitable buttered moulds and poached, and served with a rich sauce.

Pilau or **Pillaw.** Minced meat or poultry, with savoury rice.

Rissoles. Small half-moon shapes of short crust or puff paste which are filled with prepared minced fish, game, meat, then egged, crumbed and fried in clarified butter.

Ravioles. Small, flat, round patties which are made of noodle paste and filled with a mixture of grated parmesan cheese, egg yolks, and cayenne, poached and baked in the oven.

Timbales and **Darioles.** Certain kinds of light fish, game or meat or poultry soufflés which are cooked in cup- or *timbale*-shaped moulds, either baked or poached. Sometimes the moulds are lined with thin pastry.

Vol-au-Vent. This light puff-paste crust is made in an oval or round shape—the interior of which is filled with delicately flavoured ragouts, or chicken, fish, lobster meat, oyster, etc., and served hot.

MEAT ENTRÉES

Can be anything from a *châteaubriand*, which is a double fillet, *entrecôtes*, which are sirloin steaks, to *filet mignon* or *cœurs de filets de bœuf*, which are smaller than ordinary fillets and are more closely trimmed than the former. *Faux-filet* is the name which is given to fillets cut from other parts, such as rump, sirloin or the rib of beef. When no special sauce is suggested demi-glace or plain gravy should be poured round the base of the dish.

Tournedos de bœuf are small fillets of beef trimmed into oval shapes, and they weigh about two ounces. They are usually dressed on *croûtons* or fried bread, and unless stated, they are broiled or tossed in butter over a quick fire or under a hot grill.

Ox tongue, ox brains and ox tail are also served dressed as entrées.

Veal, lamb, mutton, kidneys and pork are cooked in specially succulent ways and served as entrées; as are chicken, duck, goose, turkey, game, pigeon, venison, rabbit and hare.

SERVICE FROID—COLD ENTRÉES

These are a collection of dishes suitable for cold collations, and either luncheon or supper buffets. Set in aspic or in savoury jellies and garnished prettily, they make attractive and appetizing fare. Among this group are either lobster or salmon set in aspic, and chaudfroid of either chicken or partridge.

RELEVÉS

These are usually large joints, e.g. saddle of mutton or lamb, leg of mutton or lamb, sirloin, ham. Turkey and capons are sometimes served. Usually some vegetable is served as an accompaniment or garnish.

ENTREMETS

Under the heading of entremets there are no less than three distinct varieties of culinary preparations which may be served:

1. The dressed vegetables, which are known as *Entremets de Légumes*.
2. The sweets, hot and cold dishes which are known as *Entremets Sucrés*. See page 66.
3. The savouries or *Entremets Savoureux*. See page 67.

ENTREMETS DE LÉGUMES (DRESSED VEGETABLES)

Dressed vegetables are sometimes served as a course. The dressing varies: sometimes just a good white sauce or oiled butter is used, with a flavouring of lemon juice; other times Béchamel, Hollandaise, Tomato, 'or a Vinaigrette sauce may be used. Vegetable soufflés, stuffed vegetables (e.g. marrow, tomatoes, onions, etc.), vegetable fritters made from cooked vegetables sliced, are served.

PUNCHES, SORBETS

Sorbets, Granites and Roman Punch are ices in a semi-liquid state. They are always served in a goblet with a stem or in punch glasses immediately before the roast; this is to refresh the palate and to prepare the guest to enjoy the succeeding dishes—the roast and the entremets.

Although they are served separately, the sorbet or punch is not given a separate heading on the menu, but simply placed on a line distinct from other courses. There are many varieties of these preparations.

RÔTIS—ROASTS

The dishes which are served under this heading form the second service of the dinner.

It is known as The Roast—Rôt or Rôti course.

On the Continent the large joints of butcher's meat are generally preferred as *relevé* (remove); but in England, especially when that course is omitted, the roast course is prepared. The essential part for this course is that the game, poultry or meat is roasted and served with richly flavoured gravy.

If a remove is served, the roast then consists of game or poultry;

if game is out of season, capons, duckling, duck, guinea fowl or pigeon are served.

Bread sauce, brown breadcrumbs, *croûtes* of bread, and chipped or other fried potatoes, garnished with watercress and a seasonable salad, form a usual accompaniment with roast birds. Relevés (roast joints) are not dealt with here but under that heading.

SALADES—SALADS

There are countless varieties of salads. Many are made of salad plants, raw herbs or plants, which are known as acetarious or succulent plants.

Hot or cold cooked vegetables, shell fish, cold fish, game, meat, poultry are mixed or blended together—sometimes fresh fruits are added—mayonnaise or a fruit-juice dressing is used. One flavour must not predominate, otherwise the salad's flavour is spoilt.

ENTREMETS SUCRÉS (SWEET DISHES)

In this group of sweet dishes, the hot sweets consist of fritters, *croûtes* of fruit, puddings, savarins, soufflés, omelettes, pancakes, etc., while the cold sweet dishes are usually composed of *bavarois*, jellies, fruit pies, *bordures*, chartreuse of fruits, compotes, macedoines, trifles, charlottes, frozen puddings, iced creams, fancy *gâteaux*, pastry, soufflés, ices, *plombières* and various other kinds of sweet-meats.

Beignets—Fritters can be made with any fruit, fresh or tinned.

Charlottes

There are two different kinds of charlottes—
  (1) those served hot,
  (2) those served cold.

They are made entirely differently. For the first group, the interiors of plain charlotte moulds are lined with slices of bread, which are dipped or slightly browned in butter. They are then filled with fruit purée and baked. In the second group the charlotte moulds are lined with finger biscuits or slices of *génoise* cake, and they are then filled with a cream or ice mixture—in the latter case *glacée* (frozen) should be placed after the name on menu.

Compotes de fruits. Stewed fruits.

Croûtes aux fruits. Compotes of fruit served on fried cake or bread *croûtons*. They are garnished with glacé fruit, almonds, angelica, cherries, raisins, and then sauced over with fruit syrup.

Gelées. Jellies may be plain with wine flavouring, or with fruit set in a design in a mould.

Compote d'Oranges Napolitaine. Orange skin filled with port wine jelly and vanilla cream in two or three layers, then cut into quarters when cold and served on vanilla ice, or rice.

Œufs Vanille à la Neige (hot). Quenelles of stiffly whisked whites of egg poached in milk. Served with vanilla custard.

POUDINGS—PUDDINGS

There are many puddings; among these are the fruit puddings, sponge puddings, suet puddings, cereal milk puddings and Christmas pudding.

SOUFFLÉS AND OMELETTES

The name 'soufflé' is always given to any light mixture which is served either hot or cold. Soufflés are either baked or steamed. Sweet omelettes are made soufflé by whisking the whites of egg until stiff and then these are folded lightly (with a metal spoon) into the other ingredients. Sweet omelettes are usually made in an omelette pan, over a quick heat. Sometimes they are baked in the oven to brown the topside and to help the rise, and so make them light and fluffy.

Flans. Round or oval-shaped tarts. They are filled with cream or fruit.

Tarte aux Fruits. Open fruit tart.

Éclairs. Finger-shaped pieces of choux paste baked and filled with cream and iced with chocolate or coffee icing.

ENTREMETS SAVOUREUX (AFTER-DINNER SAVOURIES)

These dishes may be served hot or cold, although the former is the more usual. They must always be dressed in very small portions, and the most popular ingredients are cheese savouries, egg savouries, or smoked fish savouries. Shrimps or mushrooms are also frequently used.

OMELETTES

There are many omelettes—plain, compound, savoury or sweet—which are served either at the beginning of a meal, if they are savoury, or, if they are sweet, they are served as a pudding course.

GLACES

The word *glacé* means 'coated or masked with sugar or syrup'. But the course known as Glaces in this instance consists of ices made of juices, sweetened fruit, cream and other mixtures.

BOMBES, MOUSSES

These light preparations are made from custard, cream, fruit, or syrup with whipped whites of eggs. They are served in soufflé cases or soufflé dishes.

FROMAGE—CHEESE

Cheese is served before the fruit and it is frequently mentioned on the menu. It is usual to serve at least two varieties of cheese; small pats of fresh butter and dry plain biscuits are served with it. Curled celery and radishes are also served when in season, if desired.

DESSERT

This term is applied to the last course of a dinner—the English term being derived from the French *desservir*—to clear the table.

Dessert, as we understand it now, signifies anything but the clearance of the table (except in so far as savouries are concerned), being more correctly a service of fruits, biscuits, cakes, preserves, and other sweetmeats accompanying the service. Modern customs have decided that sometimes the dessert, with flowers, shall occupy the centre of the dining or banquet table forming a kind of ornamentation that cannot be excelled. As soon as the dinner is at an end, and all the dishes have been removed (a salt cellar is left for those guests who like their walnuts with salt), a few small glasses containing crystallized fruits and other tasty morsels are added to the fine dishes already in position (or just placed to enhance the floral decoration).

Each guest is given a dessert plate, fruit knife, fork and spoon, wine glasses to suit wines, and fingerbowls.

CAFÉ

The last item of a menu is coffee. It is usually served black (*café noir*), but there are some people who cannot drink black coffee; then, of course, it is served with cream or hot milk. Coffee is served in very small cups.

Liqueurs such as Cognac, Liqueur Brandy, Cointreau, Kümmel, Drambuie, Crème de Menthe, or Benedictine are served in large brandy glasses, or in very small goblet-shaped glasses.

AFTER-LUNCH COFFEE

This is served either at the table or in the living-room. (See below.)

AFTER-DINNER COFFEE

This is always served in the living-room at formal dinners. It is correct to let the guests help themselves, or it may be served, the server holding the tray in one hand and pouring the coffee with the other.

The after-dinner coffee cups (each standing in its own saucer, all handles to the right, with the spoons lying in each saucer parallel to the cup handle) are placed on a silver or other tray, with sugar, cream or hot milk and coffee-pot—or cups on one tray with sugar and cream and coffee pot on another.

With one maid or no help, coffee is sometimes served at the table while others prefer to serve it in the living-room.

> *Coffee, which makes the politician wise,*
> *And see thro' all things with his half-shut eyes.*
>   POPE, *The Rape of the Lock*

Meal Planning

In order to know whether a human being is young or old, offer it food of different kinds at short intervals. If young, it will eat anything at any hour of the day or night. If old, it observes stated periods.

O. W. HOLMES,
The Professor at the Breakfast Table

F

*If medicine be marked among those Arts which
dignify their professions . . . Cookery may lay claim
to an equal, if not superior distinction; to prevent disease, is surely a more advantageous Art to
Mankind than to cure them.*

OWEN MEREDITH,
The Art and Science of Cookery

A carefully planned menu is the first step to ensure a successful meal.
The usual dietetic principles must be observed, and emphasis must
be placed on the following points:

Choose the type of food which is most suitable for the age, sex and
occupation of those to be served.

Watch the season and climate: always serve heavier foods in cold
weather and the cool, fresh foods in hot weather. Use foods at their
best season both for availability and cost. Always plan to serve the
traditional foods at festive seasons, and take care to choose colours
which vary, and do not repeat either flavour or garnishes.

The number to be served influences both the preparation of food
and the cost.

Remember that appetites vary, so try to provide enough, but not
too much.

The amount to be spent on the meal must be kept within limits.

Take into consideration the equipment, which includes the china,
glass, cutlery, linen and silver.

Consider the type of kitchen, the help available (try to avoid last
minute preparation), and the service if help is limited.

See that the appearance of the food is attractive and that there is
colour and harmony in the choice of foods.

Be sure that there is no dominating food in the menu, and never
serve two foods which are identically prepared.

Never serve the same coloured food in succeeding courses—great
care should be taken to have a blended variety in colours.

Avoid serving two pronounced flavours or two dishes which taste
the same. Try to have definite contrasts of both texture and flavour
in each course.

Choose the recipes carefully; be familiar with them and allow time
for preparation and cooking.

Since what we love has always found
Expression in enduring sound,
Music and verse should be competing
To match the transient joy of eating.
LOUIS UNTERMEYER

BREAKFAST

Before breakfast, a man feels but queasily.
And a sinking at the lower abdomen
Begins the day with indifferent omen.
ROBERT BROWNING,
Flight of the Duchess

There is not the slightest doubt that the charm of a well-set table can do much to overcome the early-morning grumps of some people. Choose the simplest linen cloth, white or coloured, or table mats which harmonize with the china. Use coloured pottery for the marmalade or honey pots, or pastel-coloured or plain crystal in gay colours. Low, simple floral decoration, or perhaps a bowl of fruit as centre piece.

Many families have a breakfast nook or corner in their kitchen. A gaily spotted or checked cloth which can be obtained in a range of colourings has been found ideal for breakfast setting. Wooden or coloured pepper and salt cellars may be used. Ring the changes for the small glasses used for orange juice or cereal bowls. Use reds, blues with white, or harmonizing linen; and with yellow checked or spotted cloths, or plain yellow mats on a scrubbed table, use amber. If green is the chosen colour scheme, see that the greens match or harmonize.

The silver used is dependent upon the food that is to be served. Teaspoons for fruit, dessertspoons for cereals, breakfast knife and fork, or fish knife and fork.

When serving breakfast for four persons, the table is usually sufficiently large for the hostess to preside at one end of it; and the coffee pot or teapot, milk and cream jug, sugar basin, cups and saucers are placed before her, either on a silver tray or on one of the gay coloured trays which are available to-day.

Orange juice is served well chilled, and the cut half-grapefruit in a small glass bowl (this is sometimes set in a plate filled with cracked ice).

It is wise to provide an ash-tray either on the table or at some convenient place, as nothing is so unpleasant as ash in the tea or coffee cups and saucers.

If preferred, the individual places are set at the table, and the tea, coffee cups and a hot-plate to keep food, serving dishes and plates warm, are set on a side-table.

When boiled eggs are served, a small-sized plate, plus egg spoon, must be available. Usually the eggs are brought into the room in their egg cups. Small silver egg cups fixed into a carrying stand, or wooden egg-cup sets, are favourites because they are labour-saving.

When fresh fruit is served, a fruit knife should be laid at the side of the fruit plate. Stewed fruit is served in an individual glass bowl, and the family and guests help themselves.

> *When work seems*
> *Rather dull to me*
> *And life is not so*
> *Sweet,*
> *One thing at least can*
> *Bring me joy—*
> *I simply love*
> *To eat!*
>
> REBECCA MCCANN

For a Breakfast Tray in Bed

Special trays are quite inexpensive. If one is not available, use a light convenient-sized tray. Always be sure to see that the tray cover is free from wrinkles and that it is dainty. Very pretty sets which include coffee pot, teapot, milk jug, sugar bowl, covered dish, cereal plate, breakfast plate, bread and butter plate with matching egg cups, and pepper and salt, are now available.

Setting the Table for Breakfast

The arrangement of the tea or coffee pots, milk, cream, sugar, also breakfast cups and saucers is dependent upon the size of the table. Sometimes these are placed on a tray in front of the hostess, at other times they are set on a side-table where the family or guests may then help themselves. But in many families, a 'family' method of table appointments can be—a teapot or an electric coffee pot and toaster, a sugar bowl, cream jug, cups and saucers and teaspoons, a service plate of breakfast size at each place, a grapefruit all cut ready for eating, or an apple, pear or slice of melon, or if preferred, a glass of orange juice. To follow fruit—a cereal dish; and when this is removed, a hot service plate for bacon, tomato, eggs, etc.

When breakfast is a self-service meal, as it is with so many families, the fruit may be placed on the table before anyone comes in to breakfast. Set the breakfast table as follows:

The teapot and hot-water jug, or coffee pot and hot-milk jug are just placed on heat-proof mats, and the breakfast cups and saucers put in a convenient position. The salt and pepper may be set either at the corners or farther in from the corner nearer the centre piece. Marmalade, honey, jam and butter dishes are all placed as desired.

A bread-and-butter plate and small knife are placed for each person. When a cereal is to be served, a dessert spoon must be set for this, also a cereal bowl or deep plate. When fish is to be served, a fish knife and fork must be set. When bacon and egg, cold ham or other meat dish, tomatoes, mushrooms, etc., are to be served, a small knife and fork or large knife and fork, according to choice, must be set.

You may serve: Fruit juice, fresh fruit, or a cereal—followed by a main dish, then toast with marmalade, honey or jam, and tea or coffee.

See EGG DISHES, p. 94.

See GRAPEFRUIT, p. 137.

> *A meagre unsubstantial breakfast causes a*
> *sinking sensation of the stomach and bowels.*
>
> P. H. CHAVASSE,
> *Advice to a wife*

These recipes will help you to vary the breakfast menu.

Bacon and Kidneys

Rashers of bacon	1 *saltspoonful salt*
Kidneys	½ *saltspoonful pepper*
1 *tbsp. flour*	*Butter or margarine and bacon fat*

Remove with scissors the rind of bacon and halve rashers. Trim away the fat. Skin and cut each kidney into slices the round way. Mix the flour, salt and pepper, dip each slice into this mixture. Melt the butter and bacon fat. Add the bacon rashers.

Fry gently over a low heat, turn them repeatedly. When done enough, put on hot dish. Fry the sliced kidney in the same fat. Turn every minute for four minutes, when they will be done and can be put with the bacon. Sprinkle a little flour into fat, mix well, add a spoonful or two of water. Stir till boiling, pour over serving dish.

Baked Fish in Scallop Shells

1 *lb. cooked cold fish*	1 *saltspoonful salt*
6 *oz. white breadcrumbs*	*Finely minced parsley*
1 *saltspoonful spiced pepper*	*Raspings*
Butter	

Butter the scallops. Lay flaked fish and crumbs in a medium-sized baking dish, then scatter a fine layer of minced parsley over them. Moisten thoroughly with sauce. Strew a layer of crust raspings over the surface. Dot with butter. Place in a moderate oven, 350° F., and heat through. This takes about 20 minutes.

For Sauce

1 *onion*	*Milk and water*
1 *tsp. salt*	1 *tsp. anchovy sauce*
6 *black peppercorns*	½ *oz. butter* } *to each break-*
The fish bones and skin	½ *oz. flour* } *fast cupful stock*

Put skin and bones into saucepan with onion, salt and peppercorns. Cover with milk and water. Add anchovy essence, set to boil, then simmer for 15 minutes. Strain, slightly thicken with blended flour and butter. Add any liquid left over from fish.

Baked Sole

1 *large or 2 medium-sized soles*	*Finely chopped parsley*
A little butter or margarine	*The juice of a lemon*

Skin and leave the fish whole. Butter a flat *Gratin* dish, sprinkle this over with finely chopped parsley. Lay the sole upon it and moisten the upper side of the fish with a little melted butter. Place in a moderate oven, 350° F. After eight minutes carefully turn the sole and baste with butter. Return to oven and cook for six further minutes, when the fish should be done. Lift the fish with a slice and put it upon a hot dish prepared for it. To the butter in the *Gratin* dish add a tablespoonful of minced parsley and the juice of a lemon; pour this over the dished sole and serve immediately. (This dish must be served very hot to prevent greasiness.)

Cod in Custard Sauce

1¼ *lb. cold boiled cod*	*A grating of nutmeg*
Salt and pepper to season	*2 yolks of eggs*
	½ *pt. milk and fish stock*

Put the flaked fish into a saucepan, add seasonings and add sufficient milk or fish stock to just cover. Place in a double saucepan and heat up slowly. Make a custard with the yolks of eggs and milk or stock. When fish is warmed, drain off milk. Arrange on dish and smother with custard.

Eggs to boil

Put the eggs into a small saucepan—

(1) In cold water and bring to the boil.

(2) Place in boiling water and simmer for 3–5 minutes.

(3) To hard boil—boil for at least 15 minutes.

Finnan Haddock

2 *haddocks—if small*	1 *tbsp. cornflour*
Eggs	*Black pepper*
1 *pt. milk*	*Finely chopped parsley*

Soak and simmer the haddocks in milk (until the meat can be easily removed from bone). Remove from the bone, season with black pepper, place on dish. Thicken the liquid with blended cornflour. Serve garnished with poached eggs and parsley.

Broiled Mackerel

Allow one mackerel per head   *1 tbsp. of horseradish cream*
if small, otherwise one large   *1 yolk of raw egg*
one between 2 persons   *1 doz. mushrooms*
½ pt. melted butter sauce   *Pinch of pepper and salt*

Split open the mackerel and broil under the grill. Grill or fry
the mushrooms. Add the horseradish to melted butter sauce.
Remove from heat and stir in the yolk of egg. Add pepper and
salt to season, and serve.

Fresh Haddock

1 haddock   *Raspings*
Veal stuffing (use half the   *Chopped parsley*
recipe on p. 204)   *Butter*

The fish can be stuffed the previous day and kept in a cold
place all night. When required for breakfast, strew a thin layer
of raspings over a fireproof dish sufficiently large to hold it.
Sprinkle a layer of chopped parsley over the dish and lay the
fish upon it. Pour over a little melted butter. Place in a moderate oven, 350° F., for 30 minutes, try with skewer to see if
tender, and serve.

Fresh Herrings au Gratin

4 herrings (trimmed and cleaned)   *Chopped parsley*
Butter   *Pepper and salt*
Raspings or oatmeal

Butter a flat *Gratin* dish, sprinkle a layer of chopped parsley
over its surface, lay the herrings upon this, season well with
pepper and salt and cover with raspings or oatmeal, pour on a
little melted butter. Place under grill, watch them and baste well.
Serve the dish and cover on a folded napkin, or garnish with a
little finely chopped parsley.

Fried Plaice

A plaice   *Breadcrumbs*
1 beaten egg   *Sprigs of parsley*

Skin and trim a plaice, dividing it into fillets 2½ inches long and 1½ inches wide. Egg and crumb them and fry them one by one in very hot fat, drain on blotting paper and set them dry and crisp upon a doily. Garnish with slices of lemon and small sprigs of parsley.

Fried Sprats

Sprats

Seasoned flour

Lemon

Brown bread and butter

Toss the prepared sprats in seasoned flour and flour well, fry at a gallop in boiling fat. Drain well. Sprinkle with salt, garnish with lemon quarters and serve with brown bread and lemon quarters.

Kedgeree

½ lb. salmon or tinned salmon   2 oz. butter or margarine

Cooked boiled rice (½ lb.)   Salt, pepper, cayenne

2 well-beaten eggs

Remove skin and bone from fish, and flake. Mix the fish and rice together, using a fork. Melt butter, add fish mixture and seasoning. Stir in the well-beaten eggs and serve very hot (on a silver dish if possible).

Salmon Cakes

1 pound tin salmon

½ bkcp. mashed potato
and breadcrumbs

2 beaten eggs

½ tsp. salt

⅛ tsp. paprika

Butter or margarine

Finely chopped parsley

Mix all ingredients well together and form into cakes. Sauté in butter until brown.

Kippers

Kippers   Butter   Pepper

Trim off the head and tail. Plunge the kippers into boiling water, then drain and place on grill tray with a knob of butter on each. Cook quickly under a hot grill, and just before serving add a shake of pepper.

Sausages and Tomatoes

Sausages Dripping Tomatoes

Melt a little dripping in a frying pan. Prick sausages, add to the dripping. Cook over low heat until brown (about 20 minutes). Serve with grilled tomatoes.

Trout Fried

Trout   Butter

Clean the trout (do not split), and sprinkle them with salt and fry in butter in a sauté pan. Serve very hot.

Whitings Fried

Whitings   Butter

Breadcrumbs   Chopped parsley

Breadcrumb the whiting and fry in the hot fat. Dish them on fish paper. Garnish with parsley. Serve a little melted butter with them in a hot sauce-boat.

Marmalade

6 *Seville oranges*, 1 *sweet orange* 6 *pts. water*

1 *lemon*   6 *lb. sugar*

Slice the fruit thinly, place pips in cupful of water to soak. Place fruit in water and allow to stand for 24 hours. Then boil until fruit is tender. Add strained pip water with sugar, boil until the marmalade thickens. Test for setting, pour into heated jars and cover when cool. For a slightly sharper flavour add the juice of 1 lemon.

LUNCHEON

The custom of saying Grace at meals had, probably, its origin in the early times of the world, and the hunter-state of man, when dinners were precarious things, and a fine meal was something more than a common blessing.

CHARLES LAMB

Luncheon is usually an informal meal—but sometimes it is given for some special guest. Then it may assume more formality. For family luncheons, the number of courses served varies greatly according to the likes and dislikes of the family, economic conditions, and also whether the family are all at home or out at work and just home for an evening meal.

When setting the luncheon table the same conditions are observed as for an informal dinner. Candles are not used unless the room is particularly dark. Use dainty mats, or cloth with matching napkins which can be folded into neat, but not fancy shapes.

Should the luncheon be a formal one it resembles the formal dinner, though generally the menu is somewhat simpler. It is therefore not necessary to describe it. Naturally the floral decorations will be more elaborate than for an informal luncheon, but the table must not be over-decorated. The silver shining on a well-cared-for polished table-top, if mats are used, makes an excellent background for beautiful china and appointments. The service for luncheon is the same as for dinner. Four courses are served for formal luncheons. These could include:

FRUIT COCKTAIL or MELON or SHELLFISH COCKTAIL

HOT or COLD SOUP according to season.

A MAIN COURSE—which can be meat, fish, cheese or an egg dish, with a salad and vegetables.

AN ICE or some specially chosen sweet

CHEESE, if desired

DESSERT

COFFEE.

Coffee cups and saucers are set on a tray with cream and sugar, ready to serve when required.

The selection of glasses is according to beverages chosen. If the hostess knows any special preferences of her guests for flowers or food, she would be wise to make notes of their likes and dislikes.

MENU I

ŒUFS DURS—SAUCE TOMATE

ESCALOPES AU NATUREL

PETITS POIS AU NATUREL: POMMES DE TERRE SAUTÉS

SOUFFLÉ AU CARAMEL

Œufs durs—Sauce Tomate (*See p.* 95)

Escalopes au Naturel (*Veal escalopes*)
Flour the veal *escalopes* and put them into a frying-pan containing very hot butter. Fry over a brisk heat, till they become golden brown. Then turn and brown on the other side. If they are thin they will easily cook in 5 to 8 minutes. Sprinkle with salt and remove from pan. Rinse pan with a little hot water to make gravy and pour it on *escalopes* before serving.

Petits Pois (*Green peas*)

2 *lb. green peas* (*shelled*)	1–2 *oz. butter*
¼ *lb. spring onions*	*A little sugar*
Pinch of salt	*A sprig of mint*

2 lb. peas in the pod should serve 2 people. Shell them and place them in a pan, butter peas and peeled onions and moisten with a glass of cold water. Add salt, sugar and mint. Cover pan, boil slowly for about ½ hour. Toss in butter.

Pommes de terres sautées (*Sauté potatoes*)
Cook the potatoes in their jackets. When cooled peel and slice them. Put some butter or lard in a frying pan, and when the fat has melted and smokes, throw in the sliced potatoes. If the fat is not too plentiful, the potatoes may stick to the pan. Turn over from time to time with a wooden spoon, or toss them up

and catch them in the pan. When the potatoes are golden brown serve them, garnished with chopped parsley.

Soufflé au Caramel (*Caramel Soufflé*)

3 *whites of eggs*	2 *oz. caster sugar*
3 *yolks of eggs*	1 *pt. cream*

Caramel

Whip the whites of eggs until very stiff. Add the caster sugar and mix very lightly. Have ready a mould with plenty of caramel, put the mixture into the mould, and steam for an hour. Leave it in the pan in which it has been steamed, until it is nearly cold. Then turn it out, and make a good sauce with the yolks of eggs and cream. Pour round the soufflé.

MENU II

TARTE AU FROMAGE
HOMARD À LA NEWBURG
CÔTES PANÉES AU RAIFORT
POMMES DE TERRE À LA VAPEUR
TOPINAMBOURS FRITS
SOUFFLÉ À LA BÉCHAMEL

Tarte au fromage (*Cheese tart*)

1 *pt. milk*	¼ *lb. grated gruyère cheese*
¼ *pt. thick cream*	3 *eggs*

Salt and pepper

Line a buttered tart tin with short crust pastry ¼ inch thick, fill it three-quarters full with a cream made of the above ingredients. Bake well in a hot oven at 400° F. Serve hot.

For the Short Crust Pastry

4 *oz. butter or margarine*	*Pinch of salt*
6 *oz. flour*	*A little milk*
Squeeze of lemon	*Yolk of egg, if desired*

Cut butter into sifted flour and salt. Work with fingers until crumbly. Add egg yolk, and sufficient liquid to make a stiff dough.

Homard à la Newburg (*Lobster Newburg*)

1 *lobster (boiled)*	1 *oz. flour*
3 *oz. butter*	¼ *pt. cream*
2 *tbsp. whisky*	*Rice*
Clear stock	*Curry powder*
	Cayenne

Cut the lobster meat into neat chunks. Reserve the coral. Fry the lobster in melted butter until the shell is red. Moisten with clear stock. Add a little curry powder and cayenne. Mix the coral with flour and butter and moisten the paste with a little luke-warm stock, pour this over the lobster. Cook 10 minutes, then add 2 oz. whisky previously set on fire. Boil 1 minute. Add ¼ pt. of cream. Re-heat (without boiling). Serve with a border of well-dried rice, cooked Creole way.

Creole Rice

Wash and drain a cupful of rice. Boil 2 quarts water, add a teaspoonful salt, stir the rice slowly into the water so as not to disturb the boiling, and cook until tender—about 25 minutes. Turn into a strainer and drain, pour 2 cupfuls of cold water over. Return to pan, add sauce made as follows:
Melt 2 tablespoonsful butter over a low heat, add 1 table-spoonful chopped onions, 1½ cups tomatoes, ½ a green pepper sliced, 6 olives shredded. Cook till thick, season with ¼ tea-spoonful salt, a few grains cayenne pepper, a teaspoonful brown sugar, and thicken with 1 tablespoonful cornflour blended with 1 tablespoonful water.

Côtes panées au Raifort (*Chops with horseradish*)

Dip the lamb chops into melted butter. Breadcrumb them well, pressing down the breadcrumbs with the finger tips. Grill with brisk heat, sprinkle with salt and pepper. Serve with grated horseradish.

Pommes de terre à la vapeur (*Steamed potatoes*)

Peel the potatoes, sprinkle with salt and pepper, and steam them, and then pass them through a ricer.

Topinambours frits (*Fried artichokes*)

Peel the artichokes and slice thinly, and fry in deep boiling fat. Sprinkle with salt.

Soufflé à la Vanille (*Vanilla soufflé*)

2 oz. flour	Just on a pint of milk
4 eggs	1½ oz. butter
3½ oz. sugar flavoured with vanilla	Pinch of salt

Make a Béchamel sauce with butter, flour and milk. Add salt and sugar. Set aside until it is cooled a little. Mix in the yolks. Beat the whites to a snow and add this to the sauce. Turn into a well-buttered soufflé case. Bake in a moderate oven, 350° F., till nicely browned. Serve at once.

MENU III
MOULES MARINIÈRE
JAMBON RECHAUFFÉ
POMME FONDANTE
SALADE DE LAITUE
CROÛTE À LA PARMESAN

Moules Marinière (*Mussels*)

Put into a saucepan a glass of white wine, an onion cut small, some slices of carrot and a little fennel or parsley. Cook for ½ hour. Strain the decoction—and return to pan and add 3½ pints mussels previously scraped and washed. Cover the pan and boil for 5 minutes. The shells open and give out liquor. Serve in a deep dish, adding 2 oz. butter to sauce made from the liquid in which the mussels were cooked.

Jambon réchauffé (*Grilled cold boiled ham*)

Take thin slices of cold boiled ham and place under a hot grill —when lightly browned serve garnished with a poached egg.

Pomme fondante (*Creamed potatoes*)

3½ cups mashed potatoes	½ cup heavy cream
¾ cup coarse, stale breadcrumbs	

Put potatoes in buttered baking dish. Pour cream over them, and sprinkle crumbs on top. Bake at 425° F. until crumbs are brown.

Salade de laitue (*Lettuce salad*). *See p.* 99

Croûte à la Parmesan (*Parmesan and asparagus on toast*)

Take some cooked asparagus tips, prepare some buttered toast; put a layer of grated cheese, gruyère and parmesan in equal quantities mixed with a little butter, then a layer of asparagus tips seasoned with salt and pepper. Finish top with a layer of grated cheese and brown under the grill.

MENU IV

POTAGE DE CÉLERI

COQUILLES ST JACQUES

LEVRAUT AU VIN BLANC

PURÉE DE POMMES DE TERRE

MONT BLANC AUX MARRONS

Potage de Céleri (*Celery soup*)

2½ pt. clear soup	1 small head of celery
¾ oz. butter	1 gill cream

Brown the butter in the frying pan. Throw in the celery, cut into small cubes, and fry to a golden brown, put in the pan and add the soup. Cover and boil 20 minutes, pass through a sieve, then add cream.

Coquilles St Jacques (*Scallops*)

Open the shells, remove the scallops, being careful to cut out the black glands. Cook in white wine, and put them back into the lower half of the shell and season. Garnish with grated parmesan, chopped chive or mushrooms, and top with sauce—Tomato, Béarnaise, or Hollandaise sauce—and breadcrumbs, and brown under the grill.

Levraut au vin blanc (*Leveret in white wine*)

1 young hare	2 tbsp. butter
Salt and pepper	¼ tsp. powdered thyme
Pinch nutmeg	1 tsp. chopped parsley
2 tsp. chopped onion	¼ pt. dry white wine
	¼ pt. stock or water

Joint the dressed and cleaned hare into serving pieces. Melt the butter in a large frying pan and brown the pieces well on both sides—this will take about 20 minutes. Add seasonings, wine, stock, water, cover and simmer 25 minutes. Serve in sauce.

Purée de pommes de terre (*Potato purée*)

3 *lb. potatoes*	8 *oz. milk*
3 *oz. butter*	2 *oz. thick cream*
4 *oz. grated cheese*	*Salt and pepper*

Peel the potatoes and cut them into quarters, put them into a saucepan and barely cover with salted water. Cover the pan and boil until the potatoes break easily when tested with a fork. Drain carefully and mash, and bring the purée to a consistency of thick cream by adding hot milk little by little, and stirring with a whisk. Reheat and add cream and cheese. Add pepper and salt to season.

Mont Blanc aux Marrons (*Chestnut purée with cream*)

2 *lb. chestnuts*	1 *oz. butter*
3 *oz. sugar*	$1\frac{1}{8}$ *pt. milk*
Vanilla	*Chantilly cream*
	1 *egg yolk*

Boil the chestnuts 10 minutes in salted water. Set aside to cool a little. Remove both skins, cover the chestnuts with milk, add the vanilla and sugar, and cook until done. Pound the chestnuts in a mortar with a pestle. Add hot milk to obtain a good consistency. Then add the butter and lastly the egg yolk. Shape in the form of a mound and set aside to cool. Serve cold with chantilly cream (whipped cream flavoured with vanilla and slightly sweetened with sugar).

MENU V

SAUMON FUMÉ

DUCKLING À LA PRESSE

SALADE DE LAITUE À L'ORANGE

CHARLOTTE RUSSE

Saumon fumé (*Smoked salmon*). *See p.* 133

Duckling à la presse

Take a roast duckling and carve into neat slices; keep these hot. Chop up the carcass and put it into a press. Extract all the juices. Add to these a glass each of red wine and brandy—together with the finely minced liver. Pour this liquid over the fillets and serve very hot, but do not boil.

Salade de laitue à l'orange

Make a salad (see p. 99). Add sliced oranges.

Charlotte Russe

Lemon jelly	*Cherries and angelica*
¼ lb. sponge fingers	*¼ oz. gelatine*
⅛ pt. water	*¼ pt. each cream and custard*
2 tbsp. sherry	*1 tsp. vanilla essence*

1 or 2 tbsp. sugar

Pour a little jelly into the bottom of a soufflé tin. Decorate with cherries and angelica. Add a thin layer of jelly and set. Line the tin with sponge fingers, pressing them well together. Dissolve the gelatine in cold water. Half whip cream and add custard, lightly fold in other ingredients. Add the gelatine last. When on point of setting pour carefully into prepared mould set. Trim edges of sponge fingers level with cream. Turn out, and arrange chopped jelly round. (In hot weather allow a good measure of gelatine.)

MENU VI

SOUPE AUX TOMATES
OMELETTE AU JAMBON
POULET AU CRÈME
SALADE DE POMMES DE TERRE
TARTE LYONNAISE

Soupe aux Tomates (*Tomato soup*)

This soup may be served hot, or in very hot weather it may be served iced.

2 lb. fresh tomatoes	*2 oz. butter*
3 oz. fine semolina	*3½ pt. cold water*
	or
3½ oz. concentrated tomato purée	*1 gill thick cream*

Salt

Mash the tomatoes and cook them in butter. Add water and pinch of salt, simmer 20 minutes in covered pan. Pass through a sieve—boil again, sprinkle in the semolina and stir, boil another ¼ hour. Add cream and serve.

Omelette au jambon (*Ham omelette*)

¼ *lb. boiled ham*	1 *tbsp. butter*
6 *eggs*	1 *tsp. water*
⅛ *tsp. white pepper*	½ *tsp. salt*

Remove the fat from the ham. Dice and fry it in butter. Add to well-beaten eggs. Melt the butter in a light frying pan and when it is sizzling hot, but not brown, pour in the eggs—and as the egg mixture begins to set on the bottom, prick it with a fork, and raise a little; this allows the uncooked egg to seep through; continue to prick and raise until almost all the liquid has disappeared. Remove from heat and loosen the edges of half the omelette from the pan with a palette knife, fold one half over the other. Turn upside down on a heated platter. In a French omelette the centre should always be 'runny'.

Poulet au Crème (*Cold sauté chicken*)

Carve the chicken in the ordinary way—that is, divide it into 2 wings, 2 legs, one piece of breast. Season these and *sauté* them in butter in a flat saucepan with the lid on; when the pieces are well coloured on one side, turn them on the other side. Finish cooking slowly; when ready, remove the pieces and put aside the butter in which they have cooked. Put in the saucepan a glass of dry white wine, stirring well to melt the essential juices left on the bottom and the sides of the pan. Cook a few minutes and then add two tablespoonsful of cream and one of rich white sauce. Put the pieces of chicken in another saucepan, squeeze the sauce over them through muslin, and let the whole thing cook over a slow heat for a few minutes only—but do not boil. Arrange the pieces in a deep glass dish, add a few peas, French beans and young carrots, which have been previously sliced, boiled and seasoned. Pour sauce and serve cold. Put into refrigerator until wanted for use.

Salade de pommes de terre (*Potato salad*)

For this salad use the yellow waxy kind of potato. Boil them in their skins; when cooked peel and slice them. Dress while still hot with plenty of vinegar and oil, add a few chopped spring onions and season with pepper and salt.

Tarte Lyonnaise

Line a flan tin with plain pastry ¼ inch thick. Fill with the following mixture:

3½ oz. breadcrumbs	1 tbsp. Kirsch
½ pt. milk	3 chopped bitter almonds
3 oz. sugar	4 egg yolks
2 egg whites (stiff-beaten)	

Moisten the breadcrumbs with milk, add sugar, Kirsch and almonds. Mix in the yolks, then fold in the whites. Bake for ½ hour in a hot oven, 400° F.

LIGHT LUNCHEONS

Even the headless oyster seems to profit from experience
DARWIN

In planning light meals, always choose as the final course the dish demanding the longest time to cook—so that this can be cooking while the meal is being eaten—and plan meals that will use one kind of oven heat. Always start the dishes which require the longest cooking-time first. Set the table and get out serving dishes. Prepare the salad or cold course and place in the refrigerator to chill well. (Always use up canned food, when it has been opened.)

Choose a soup, and follow with an egg dish (p. 94), noodle or spaghetti (p. 97) or savoury (p. 97), and a salad (p. 99).

SOUPS

Cabbage soup

1 good-sized cabbage	Salt
4 carrots	1 rasher bacon
2 turnips	Chopped parsley
1 leek	2 heads garlic
1 clove	Salt and pepper to season
2½ pt. water	

Break up the leaves of the cabbage, wash them well, and cut them into pieces about 3 inches long. Clean, scrape or peel the carrots, leeks and turnips, remove root and any discoloured leaves from the leek. Slice into neat pieces. Bring water to boil, add vegetables, the clove and salt (2 teaspoonsful) and simmer for 2 to 3 hours.

About half an hour before serving add bacon, parsley, garlic, all chopped fine. Re-season with salt and pepper. Stir occasionally and serve accompanied by a bowl of grated cheese.

Cream Soup

This white sauce makes a very good base for cream soup.

2 tbsp. butter	1½ pt. milk
2 tbsp. flour	½ tsp. salt

Melt the butter, add flour and blend well. Add milk and salt, cook until slightly thick, stirring constantly.

FOR VARIATIONS (*appx. 6 servings*):

Cream of Celery. 2 bkcp. chopped celery. 1 diced onion cooked in just sufficient water to cover. Cook quickly until tender. Add pepper and salt to season. Garnish with a little chopped celery leaf.

Cream of Carrot Soup. Scrape 1 lb. carrots. Peel 1 onion, season with pepper and salt. Put into a saucepan with ½ pt. water. Cook till tender and pass through sieve. Add to sauce.

Cream of Onion. Fry 3 large onions (sliced) in 2 tbsp. melted butter until light brown. Add ½ pt. milk. Cook in a double saucepan for 30 minutes and add to the white sauce.

Cream of Potato Soup. Add 2 bkcp. cooked potato, and 1 tbsp. of finely chopped parsley to sauce. Season with pepper and salt just before serving. (If desired add ½ pt. cream or evaporated milk just before serving.) Garnish with chopped chives.

Cream of Mushroom Soup. 2 bkcp. chopped mushrooms. Cook quickly till tender in ½ pt. milk. Add pepper and salt to season. Pass through sieve and add to sauce.

Barley Soup

2 *tbsp. barley*	1 *piece turnip*
1 *qt. bacon-bone stock*	3 *potatoes*
2 *carrots*	*Salt, pepper to season*
1 *parsnip*	1½ *pt. milk*
1 *piece celery*	

Rinse the barley in cold water, cook in stock until half done, prepare the vegetables and cut them into even-sized cubes. Add to the barley and stock. Cook until tender. Add milk, season and serve immediately.

Vegetable Soup

½ *head cauliflower cut*	*Salt and pepper to season*
into small pieces	1 *tbsp. butter or margarine*
1 *bkcp. shelled peas*	2 *tbsp. flour*
4 *small sliced carrots*	1 *egg yolk*
2½ *pt. water or stock*	3 *tbsp. cream or evaporated milk*

Cook the vegetables until tender in water or stock. Roll the butter and flour together; add slowly to the soup. Simmer for about 10 minutes, stirring frequently. Beat the egg yolks and cream together in a soup tureen, stirring. Pour in the hot soup. Add seasoning, sprinkle with finely chopped parsley and serve. Accompany by a bowl of grated cheese.

Celery Tomato Soup

1 *small onion*	½ *cup finely chopped celery*
2 *tbsp. margarine*	1 *tbsp. lemon juice*
1 *10-oz. size tin condensed*	1 *tsp. sugar*
tomato soup	¼ *tsp. salt*
½ *pt. cold water*	⅛ *tsp. pepper*
1 *tsp. minced parsley*	

Simmer all together for about 5 minutes. The celery remains crisp.

Split Pea Soup

½ cupful dried split peas	2 tbsp. melted butter (or margarine)
2 rashers bacon, diced	Pepper and salt to season
2 qt. water	¼ pt. cream, or evaporated milk
1 medium-sized onion	1 tsp. finely chopped mint or parsley
1 tbsp. flour	

Soak the peas in the water overnight. Add the diced onion, bacon, and cook until the peas are tender. Pass through a sieve and bring to the boil. Blend the flour with the melted margarine. Add to soup. Season with salt and pepper. Add cream just before serving. Serve garnished with mint or parsley.

Egg Dishes

The French menu terms are given for the egg dishes because as well as being good light luncheons they are sometimes used as a first course in formal luncheons. They make good light luncheons or main dishes. For emergency meals they are quickly and easily made. They are useful, too, for either breakfasts or high teas.

Most of these recipes are meant for four or five people of average-sized appetites. So should you want to make the dishes for more, you increase the quantities proportionately. A bowl of soup (see pp. 91–94) is a good beginning on a cold day, for a quick meal. Some people prefer to finish their meal with fresh fruit, or cheese and biscuits. Remember, too, to provide a fresh brown loaf, and cream cheese to spread in place of butter—a glass of fruit juice and a cup of coffee helps to make the meal; sometimes for special occasions, a bottle of wine.

Œufs durs (Hard-boiled eggs)

Boil the eggs quickly for 15 minutes, then crack them (this prevents the black rim between the white and the yolk) and place them in cold water. It is best to leave them until they are completely cold before peeling.

Œufs durs Béchamel (Hard-boiled eggs with Béchamel sauce)

Cut into halves, and cover with Béchamel sauce. Serve with a garnishing of finely chopped parsley.

Œufs durs sauce tomate (*Hard-boiled eggs with tomato sauce*)

Cut into halves, and cover with tomato sauce. Serve garnished with triangles of fried bread round the dish and a little watercress, parsley, or finely chopped chives.

Salade d'œufs durs (*Hard-boiled-egg salad*)

Take some hard-boiled eggs (allow 3 for 2 people), cut them in half and remove the yolks. Put on a plate with salt, freshly-ground pepper. Add a dessertspoonful of wine vinegar. Squash the yolks well with a fork, mix well, add 2 dessertspoonsful of olive oil; beat till smooth, then add the diced whites and cut small, two or three spring onions finely chopped.

Œufs durs au gratin (*Hard-boiled eggs au gratin*)

Cut the eggs into halves, remove the yolks without damaging the whites, pound them, add a few chopped mushrooms, a finely chopped shallot and a little chopped parsley. Add a tablespoonful each of tomato sauce and consommé (or milk), season with pepper and salt, add a small piece of butter the size of a walnut and cook together for a few minutes. Arrange the whites on an oven glass or fireproof dish, fill them with the mixture, sprinkle with breadcrumbs, put a small knob of butter on each, and brown in the oven. Serve garnished with sprigs of parsley or watercress.

Œufs durs en salade (*Hard-boiled eggs with salad*)

Cut the required number of hard-boiled eggs into quarters, chop a little chervil and spring onion together, mix well, add half the number of yolks pounded and the usual seasoning of vinegar, oil, salt and pepper. Serve garnished with heart-of-lettuce leaves.

Œufs sur le plat (*Baked eggs*)

Put a small piece of butter in a fireproof dish, break your eggs carefully and season with salt and pepper, place in the oven to set. The yolk should be quite liquid, and the white set but creamy before serving.

Œufs au beurre noir (*Eggs with black butter*)

Melt some butter and add 2 or 3 drops Worcester sauce, break your eggs in, season with salt and pepper and cook quickly.

Œufs au jambon (*Eggs with bacon or ham*)

Remove the rind from 2 or 3 rashers of bacon (or gammon), place them in a fireproof dish with a very small piece of butter; place in hot oven, 400° F., and when nearly cooked, break your eggs over them—return to oven until the eggs are cooked. Serve garnished with chopped parsley.

Œufs pochés (*Poached eggs*)

Fill a large saucepan with salted water, add a little vinegar and bring to the boil. Break your eggs one by one in a saucer and drop them, also one by one, carefully into the water. Cook for few minutes only (as the inside of the egg must be soft). Among alternatives—

Serve on rounds of freshly buttered toast.
Serve on spinach purée.
Serve on mashed potatoes.
Serve with tomato sauce.
Serve on sweet corn.
Serve on finnan haddock.
Serve on slices of cold ham with finely chopped mint.

Œufs en Cocotte (*Eggs cocotte*)

Put a little melted butter in an individual *cocotte* or fireproof dish. Break your eggs over it, one into each *cocotte*. Cook *au bain marie*, seasoning with salt and pepper and adding, just before serving, a little cream or tomato sauce. Serve with a garnish of finely chopped parsley.

Œufs Brouillés (*Scrambled eggs*)

Break your eggs separately and turn into a basin, add salt and pepper to season, beat them well; put a teaspoonful or two of milk into a saucepan, add a knob of butter and, when well heated, add egg. Cook over a low heat, stirring occasionally (see that it does not stick to the side or bottom of the saucepan). Add a spoonful or two of cream just before serving on:—

Rounds of buttered toast.
Spinach purée.
A slice of grilled ham.
Split toast sandwiches.
Bridge rolls.

MACARONI AND SPAGHETTI

Macaroni, spaghetti and noodles all make good light dishes. They should be cooked by throwing them into a pan of boiling water and boiling. When tender they should be drained and rinsed in cold water, under a running tap, and then re-heated and served with sauce or dressing, or in any of the ways given below. Garnish these savoury dishes with chopped parsley, chives and watercress.

Uses for Macaroni

Cold, with raw grated carrot, cheese and celery, garnished with lettuce.

In batter and fried as fritters, with diced cheese and apple added.

In curry sauce, garnished with peas.

With melted butter and sweet pickle.

With tomato purée and parboiled onion, all mixed together and re-heated.

With white sauce and grated cheese, a sprinkle of mustard, pepper and salt.

In a milk pudding.

As garnish in a clear soup.

As a garnish (see Garnishes).

Uses for Spaghetti

Plain, with butter and grated cheese and tomatoes.

With cooked diced celery and grated cheese.

With fried onion and cheese.

With curry sauce and parboiled vegetables.

With parsley sauce, garnished with tomatoes.

With grated beetroot and onion.

Cold, dressed with mayonnaise.

In a milk pudding.

SAVOURIES AND SAVOURY TOASTS

Delectable savouries may be quickly and easily made, and if served in larger portions than for a dinner menu they will make good light luncheon or supper dishes, especially when accompanied by a good green salad.

Remember that hot savouries must be served really hot, and see that the plates, too, are piping hot. Many a good savoury has been ruined by being lukewarm.

Cold savouries should always be served with a garnish.

Savoury toasts may be made by spreading slips or rounds of toast with margarine, or frying bread in fat, and adding any of the following:

A pile of savoury scrambled egg, garnished with chopped olives or anchovy (on small toasts).

Asparagus tips with a dollop of mayonnaise.

A tablespoonful of chutney, a pinch each of curry powder and mustard, a few drops of Worcester sauce, blended together. After spreading on the toast, it should be placed under the grill to brown, and served garnished.

Chopped ham or tinned meats, pounded with a little margarine to soften, seasoned and garnished with paprika and chopped parsley.

Chutney, garnished with grated cheese.

Curried rice, garnished with shrimps.

Fillets of anchovy, garnished with chopped olives.

Flakes of cold or tinned fish and mayonnaise, garnished with chopped walnuts.

Fried apple rings, with chopped pickled walnuts.

Fried slices of beetroot, garnished with cream cheese.

Grilled mushrooms.

Mayonnaise and capers, creamed together.

Prunes, cooked with a little spice in vinegar, stoned and pounded, and a layer of thick cream cheese.

Raw cheese in a slice, sprinkled with pepper, salt and mustard, and placed under the grill to heat through.

Shelled prawns with a little curry sauce, garnished with chopped parsley.

Small cubes of cheese dipped into batter and fried in deep fat.

Small dollops of creamed mushrooms.

Spiced prunes rolled in bacon.

Toasted cheese.

Tomatoes and grated cheese, placed under the grill and garnished with parsley.

Tomatoes, cut into halves and with the centres scooped out and filled with a mixture of tomato pulp and scrambled egg.

Many of these savouries can be adapted as sandwich fillings.

SANDWICHES

Bread should be at least 24 hours old before it is cut for sandwiches. It is easier to spread certain types of sandwich fillings if the butter is slightly warmed and pounded together with them.

Layer sandwiches should be so arranged that the colours vary. Savoury sandwiches should always be garnished with cress or a sprig of parsley before they are served.

Sandwiches may be in the form of rolls and cut into small sections.

Suggestions for sandwich fillings are given below. They may either be spread on bread, or in split toast as larger sandwiches.

Lettuce leaves, shredded spinach, cress or watercress may be used to give an extra layer inside the sandwich.

Rainbow sandwiches are made with a cut loaf and layers of tomato, cream cheese, chutney and watercress or lettuce.

Suggestions for fillings:

Asparagus tips in mayonnaise.

Chopped cooked bacon and tomato.

Chopped hard-boiled egg and a layer of mustard and cress.

Chopped pickled walnuts and cream cheese with a layer of cress.

Chutney.

Cooked sage and onions.

Cooked sausage meat.

Creamed mushrooms.

Creamed sardines.

Curry powder, mixed with onion and fried in margarine, used with cress in split toast sandwiches.

Diced vegetables creamed with mayonnaise.

Grated cheese creamed with Worcester sauce.

Minced ham creamed with a little mayonnaise.

Pilchards and tomato.

Scrambled egg with tomato or chutney added.

Slices of cold cooked meats with a spread of mayonnaise.

Slices of smoked salmon.

Tomato, grated cheese and mayonnaise, creamed together.

Tomato sauce with a layer of grated cheese on top.

SALADS

Salade de Laitue (*Lettuce salad*)

Lettuce with the heart of chopped chervil and spring onions, oil and vinegar dressing (no mustard), a pinch of sugar, and seasoned with salt and pepper.

Salade de Chicorée (*Chicory salad*)

Chicory, sliced or in pieces. Plain dressing, and rub the salad bowl with a little garlic.

Salade de Tomates (*Tomato salad*)

Blanched, peeled tomatoes cut into thin slices, seasoned with plain dressing and garnished with chopped parsley.

FORK LUNCHEONS

A cup of soup may be served—then follow with food which can be easily eaten with a fork only. With this type of luncheon one can invite more people.

The choice of food varies according to the party.

Have a serving table so that guests may help themselves, and do remember to provide a few chairs so that some people may sit down to eat if they prefer it.

See SOUPS, p. 91; HORS D'ŒUVRES, p. 56; BUFFET LUNCHEON, p. 152; EGGS, p. 94; LIGHT LUNCHEONS, p. 91; SPAGHETTI, p. 97; SANDWICHES, p. 99.

THE TEA TABLE

> *Now to the banquet we press*
> *Now for the eggs and the ham,*
> *Now for the mustard and cress,*
> *Now for the strawberry jam,*
> *Now for the tea of our host!*
>
> W. S. GILBERT

The tea table is not usually a permanent feature in a room. In some homes tea is served from a trolley. As a tea table is a focal point where guests seat themselves, care should be taken to see that the chairs are conveniently placed for it.

A kettle with a spirit lamp or an electric kettle are useful. A teapot with a tea caddy, milk jug, sugar bowl and a small glass dish to hold sliced lemon for those who prefer lemon in their tea will be needed.

Teacups and saucers and spoons, also a pile of small tea plates with a small 12-inch napkin folded square under each plate. There can be sandwiches neatly cut, with crusts off and bread of wafer thickness, a round cake, a plate of small cakes and perhaps a covered dish with hot scones. If toast and jam or honey are served, small tea knives will be required, and, where possible, individual tables are useful (a nest of tables all varying in both size and height). In the summer, strawberries and cream or ice-cream are sometimes served.

The linen cloth on the tea table or trolley should be dainty and have matching napkins; it should have a drop around the table top of from 12 to 15 inches. Beautiful china makes a gay, cheerful and cosy table, and tea time becomes again, as in ages past, a favourite time of day, especially where the cakes and buns are home made. Here are some suggestions:

CAKES AND SCONES
Currant Buns

1 *lb. flour*	¼ *lb. currants*
¼ *lb. margarine*	½ *pt. milk*
6 *oz. sugar*	2 *tsp. baking powder*
	1 *tsp. spice*

Mix together the flour, baking powder, sugar and a pinch of salt (and a teaspoonful of spice, if desired). Melt the margarine in ½ pint of warm milk and add it to the dry ingredients. Mix to a dough and add currants. Divide the dough and form into small rounds, and bake on a well-greased tin for about 45 minutes in a hot oven.

Drop Scones

4 *oz. plain flour*	2 *tbsp. sugar*
¼ *tsp. bicarbonate soda*	1 *egg*
½ *tsp. cream of tartar*	*Lard*
Pinch of salt	¼ *pt. milk*

Break egg into a saucer to ensure that it is fresh. Sift flour and other dry ingredients and raising agents, add sugar. Make a well in the centre, drop in egg. Add a little milk and beat well. Gradually draw in the flour and add the remainder of milk. If desired ½ teaspoonful golden syrup can be beaten in. After adding the milk, turn the mixture into a jug. Heat the girdle and rub over with lard. If you have no girdle, use a heavy frying pan. Only pour sufficient batter to leave good space between scones, keeping them well apart to give size of scone desired. Cook over a moderate heat 1–2 minutes. When the top of the scone is covered with small bubbles turn quickly with a spatula or fish slice. Then cook for 1–2 minutes on the other side. It is best not to raise heat above moderate, or the underside is apt to burn before the mixture is heated through. As each batch of scones is cooked, remove from girdle pan and keep warm in a cloth. If syrup is included, the scones must be turned as soon as the top side bubbles, or the underside may burn.

Dundee Cake

½ *lb. fresh butter*	¼ *lb. each currants, sultanas, raisins*
Finely grated rind of lemon	*2–3 oz. candied peel, shredded*
½ *lb. caster sugar*	*1 tbsp. rum and sherry*
3 large eggs	*9 oz. flour*
3 oz. ground almonds	*Pinch of salt*

2 oz. Valencia almonds, bleached and sliced

Sieve flour and salt. Cream butter, add lemon rind and sugar, cream again. Add one unbeaten egg at a time (break each into a cup first to see that it is good). Beat well between each addition of egg. Add one-third flour, mixed almonds and prepared fruits. Add sherry and rum lightly, if desired. Lastly, add remaining flour, mixing lightly. Put the mixture in an 8-inch cake tin lined with ungreased double greaseproof paper. Sprinkle over the sliced almonds. Put into a very moderate oven, 250° F., for about 3 hours.

Ginger Snaps

4 oz. golden syrup	*1 tsp. grated lemon rind*
3½ oz. flour	*1 tsp. ground ginger*
3½ oz. caster sugar	*4 oz. butter*

Tsp. brandy or rum, if desired

Melt the syrup, sugar and butter in a small saucepan. Stir in the flour, sieved with ground ginger and the grated lemon rind and brandy. Drop the mixture in small teaspoonsful on a greased baking sheet and spread thinly in rounds. Bake in a cool oven, 200° F., for 7–10 minutes. When evenly browned and just set, remove from the tin and roll the 'snaps' in turn on the lightly greased handle of a wooden spoon. Store as soon as the snaps are cool in an airtight tin.

Lardy Cake

1 *lb. bread dough*   3–4 *oz. best lard*
2 *oz. sugar*   *A little spice*

Turn the dough on to a floured board and * roll out into an oblong shape. Spread on it half the lard and half the sugar, mixed with spice, covering only two-thirds surface (as for flaky pastry), dredge lightly with flour. Fold up as for flaky pastry and give dough half turn.** Repeat from * to **, using the remainder of the lard and sugar and spice. Repeat after giving only a dredging of spice.

Then roll out again about ½ inch thick, round off the corners with the hands. Score the top with a knife. Put the dough on to a warmed floured tin. Leave for 15 minutes. Brush with a little warm milk. Bake in a hot oven, 400° F. Serve hot with butter.

A Loaf of Bread

1 *lb. flour*   1 *tsp. salt*
½ *oz. yeast*   1 *tsp. caster sugar*
              ½ *pt. tepid water*

Sift the warmed flour and salt into a warm basin, then make a well in the centre. Mix together carefully, then knead for 10 minutes (this helps to distribute the yeast thoroughly). Press lightly into a warmed lightly greased tin, and leave to rise until the dough has doubled its bulk. Brush with a little warm milk (if a glossy surface is liked), and bake in a hot oven, 400° F., for 15 minutes, then reduce heat and leave to cook for about 45–50 minutes.

Madeleines

2 *eggs*   2 *oz. butter*
2 *oz. caster sugar*   *Apricot marmalade*
2 *oz. flour*   *Desiccated coconut*

Beat the eggs, add the sugar, and beat until the mixture is thick and spongy. Fold in the sieved flour lightly with an iron spoon and then add the oiled butter and vanilla essence. Put the mixture into greased and floured madeleine moulds, fill the tins almost level. Bake in a hot oven, 400° F., for about 10 minutes. If desired, when cold, brush with apricot marmalade and roll in desiccated coconut.

Potato Cakes

10 *oz. cooked potatoes*	½ *tsp. salt*
4 *oz. flour*	2–3 *oz. oiled butter*
	A little milk

Use freshly boiled potatoes and while still hot mash them thoroughly. Add flour and salt and a little oiled butter and milk. Turn on to floured board, roll out ¼ inch thick and cut in rounds of 2½-inch diameter. (This makes about a dozen cakes.) Cook on a girdle for 5–6 minutes until browned on both sides, or in the oven and turn to brown the underside.

Queen Cakes

3 *oz. butter or margarine*	2 *small eggs*
The grated rind of half a lemon	2 *oz. currants*
or a little nutmeg	4½ *oz. flour*
3 *oz. caster sugar*	*Almost ½ tsp. baking powder*

Sift flour, salt and baking powder. Cream the butter, add lemon rind and sugar, and cream again. Add the well-beaten eggs slowly, then currants, and mix the flour lightly in. Fill mixture into 18 queen-cake tins. Bake at 400° F., for 15–20 minutes.

Rice Loaf

¼ *lb. butter or margarine*	5 *oz. flour*
Grated rind ½ lemon	*Pinch of salt*
¼ *lb. caster sugar*	2 *oz. ground rice*
3 *eggs*	½ *tsp. baking powder*
	2 *slices thin citron*

Sieve the flour, ground rice and baking powder. Cream butter or margarine thoroughly with grated lemon rind. Add the sugar and cream again. Add the well-beaten eggs by degrees, beating well between each addition. Add the flour, folding it in very lightly, about one-third at a time. Pre-grease an oblong tin, dust out with a little icing sugar and cornflour sieved together. Put in the mixture and lay 2 thin slices of citron on top. Place in a moderate oven, 350° F., and bake for about 1¼ hours.

Oatmeal Scones

¼ lb. oatmeal	1½ tsp. cream of tartar
¼ lb. flour	1 tsp. bicarbonate of soda
2 oz. fat	2 tbsp. golden syrup

Buttermilk or sour milk

Mix together the fine oatmeal and flour and rub in the fat. Add bicarbonate of soda, cream of tartar, a good pinch of salt and golden syrup. Mix well together and moisten with buttermilk or sour milk to make a soft firm dough. Place on a well-floured board and form into small rounds of not more than ½ inch thickness, and bake on a girdle or hot-plate.

Scones

½ lb. flour	¼ tsp. salt
* ½ tsp. bicarbonate soda	1 tsp. caster sugar
1 tsp. cream of tartar	2 oz. butter or margarine

About ¼ pt. milk

Sieve flour, bicarbonate of soda, cream of tartar, salt and caster sugar together. Cut and rub in the butter lightly with the fingertips. Then add milk. Mix to a pliable dough, handling the mixture as little as possible. Turn on to a floured board and roll out ¼ inch thick, prick with a floured fork. Cut into rounds of about 2-inch diameter. Brush with milk just before cooking.

When the scones are to be cooked on a girdle, the dough should be rolled out thinner.

Bake in a hot oven, 400° F., until well risen and the scones begin to brown, then reduce heat and allow them to cook through. Split, butter and serve hot at once, or leave to cool and serve with butter.

*I. If preferred use 2 heaped teaspoonsful of baking powder.
II. When sour milk is used, use half the cream of tartar.

III. When self-raising flour is used, delete the bicarbonate of soda and cream of tartar. Add ½ teaspoonful baking powder.

IV. For wholemeal scones use half wholemeal and half white flour.

V. For sultana scones add about 2 oz. clean stoned sultanas.

Wholemeal Scones (Fatless)

8 oz. wholemeal flour	Milk
2 tsp. baking powder	Pinch of salt

Sift together into a basin the flour, salt and baking powder. Mix to a stiff consistency with milk, or milk and water, and turn on to a well-floured board. Divide into two portions, form each into a round, roll out and cut into four. Bake in a hot oven 400° F.

Sly Cake

½ lb. flaky pastry	4 oz. currants
2 oz. chopped peel	A little spice and sugar

Roll out the flaky pastry into an oblong and cut in half. Sprinkle one half with currants and peel, and scatter over spice and sugar. Put on the second piece of pastry and roll lightly so that the pieces join together. Bake until the pastry is set, in a hot oven, 400° F., about 20 minutes. Dredge with caster sugar and cut in slices.

Sponge Cake

3 oz. flour	3 large eggs
1 small tsp. baking powder	3 oz. caster sugar

Sieve the flour and baking powder. Separate the yolks and whites of eggs, work the egg yolks with the sugar until they become thick and creamy and light in colour. This may take about 20 minutes. Fold in the stiffly whisked whites and flour alternately and lightly, about half at a time. Pour into a prepared tin and bake in a moderate oven, 350° F. (This sponge is good for larger cakes.)

Tea Cakes (Yorkshire)

1 lb. flour	3 tbsp. tepid water
1 tsp. salt	2 oz. lard
1 oz. yeast	½ pt. milk and water
1 tsp. caster sugar	4 oz. currants
	1 oz. candied peel

Sieve the warmed flour into a warm basin with the salt. Make a well in the centre and add the creamed sugar and yeast and 3 tablespoonsful of tepid water. Stir in a little flour to make a thin batter, leave about 20 minutes to rise. Put the lard into a ½-pint measure. Add sufficient boiling water to fill the measure one-third full. Stir until the lard has melted, fill up the measure with cold milk. Add this gradually to the flour, work to a smooth dough, add currants and peel and knead thoroughly. Cut in 6 pieces. Make each into a ball, flatten with a floured rolling pin and prick with a fork. Put the cakes on to a warmed, greased, floured baking sheet. Leave to rise 1 hour, then bake in a hot oven, 400° F., for about 20 minutes. Just before the cakes are quite cooked, brush them with beaten egg and milk.

Walnut Cake

2½ oz. butter	1 tsp. baking powder
3 oz. caster sugar	Pinch of salt
2 smallish eggs	½ tsp. vanilla essence
1 oz. chopped walnuts	Frosting
5 oz. flour	A few walnut halves

Sift together flour, salt, baking powder. Line a 6-inch cake tin with greaseproof paper. Cream the butter, add sugar, and cream again. Add the well-beaten eggs by degrees—beating well after each addition. Add the chopped walnuts and the vanilla essence. Lastly, add flour. Put the mixture into the cake tin. Bake in a moderate oven, 350° F., for about 1¼ hours.

When the cake is cold, cut it in half and sandwich together with American frosting, and coat with frosting and decorate with the halved walnuts. This mixture may, if preferred, be baked in 2 × 6-inch sandwich tins and sandwiched together with lemon- or vanilla-flavoured butter icing.

For Icing

½ lb. granulated sugar	¾ gill water

2 egg whites

Put the sugar and water into a saucepan and brush down any crystals found just above the liquid level, using a pastry brush and warm water. When the sugar is quite dissolved place the lid of the pan on and boil to 240° F. If the sugar is under-boiled the icing will not set, if it is over-boiled it will be too hard. So care should be taken to boil to the correct degree. Put the egg whites into a deep earthenware bowl, and whisk until the whites are stiff. Pour the syrup in a slender line into the bowl, holding the saucepan at a good height to cool the sugar slightly while pouring (if too hot it will curdle the egg whites). Whisk briskly the whole time the syrup is added and continue to whisk until the mixture loses its shiny appearance and begins to look dull like cotton wool. Spread the icing on the cake at once. Sweep it over in quick strokes. Decorate with walnuts.

For Vanilla Butter Filling

1½ tsp. cornflour	1½ oz. butter or margarine
½ teacup milk	3 dsp. icing sugar
Vanilla flavouring	A few walnuts

Blend and boil cornflour with milk. Leave to cool. Add flavouring, cream the butter and sugar and beat in the thickened cornflour until the mixture is creamy. Add walnuts and use for filling.

Wine Biscuits

5 oz. flour	Pinch of salt
¼ lb. butter	3 oz. caster sugar
1 yolk of egg	1 tbsp. sherry

Sieve the flour and salt together and rub the butter into it with the finger-tips. Add sugar, and mix all to a firm dough with the egg yolk and sherry. Turn on to floured board and roll out to ⅛ inch thick. Prick well and cut into shapes. If desired brush some of the biscuits with slightly beaten egg white and sprinkle them with chopped almonds or decorate them with small pieces of cherry. Bake in a fairly hot oven, 425° F., for about 12 minutes, until they are set and a golden brown colour. If desired these biscuits may be iced with Royal icing.

PRESERVES
Strawberry Jam

6 lb. strawberries	6 lb. sugar

Pick over the fruit and remove stems. Boil the sugar in preserving pan until it candies when dropped into cold water. Add fruit and boil quickly for 10 minutes. Pour into heated jars and cover immediately.

Marrow Jam

| 6 lb. vegetable marrow | 2 lemons |
| 6 lb. sugar | 1½ oz. bruised ginger |

Peel marrow and cut into 2-inch cubes. Squeeze the juice from lemons and cut the rind thinly. Place marrow and lemon and rind in a large bowl with the sugar and allow to stand for 24 hours. Place mixture in preserving pan, add ginger and boil 1½ hours. Pour into warm jars, cover when cold.

Apricot Jam

| 2 lb. dried apricots | 6 lb. loaf sugar |
| 6 pt. water | A few almonds |

Cut each apricot in half and place in a large bowl with water and allow to stand for 3 days and 3 nights. Then place all in preserving pan with a few finely chopped almonds. Bring to the boil slowly and allow to boil for 30 minutes, until the jam thickens. Test for setting. Pour into warm jars and cover.

HIGH TEAS find a special place for those who have a light lunch or snack and are hungry before the time of the evening meal. Many tempting dishes may be made for this meal. They may be hot or cold fish, cold fish with salad, finnan-haddock, fish mayonnaise or salads or mousse; cold ham, tinned meats and a green or vegetable salad; egg dishes—savoury toasts, fruit or jelly, and in some homes coffee is substituted for the tea.

One great advantage of it is—to some householders whose family are home early—that they can eat early. The meal is cleared away and dish-washing done and there is a long evening ahead either to go out or settle indoors.

See EGGS, p. 94; SALADS, p. 99; PASTA, p. 97; SAVOURIES, p. 97; SANDWICHES, p. 99.

COCKTAILS
THE COCKTAIL HOUR

I drink when I have occasion, and sometimes when I have no occasion.

CERVANTES, *Don Quixote*

The 'cocktail hour' has been found by many people an ideal time to return hospitality. This is especially so for those who live in a small flat or who are unable to spend time preparing a dinner, as they are at work all day.

Cocktail parties are an easy informal form of entertaining, for no table need be set, or if one sets a table this is utilitarian. Trays of canapés and cocktails are passed by an assistant, or by the host himself, who with a shaker in hand circulates amongst the guests refilling the glasses when necessary.

The drinks, which do not take long to make, are usually prepared in advance. Have two sorts available. The 'titbits' need not be elaborate, but they need to be slightly more filling than those served for the pre-dinner cocktail. Cubes of cheese gaily stuck with a toothpick, slivers of smoked salmon, rolled Salami or cold shrimps in a cocktail sauce—using a toothpick to spear. Button onions, olives, salted nuts and crisp celery stuffed with cheese make an appetizing array.

Cocktail parties can easily develop into buffet suppers. This is not really what the cocktail hour was meant to be, for the party is sometimes too big for the hosts to enjoy the company of the guests.

For an informal party provide olives, nuts, salted almonds, tiny sausages and an assortment of 'titbits'. Always have a tomato-juice cocktail ready, as there are some guests who prefer this to alcoholic mixtures. It is wise to provide a decanter of sherry as this is sometimes preferred to a mixed drink.

Shakers vary in types according to choice and usually have matching glasses. Ice cubes must not be forgotten.

Cocktail glasses are of two types—those which are intended for such drinks as Martinis and Manhattans, or for gin and lime. The first type of cocktail is prepared in a shaker or mixer. 'Old Fashioneds' and other cocktails which are of ample proportions, with the addition of ice and sliced orange and other fruits, are mixed in the individual larger glasses.

Pre-Lunch Cocktails

> *There are two reasons for drinking; one is, when you are thirsty,*
> *to cure it; the other, when you are not thirsty, to prevent it. . . .*
> *Prevention is better than cure.*
>
> T. L. PEACOCK, *Melincourt*

Both informal and formal luncheons are preceded by cocktails in the living-room. (Always have tomato juice or a pure fruit-juice cocktail for those who do not care for liquor.)

There should be another tray for the potato chips, canapés, olives, almonds, nuts or whatever delicacies you have decided to serve. They should not be filling—like those served at a cocktail party—as they precede a meal.

The cocktail tray should hold the number of filled glasses required and the shaker should have a dividend—in case of request.

On ordinary occasions no precedence is observed unless there is a guest of honour—when he or she and the hostess leave the room first together.

Pre-Dinner and Buffet-Meal Cocktails

> *What's drinking? A mere pause from thinking.*
>
> BYRON

The cocktails preceding dinner are mixed outside by the host, butler or maid and they are brought in on a tray with the shaker containing the dividend.

Olives, salted nuts or canapés are served with them as at luncheon.

Before a buffet luncheon or supper, cocktails may or may not be served according to taste.

When the cocktails are placed on the table they are apt to disturb the setting. Appetizers may accompany the cocktails: cubes of cheese, olives, salted nuts and potato chips are very little trouble to get ready and they are popular accompaniments to cocktails.

Essentials in Cocktail Mixing

Ice is an essential in most cocktails—and this should only be used once.

The shaker should be large, as the ingredients mix better in a good-sized shaker. Always shake just as *hard* as you can. Ice the glasses before use when possible. Mix and drink a cocktail—don't mix and leave it, as it loses its 'body'.

Most people have their own particular specialities. Here are a few suggestions. Remember—*shake well and strain.*

Absinthe	$\frac{1}{2}$ each absinthe and water, 1 dash each syrup and Angostura bitters.
Bacardi	$\frac{1}{4}$ each of lemon or lime juice and Grenadine, $\frac{1}{2}$ Bacardi rum.
Brandy	2 dashes curaçao, $\frac{3}{4}$ wine glass brandy, $\frac{1}{4}$ each of orange juice, French and Italian vermouth, $\frac{1}{2}$ dry gin.
Canadian Whisky	1 glass rye whisky, 2 dashes Angostura bitters, $\frac{1}{2}$ tsp. Gomme syrup.
Champagne	1 lump sugar saturated with Angostura bitters. Add ice, fill glass with champagne, squeeze of lemon—serve with slice of orange.
Clover Club	Juice of $\frac{1}{2}$ lime or lemon, $\frac{1}{3}$ Grenadine, $\frac{2}{3}$ dry gin, 1 white of egg.
Clover Leaf	As above, add leaf of mint.
Dubonnet	$\frac{1}{2}$ each Dubonnet and dry gin.
Gimlet	$\frac{1}{4}$ lime juice, $\frac{3}{4}$ dry gin—fill glass with soda water.
Manhattan	1 dash Angostura bitters, $\frac{1}{3}$ Italian vermouth, $\frac{2}{3}$ rye whisky.
Martinez	3 parts gin, 1 part French vermouth, 1 dsp. orange bitters or 2 dsp. Maraschino.
Martini (Dry)	$\frac{1}{5}$ French vermouth, $\frac{4}{5}$ dry gin. Add a squeeze of lemon rind.
Martini (Medium)	$\frac{1}{2}$ dry gin, $\frac{1}{4}$ each French and Italian vermouth.
Martini (Sweet)	$\frac{2}{3}$ gin, $\frac{1}{3}$ Italian vermouth.
Old Fashioned	1 glass rye whisky, 2 dashes Angostura bitters, 1 lump sugar, crushed ice, twist lemon, slice orange.
Pink Gin	1 dash Angostura bitters, 1 glass gin.
Pink Lady	1 tbsp. Grenadine, 1 glass Plymouth gin, 1 egg white.
Port Wine	1 dash brandy, 1 glass port wine.
Prairie Oyster	1 yolk egg (unbroken), 2 dashes vinegar, 1 tbsp. each Worcester sauce and tomato ketchup, 1 dash pepper.
Rum	$\frac{3}{4}$ rum, $\frac{1}{4}$ Italian vermouth.
Rye Whisky	1 glass rye whisky, 1 dash Angostura bitters, 4 dashes syrup.

Sidecar	¼ each lemon juice and Cointreau, ½ brandy.
Vermouth	1 glass Italian or French vermouth. A dash of Angostura bitters.
White Lady	½ of dry gin, ¼ each lemon juice, Cointreau.

For the non-drinker, serve this 'soft' cocktail:

Tomato-juice Cocktail

Put a little crushed ice in shaker. Open a can of tomato juice and pour into shaker. Add a sprinkle of celery salt, a squeeze of lemon juice, a few drops of Tabasco or Worcester sauce. For young people do not add the two latter. Shake well and serve well chilled.

DINNER

THE HOUR BEFORE DINNER

Wherever the dinner is ill got up, there is poverty or there is avarice or there is stupidity; in short, the family is somehow grossly wrong.

DR JOHNSON

I am a firm believer that the hour before dinner should be peaceful and that there should be no domestic upsets or frantic and frequent trips to see 'what is cooking'. The menfolk are home from work, and before this meal—which should be planned for pleasure—most of us like to enjoy a cocktail, sherry or a quiet chat, unhindered. When you keep this hour each day, you can be calm and relaxed when guests are present (even if you don't possess any domestic help). The feeling of panic, wondering if the evening will be successful and if the guests will enjoy themselves, is eased when you're not rushing round with one eye on the clock and one eye on the food which you are preparing. When you know that nothing in the kitchen needs preparation or attention, you can be placid and receive your guests and enjoy a cocktail with them.

The secret of leisure is careful planning. So several days before a party write down a menu which is seasonable, check supplies in hand and make a list of what to buy. As it is usually quite impossible to give an entire day to party preparation, set the table beforehand, when you can, for a sit-down or even a buffet meal. This will help to prevent a rush at the last minute.

In a cook, the most essential quality is punctuality; it should also be that of the guest.

Never attempt a formal dinner without proper equipment and

service, and never attempt to serve a meal to more guests than you can comfortably cook for and serve. It is much wiser to give two or three small successful informal dinners than to attempt a formal dinner that cannot be properly served.

The lustre of the glass, the friendly glow of the candlelight give glamour to a table. A well-appointed table goes a long way towards helping the hostess to create an atmosphere of real enjoyment.

Contrasts or harmonizing colour-schemes may be planned. And remember ·not to overcrowd your table. Some people have a flair for table setting. It is easy to teach a maid to set a table, but it is that little something which the hostess or her daughters or the caterer can add to the table that helps to make the dinner.

For informal dinners, glass, silver, plates, and so on, are all arranged in the same way as at formal dinners, except that possibly the hostess may choose to serve fewer courses at times. (See TABLE SETTING, p. 13.) To-day, with simplified settings, usually there are not more than three pieces of silver on either side of the plate. The extra pieces, such as dessert spoon and fork, and dessert knife and fork are brought in on the dessert plates. A finger bowl can be placed on the dessert plate, which may be china with a fruit decoration on it, or a crystal plate with matching finger bowl. A charming touch is to add to the bowl—floating delicately in the water—a smaller flower.

Peppers and salts should be conveniently placed round the table, preferably one between two persons. This saves the guests from having to pass them to one another.

Carving at the table takes much longer than when done in the kitchen beforehand, and also requires more space, but it also allows more time for conversation between guests.

When a dinner is served without domestic help, a trolley will be found to be most useful.

INFORMAL DINNERS

Informal dinners are far more popular than a formal dinner party, which is really only suitable when a number of servants are employed. It would be far better to plan a strictly informal dinner party than to spoil the charm of a well-appointed dinner by the uncomfortable mistakes that occur through nervousness, careless serving or over-ambitious dishes badly cooked.

It is quite easy to vary your favourite dinner menu. Change the first course—serve soup, fruit, fruit cocktail, or hors-d'œuvres. Then vary your sweet. Perhaps you prefer a fresh fruit salad (this can be varied according to the season) enriched with a little sherry or Kirsch; or perhaps a meringue, ice-cream and hot sauce—chocolate and fudge, or a different savoury (see p. 97). Perhaps just blue cheese, Camembert—with radishes and celery. In all menus it is easy to add or delete a course.

> *He may live without books, what is knowledge but grieving?*
> *He may live without hope, what is hope but deceiving?*
> *He may live without love, what is passion but pining?*
> *But where is the man that can live without dining?*
>
> OWEN MEREDITH, *Lucile*

SIX INFORMAL DINNER MENUS

MENU I

SOLE NORMANDE

CANARD AUX PETITS POIS

POMMES DE TERRE NOUVELLES AU BEURRE

ŒUFS À LA NEIGE

FROMAGE

CAFÉ

Sole Normande (*Sole Normandy*)

A good-sized sole	A few prawns and mussels
Salt and pepper	2 tbsp. water
Butter	A little flour
1 glass white wine	A little fresh cream

Remove both skins from the sole, put it in a fireproof dish with salt, pepper, a piece of butter and the wine. Cook at 350° F., then remove the dish and keep it hot. In a small saucepan cook the prawns and mussels. When they are nearly cooked put them round the sole.

Mix together 2 tablespoonsful of water in which the prawns and mussels were cooked with the wine and butter used for the sole. Reduce it and add a small piece of butter previously rolled in flour, and later add the cream. Cook very slowly, and pour over the sole through a fine sieve. (The consistency should be cream-like.)

Canard aux petits pois (*Duck with green peas*)

A young duck	Newly shelled green peas
2 rashers of bacon	Pepper and salt

Pluck and truss the duck, and put it in a braising pan. Add bacon fat and rashers and fry it in melted fat. Put aside the fried bacon—when the duck is nicely browned, moisten with a little water or stock. Add the newly shelled green peas, pepper and salt. Add bacon. Cover tightly and braise for about 30 minutes.

Pommes de terre nouvelles au beurre (*New potatoes*)

New potatoes	Butter
Chopped parsley to garnish	Salt

Wash and scrape some new potatoes. Then dry them well. Melt some butter in a pan, put in the potatoes and cook until lightly browned. Then put them into an oven-proof dish with butter and finish cooking. Season with salt just before serving and add a little chopped parsley to garnish.

Œufs à la neige (*Snow eggs*)

5 eggs	5 oz. sugar
½ pt. milk	Vanilla

Beat the whites to a snow. Put the milk in a saucepan. Add sugar and vanilla (if preferred, flavour with cinnamon, coffee or chocolate) and heat. When it reaches boiling-point put the snow into it, one spoonful at a time. It takes only a minute to cook. Then lift the poached snow out with a skimmer and place it in a deep dish. Pour over it a custard made with the milk and yolks of egg. Leave to cool. Serve with sponge finger biscuits.

MENU II

RISOTTO À LA MILANAISE

MORUE À LA CRÈME

LAPIN AUX CHOUX ROUGES

POMMES DE TERRE LYONNAISE

CRÈME AU BEURRE

Risotto à la Milanaise (*Milanese rice*)

3½ oz. beef marrow	2 oz. butter
½ lb. rice	A pinch powdered saffron
1¾ pt. clear soup or stock	Salt and pepper

Put the marrow in a saucepan and remove any solid bits left. Add the butter and, when it begins to smoke, pour cupfuls of the dry rice into the pan gradually, stir well, and when the rice is a light golden colour, moisten it with 1½ times more than its volume of hot clear stock. Season with care, add the saffron. Cover the pan and cook gently for about 20 minutes. By this time the rice will be cooked but not quite dry. Remove the lid from the pan and leave the pan over a low heat for at least ½ hour—occasionally stir the rice at the bottom of the pan. Take care not to crush the grain. Serve with a bowl of grated Parmesan and, if desired, tomato sauce.

Morue à la crème (*Cod with cream sauce*)

Cod	Water
Butter	Cream
Potatoes	Parmesan

Soak and boil some cod in water with peeled sliced potatoes. Drain, add melted butter and thick cream. Stir in some grated Parmesan. Turn into an oven-proof dish and place in a moderate oven, 350° F. Bake for ¼ hour.

Lapin aux choux rouges (*Rabbit with red cabbage*)

2 rabbits	½ bottle white wine
½ lb. fat bacon	Salt and pepper
1 small red cabbage	10 juniper berries

Wine glass of brandy

Cut up the bacon and rabbits. Fry the bacon and put it aside, fry the rabbits in the bacon dripping. Add wine, salt and pepper. Then add the blanched shredded cabbage. Cover the pan and simmer for 1 hour. Add the juniper berries. Set fire to the brandy and add it. Boil 5 minutes and serve in the pan.

Pommes de terre Lyonnaise (*Lyonnaise potatoes*)

2 *lb. potatoes*	2 *oz. lard*
7 *oz. onions*	2 *oz. butter*
Parsley	*Salt and pepper*

Melt the lard and butter. Brown some minced onions in this fat. Add the potatoes cut into very thin slices. Fry for ¼ hour. Season. Put in a moderate oven, 350° F., to brown slowly. This will take at least 40 minutes.

Crème au beurre (*Butter cream*)

¼ *lb. butter*	2 *egg yolks*
¼ *lb. sugar*	*Coffee or chocolate*

Make a syrup with the sugar. Set aside to cool. Pound the butter in a mortar till it turns white, then add the yolks, then the syrup, pounding with a pestle. For *Mocha Cream* add strong coffee to the syrup. For *Chocolate Cream* add melted chocolate to the white butter.

MENU III

FILETS DE SOLE FLORENTINE
RIS DE VEAU EN FRICASSÉE
POMMES DE TERRE BOULANGER
TOMATES À LA PROVENÇALE
FRANGIPANE

Filets de sole Florentine (*Florentine sole*)

Make a Béchamel sauce (see p. 142). Cover some fillets with this and cook over a low heat. Put some boiled (unchopped) spinach in a fire-proof dish. Dish up the fillets on this and pour the sauce over them. Glaze in the oven.

Ris de veau en fricassée (*Stewed sweetbreads*)

1 *calf's sweetbread*	*Seasoning*
1 *teacup light stock*	*Little cold water*
1 *tsp. cornflour*	1 *tsp. cream*
	1 *tsp. chopped parsley*

Steep in cold water for an hour, then blanch the sweetbreads by placing them in a saucepan of cold water and bringing to the boil. Boil 3–4 minutes, drain and put again into cold water. Remove skin and fat and break into pieces. Put sweetbread into a casserole, add stock and seasoning, simmer until tender —about 1 hour. Keep hot. Add cornflour to stock, stir until boiling, boil 5 minutes. Add cream and parsley. Pour over the sweetbreads. Serve garnished with snippets of toast.

Pommes de terre Boulanger (*Boulanger potatoes*)

Cut two large onions into thin slices. Fry only a few minutes in butter. Cut your potatoes in thin slices, arrange them in a flat dish with the onions, add a claret-glassful of consommé, a good shake of pepper and salt and place in a moderate oven, 350° F., and leave to brown for about 1½ hours.

Tomates à la Provençale (*Provence tomatoes*)

1½ lb. tomatoes	1½ oz. breadcrumbs
15 chives	2 oz. olive oil
2 pieces of garlic	Parsley
Salt and pepper	

Cut the tomatoes in halves. Mince the chives and garlic, prepare the breadcrumbs, using stale bread. Put a sauté pan to heat. Pour in the oil and wait until the smoke rises. Add chives and garlic. Cook the chives and garlic in oil, then add the tomatoes over a good heat. Five minutes before serving add breadcrumbs and let them brown in the oil. Sprinkle with chopped parsley and serve.

Frangipane (*Pastry custard*)

1⅛ pt. milk	1 oz. butter
3½ oz. flour	2½ oz. sugar
3 whole eggs	Pinch of salt
1 egg white	3½ oz. almonds

Blend the flour with a little cold milk. Add the eggs, sugar and salt. Mix well, pour the boiling milk into the mixture, stirring the whole time. Add the butter, bit by bit, and keep stirring over a moderate heat. Cook until the cream sets. Then mix in the pounded almonds.

I

MENU IV

CONSOMMÉ
TRUITE SAUMONÉE À LA CRÈME
PETITS POIS
SALADE DE LAITUE
SALADE DE FRUITS
TARTE AUX CHAMPIGNONS

Consommé (*Clear soup*)

2–2½ *lb. lean beef*	1 *lb. carrots and turnips*
Chicken bones and giblets	3 *large leeks*
½ *lb. beef bones*	*Salt and spices*

5 *pt. cold water*

Put the water into a saucepan. Add salt. Immerse the meat and bones and slowly bring to the boil. Skim before boiling and add the vegetables and spices. After bringing to the boil, leave to simmer 4 hours in a covered pan. Colour with caramel. Remove the meat and vegetables. Skim off as much fat as possible, pass the stock through a fine cloth and leave to cool. Next day skim off the surface fat; this clears the soup. Can be served in cups either hot or cold—as it is, or with various ingredients added to it.

Truite Saumonée à la crème (*Salmon trout with cream*)

A small salmon trout	*Salt*
1 *bkcp. fresh cream*	*Butter*

A glass of port wine

Take a small salmon trout, clean it well and dry it carefully with a cloth. Salt it, then dip it first in fresh cream and afterwards in flour. Melt in a long fire-proof dish a piece of butter, put in the fish, cook it a few minutes, and turn it so that it gets brown on both sides. Add a glass of port wine. Let it reduce a little, then add the fresh cream. See that it is well seasoned, and finish cooking in the oven, basting frequently.

Salade de laitue (*Lettuce salad*). See p. 99.

Petits pois (*Green peas*)

Take a saucepan allowing 1 tumblerful of water to each 1 lb. shelled young peas. Add a pinch of salt, the heart of a lettuce, two small onions and a piece of butter the size of a walnut. Bring to the boil. Put in the peas and boil in an open saucepan. When cooked remove onions and lettuce and leave only the juice. Add half a teaspoonful of sugar and a little more butter. Reboil and serve.

Salade de Fruits (*Fruit salad*)

Cantaloup melon	*Apricots*
Strawberries	*Green almonds*
Raspberries	*Sugar*
	Kirsch

Open the top of the melon, remove all seeds and scoop out the flesh with a spoon. Mix the strawberries, raspberries, apricots cut into small pieces and some melon flesh. Add the green almonds, sugar and a little Kirsch. Stand for ¼ hour before use.

Tarte aux champignons (*Mushroom tart*)

Line a buttered flan tin with plain pastry ¼-inch thick. Fill it three-quarters full with cream made with—

1⅛ pt. milk	*¼ pt. cream*
¼ lb. mushrooms	*3 eggs*
	Salt and pepper

Bake at 350° F.

MENU V

FILETS DE SOLE ORLY
GIGOT BRAISÉ AUX FÈVES
POMMES DE TERRE SAUTÉES
CHOUX AUX POMMES
MERINGUES
FROMAGE

Filets de sole Orly (*Sole Orly*)

4 soles, each about 7 oz. weight	*2 eggs*
3 oz. flour	*7 oz. stale white breadcrumbs*

Fillet the soles, roll them and then put a small skewer through
each one. Roll each fillet in flour, then in egg and lastly in
breadcrumbs. Fry, sprinkle with salt and serve with thin slices
of lemon.

Gigot braisé aux fèves (*Leg of lamb braised with beans*)

Small leg of lamb	*Fat bacon*
Bacon dripping	*1½ lb. young broad beans*
	White wine

Take a small leg and bone it. Tie it up and lard it with strips
of fat bacon. Then brown in a little bacon dripping. When it is
nicely browned place in a large earthenware casserole. Add a
little white wine. Cover closely and cook 30 minutes. Add the
beans and cook till these are tender—about 25 minutes.

Choux aux pommes (*Cabbage with apples*)

1 *white cabbage*	7 *oz. bacon*
2 *lb. apples*	*Salt, pepper and grated nutmeg*

Shred and blanch the cabbage. Put in a pan alternate layers of
cabbage and sliced apples. Season. Cut the bacon into dice,
fry, and add it with the fat to the contents of the pan. Cover
and simmer for 2 hours.

Pommes de terre sautées (*Sauté potatoes*). See p. 83.

Meringues

4 *whites of eggs*	*Pinch of salt*
7 *oz. caster sugar*	*Powdered vanilla*

Beat the whites of eggs to a stiff mixture. Add sugar, salt and
flavouring. Then put them on a buttered board and bake them
in a very low oven.

MENU VI

LES HUÎTRES
MAYONNAISE DE PERDREAU
POMMES DE TERRE EN ROBE DE CHAMBRE
SALADE DE LAITUE
BANANES CRÉOLE
CROÛTE AUX ANCHOIS

Les Huîtres (*Oysters*)

Allow ½ doz. to 1 doz. oysters per person; open them, remove beard of fringes, serve on an oyster plate (this should stand in cracked ice) with lemon quarters, brown bread and butter, white or chilli vinegar.

Mayonnaise de perdreaux (*Partridge mayonnaise*)

Cut the cold roast partridges into halves. Place them on a bed of mayonnaise sauce. Pour more sauce all over them and decorate them with small *croûtons*, stuffed olives, fillets of anchovies, chopped hard-boiled eggs, and pieces of truffles. Decorate all over the dish with chopped jelly.

Mayonnaise

2 *raw egg yolks*	2 *tbsp. tarragon, French or plain vinegar*
½ *pt. best salad oil*	*Pepper and salt*

Put the yolks into a basin with a little salt. Stir them quickly with a whisk, or wooden spoon, dropping the oil on them drop by drop, until the sauce is as thick as butter in warm weather. Then add the vinegar and the rest of the seasoning.

Pommes de terre en robe de chambre (*Potatoes in their jackets*)

Wash some firm white potatoes. Immerse them in their jackets in boiling water. Cover the pan and cook. Serve with plenty of fresh butter and salt.

Salade de laitue (*Lettuce salad*)

Take only the hearts of lettuce, or cos lettuce, keeping only the white leaves, and cut them in two. Season with salt, pepper, wine vinegar and olive oil, and serve.

Bananes Créole

Peel 6 bananas and put them in a fire-proof dish. Sprinkle over them 3 tablespoonsful demerara sugar. Squeeze the juice of a lemon and add 3 tablespoonsful of water. Bake brown in a slow oven and half-way through the baking add a sherry-glassful of rum. Serve with cream, whipped and flavoured with lemon, or rum.

Croûtons d'Anchois (*Anchovies on toast*)

Take some salt anchovies and soak them well; remove the bones, cut them and pound them in a mortar. Add a very little chopped parsley, red pepper and a good pinch of curry powder. Put them into a small saucepan with a little butter and cook for a few minutes. Then add the grated yolk of a hard-boiled egg. Spread on hot buttered toast, brown under a hot grill and serve immediately.

FORMAL DINNERS

A well cooked and well served dinner implies on the part of the entertainer a sense of the respect he owes to his guests, whose comfort and happiness he controls while they are under his roof.

DIDSBURY

A formal dinner at one time consisted of ten courses. Today we aim at perfection and it is not often that more than five courses are served. The number of courses is really dependent upon the circumstances of the host and hostess. It is not usual to serve two soups, or two or three different kinds of fish or entrées. Usually one only is served. For a five-course dinner, the courses comprise:

MENU DU DÎNER *or* BILL OF FARE

Potage	.	Soup
Poisson	.	Fish
Entrée	.	Entrée
Rôti	.	Roast
Entremets	.	Sweet

Longer dinners may consist of the following:

Hors d'œuvres	.	Side dish
Potage	.	Soup
Poisson	.	Fish
Entrée	.	Made dish
Rôti	.	Roast
Entremets	.	Sweet
Bonne Bouche	.	Savoury
	or	
Hors d'œuvres	.	Appetizer
Potage	.	Soup

Poisson	.	Fish
Entrées	.	Made dishes
Relevé	.	Remove
Rôti	.	Roast
Entremets	.	Sweets
Savoureux	.	Savoury
	or	
Fromage	.	Cheese
Fruits et Dessert	.	Fruit and dessert

The game course can be used as an entrée. Sometimes the menu is longer, at other times a shorter one. For a three-course menu serve the same foods. A salad can be served with the meat course, and coffee with the pudding course.

Six Formal Dinner Menus

MENU I

MELON CANTALOUP
SAUMON FUMÉ
SOUPE AUX CONCOMBRES
QUICHE LORRAINE
POULET RÔTI FLAMBÉ
POMMES DE TERRE AUX PIMENTS
BETTERAVES AU LAIT
BEIGNETS D'ANANAS
CROÛTE AUX CHAMPIGNONS

Melon Cantaloup (*French rock melon*)

Serve quartered, well iced, accompanied by powdered ginger and sugar.

Soupe aux concombres (*Cucumber soup*)

2 *lb. cucumber*	1 *tbsp. vinegar*
3 *oz. semolina*	*Salt and pepper*
1 *gill cream*	3½ *pt. cold water*
¾ *oz. chervil*	3 *oz. butter*

Peel the cucumbers and cut in pieces. Boil 15 minutes in a little water. Pass through a sieve previously rinsed with boiling water. Add the remaining salt and water and boil again. Sprinkle with semolina, add butter. Boil 20 minutes without lid. Add vinegar, boil 5 minutes longer. Add cream and chervil and serve—in summer serve iced if preferred.

Quiche Lorraine

Make a plain pastry, using 7 oz. flour and 3½ oz. butter. Knead on a board and add a pinch of salt and just sufficient water to form a paste that will roll out without sticking to the fingers. Set aside for an hour; line a buttered, open tart tin with this paste, which should be about ⅛ inch thick, fill with

¼ *lb. lean bacon*	1 *lb. 5 oz. thick cream*
3 *oz. ham*	5 *egg yolks*
1¾ *oz. butter*	*Salt*

Dice the bacon and blanch in boiling water for 10 minutes. Set aside. Cut the ham into small pieces. Mix the cream and egg yolks. Add ham, bacon and butter, cut up in bits the size of a hazel nut. Season with care, do not use too much salt. Fill the tart with this mixture and bake ½ hour at 350° F. Serve hot.

Poulet rôti flambé (*Roast chicken flambé*)

A roasting chicken	½ *lb. minced pork*
Pepper and salt	*Watercress*
Butter	*Pork fat*
2 *or* 3 *chicken livers*	

Salt the inside of the dressed chicken, and put in a few pieces of butter, also the minced pork, well seasoned, with the chicken liver left whole. Cook in the oven, baste frequently with melted butter. When the chicken is ready, remove it, season it well all over and *flambé* it with the pork fat—that is, have the fat at a very high temperature. Set it alight and pour it over the chicken. It will slightly char the skin and make it crisp. Serve garnished with watercress.

Pommes de terre aux piments (*Potatoes with red peppers*)

1½ *lb. cold boiled potatoes*	*Butter*
2 *red sweet peppers*	*Salt and pepper*

Cut the potatoes into pieces, and remove the seeds from the parboiled red peppers and cut into small pieces. Melt some butter in a saucepan, then addt he potatoes and pimentos, well seasoned. Break them coarsely with a fork, and stir them at the beginning, then allow the potatoes to get browned on the lower part, and turn them on to a serving dish.

Betteraves au lait (*Beetroot in milk*)

Cook some beetroot, peel them and cut into slices. Put them in a saucepan with a large knob of butter, season with salt and pepper, parsley, and chervil finely chopped. Cook slowly about a quarter of an hour. Add a sprinkling of flour, stir well, then add a glass of milk, bring to the boil, cook about 10 minutes, add a little butter, season and serve.

Beignets d'ananas (*Pineapple fritters*)

Peel and cut the pineapple into slices (halve, if large), put them in a deep dish, and sprinkle over with a small glass of Kirsch. Prepare a good frying batter with:

1 *oz. butter melted*	1 *oz. caster sugar*
3 *oz. sifted flour*	*Few drops vanilla essence*
3 *eggs*	½ *pt. milk and water mixed*

Dip the slices of pineapple into this, then drop into very hot clarified fat. Fry them to a light brown colour, drain on a paper or cloth, dredge with caster sugar or icing sugar. Dish up and serve hot.

Croûte aux champignons (*Mushrooms on toast*)

Take a stale loaf of white bread and cut slices as you would for toasting. Fry these quite crisp in butter. Prepare a rather stiff Béchamel sauce (not forgetting a little grated nutmeg). Add to it 2 or 3 mushrooms—cut in thin pieces, previously cooked. Mix well, season with pepper and salt and a little cayenne, spread the mixture thickly on the pieces of fried bread; when cold, coat with beaten egg and fry in deep fat or oil. Serve very hot.

MENU II

PAMPLEMOUSSE

POTAGE AUX FÈVES

HOMARD À L'AMÉRICAINE

FAISAN AUX CHOUX

POMMES DE TERRE DUCHESSE

TARTE AUX POMMES

CROUSTADES DE FROMAGE

Pamplemousse (*Grapefruit*)

Prepare grapefruit (*see p.* 137) and cover with brown sugar, and a few knobs of butter, place under a hot grill until the sugar melts. Serve very hot.

Potage aux l èves (*Broad bean soup*)

1¾ *lb. fresh broad beans*	¼ *oz. sugar*
2 *oz. butter*	3½ *pt. cold water*
⅛ *tsp. salt*	3 *yolks of eggs*

Cook the beans in salted water. Pass the beans through a sieve but retain the water. Melt the butter in a pan and add the bean purée, stirring well. Moisten with the water in which the beans have been boiled. Boil 10 minutes. Add sugar. Before serving stir in the egg yolks, reheat the soup without letting it boil.

Homard à l'Américaine (*Lobster American*)

2 *lb. lobster*	*Cayenne*
2 *oz. olive oil*	⅓*pt. Madeira*
2 *oz. tomato purée*	7 *oz. white wine* (*dry*)
Small bunch parsley,	*A pinch curry powder*
chervil, tarragon	2 *oz. liqueur brandy*

Cut the lobster into chunks and throw into boiling oil and fry. Add tomato purée and herbs, and moisten with white wine and Madeira. Add salt, curry and pinch of cayenne. Cook ¼ hour. Add a little white wine. Add brandy previously set on fire. Then remove the herbs and add some white breadcrumbs to thicken sauce.

Faisan aux choux (*Pheasant with cabbage*)

This is a very good way to cook old birds which might, if roasted, be very tough:

1 *pheasant*	1 *medium-sized cabbage*
Some slices of bacon	*Small sausages*
Bacon fat	*Salt, pepper, spices*

Wash and shred the cabbage—*but do not blanch it.* Fry it in bacon fat until it begins to brown lightly. Add salt and spices, cover the pan and leave on the fire ¾ hour, adding—if necessary

—a very little cold water. While the cabbage is cooking, cover the pheasant with slices of bacon and fry it in a saucepan. When it is nicely brown add the cabbage. Cover the pan and leave over the heat until the bird is well cooked. Fry the sausages and serve all together. The cooking time of the pheasant is dependent upon the age of it.

Pommes de terre duchesse (*Duchess potatoes*)

2 *lb. potatoes*	2 *eggs*
3 *oz. butter*	*Salt, grated nutmeg*

Peel the potatoes and cook in a minimum of salted water. Drain well and mash with butter. Add the egg yolks and then the whites—well beaten to a stiff froth. The purée must be very thick. Add salt and nutmeg to taste. Take up the purée little by little in a spoon and drop on a buttered tray. Flatten down each potato cake. Twirl round with a fork and brush with melted butter. Bake till brown.

Tarte aux pommes (*Apple tart*)

Line a buttered tart tin with plain pastry. Brush with apricot jam and cover with thin slices of apple. Bake in a hot oven ¼ hour. Warm a little apricot jam and pour on the top of the cooked apples—just before serving. Serve hot.

Croustades de fromage (*Cheese croustades*)

Take 2 pieces of bread 2 inches square and about ½ inch thick. Between these put a piece of gruyère cheese of about the same size but slightly thinner. Tie up with thread across and across. Fry in hot butter over a quick heat. Serve very hot, allowing 1 croustade per person. (Remove thread before serving.)

MENU III

HONEYDEW MELON

SAUMON FUMÉ

CONSOMMÉ À LA JULIENNE

TRUITE AUX BANANES

PIGEONS AU VERJUS

POMMES DE TERRE DUCHESSE

CHOU ROUGE FLAMANDE

SOUFFLÉ AU FROMAGE

Saumon fumé (*Smoked salmon*). *See p.* 133.

Consommé à la Julienne (*Julienne soup*)

14 *oz. carrots*	3 *oz. butter*
14 *oz. turnips*	5 *pt. cold water*
1 *small cabbage*	*Salt*

Cut the vegetables in thin strips, either with a knife or a special grater. Put butter in the pan and when melted add the vegetables. Turn them over often when the vegetables are coated with butter and begin to brown. Add the water and season with salt. Cover and let the soup boil 1½ hours.

Truite aux Bananes (*Trout with bananas*)

Take some trout weighing not more than ¼ lb., clean them, and having dipped them in milk, roll them in flour. Season with salt and pepper, and fry them in butter. Cut very thin some mushrooms and fry them. Peel and slice the bananas into two and fry them also in butter, and when ready, garnish the trout with them. Add just before serving a squeeze of lemon juice and finely chopped parsley.

Pigeons au Verjus (*Pigeons and green grapes*)

Pluck and draw a brace of pigeons. Stuff them with green grapes. Then cover with rashers of fat bacon. Cook in a braising pan and moisten the birds with the strained juice from some grapes. Just before serving add a few grapes to the sauce, and a tablespoonful or two of sherry.

Pommes de terre duchesse (*Duchess potatoes*). *See p.* 129.

Chou Rouge Flamande (*Flemish red cabbage*)

Cut a red cabbage into four. Blanch it and put it into an earthenware casserole containing a little lard. Season with salt and pepper. Add ½ lb. minced onions. Cover with slices of bacon. Bake 2 hours. From time to time pour in a little stock. Serve in casserole.

Soufflé au fromage (*Cheese soufflé*)

¼ *lb. grated cheese*	*4 eggs*
½ *pt. thick cream*	*Grated nutmeg*
1 *oz. butter*	*Salt and pepper*

¾ *oz. flour*

Use a fairly large saucepan, add and mix together the cream, butter, cheese and flour. Cook over a very low heat *but do not boil*. Season and let the mixture half cool. Add the yolks first, and then the whites beaten to a stiff snow. Pour the mixture into a buttered dish and bake 20 minutes at 400° F. Serve immediately.

MENU IV

PAMPLEMOUSSE

CONSOMMÉ À LA JULIENNE

HOMARD À LA MAYONNAISE

ENTRECÔTE BERCY

POMMES DE TERRE NOUVELLES EN COCOTTE

PETITS POIS AU VELOUTÉ

CRÊPES

FROMAGE

Pamplemousse, *see pp*. 127 and 128.

Consommé à la Julienne (*Julienne soup*). See *p*. 130.

Homard à la mayonnaise (*Lobster mayonnaise*)

Cook the lobster in *court bouillon* (stock, usually composed of white wine, water, pepper, salt, parsley, onions, etc. in which fish is cooked), plunging it in boiling liquid. Cook 20 minutes. Take out and leave to cool. When cold remove the coral, and using scissors cut the soft part of shell underneath and remove the flesh in one piece. Cut the flesh in scallops and dish up round the shell. Put the crushed coral into the mayonnaise to give both taste and colour. Then garnish with lettuce leaves.

Entrecôte Bercy (*Steak with white wine sauce*)

¼ *lb. chives*	1½ *oz. parsley*
½ *pt. white wine*	*Half a lemon*
2 *oz. butter*	1½ *lb. steak*

Chop the chives and cook them in white wine. Boil down well and remove from heat. Add butter and, when melted, add the chopped-up parsley and lemon juice. Grill the steak and sprinkle it with salt and pour the sauce over it.

Pommes de terre nouvelles en cocotte (*New potatoes cocotte*)

Take a shallow pan and put into it 3 oz. butter. Place on heat and, when the butter smokes, throw in 1½ lb. small new potatoes, scraped, washed and dried. Turn them over occasionally when they are nicely browned. Cover the pan and lower the heat; in 10 minutes you will have golden and well-cooked potatoes.

Petits pois au Velouté (*Peas in rich white sauce*)

Cook the peas with butter and lettuce. When almost cooked add 4 oz. thick cream into which ¾ oz. flour has been mixed. Bring to boil, then simmer for only a few seconds. Remove lettuce before dishing up.

Crêpes (*Pancakes*)

½ lb. flour	Salt, a pinch
2 eggs	1 tbsp. brandy
¾ pt. milk	3 oz. butter
½ oz. melted butter	

Prepare the pancake batter about 2 or 3 hours before required for use. Use a whisk to mix the flour, salt and eggs. Then pour in the milk little by little to avoid lumps. Add melted butter and brandy. Lightly grease the frying pan with butter and pour in just sufficient batter to spread evenly over the pan. Tip the pan so that the batter spreads evenly. Put on heat and as soon as the pancake no longer sticks to the pan, turn it over and cook it a minute more. Lay on folded napkin and make pancake. Fold into four or serve rolled, or spread with jam before rolling.

MENU V

HORS D'ŒUVRES
SAUMON FUMÉ
PAUPIETTES DE FILETS DE SOLE
FILET DE PORC AUX POMMES
PURÉE DE POMMES DE TERRE
CAROTTES VICHY
MARMELADE DE PRUNEAUX

Hors d'œuvres. *See p.* 56.

Saumon fumée (*Smoked salmon*)

Serve the sliced smoked salmon garnished with quarters of lemon and accompanied by a plate of thin brown bread and butter.

Paupiettes de filets de Sole (*Stuffed fillets of sole*)

4 *soles, each about* 7 *oz. weight*	¼ *lb. butter*
7 *oz. whiting*	7 *oz. dry white wine*
1¾ *oz. breadcrumbs*	4 *oz. cream*
1 *egg*	*Salt, pepper and nutmeg*
3 *oz. flour*	

Cook the whiting in *court bouillon* (see p. 131, lobster). Flake and mix the fish with one-third its weight of breadcrumbs, moisten in milk. Add seasoning. Cook this stuffing in a little butter and when dry, cool and add the egg. Spread the fillets with stuffing. Roll and tie them up with fine thread. Flour and fry them in a little butter. Then make a sauce by adding boiling white wine to the fat left at the bottom of the pan. Cook 5 minutes. Add cream and boil up. Remove thread and serve the paupiettes with sauce poured over them.

Filet de porc aux pommes (*Fillet of pork with apples*)

Before putting a loin of pork in the oven, surround it with whole peeled and cored apples, placing them close together. The apples cooked in the pork gravy make a choice addition to the joint.

Purée de pommes de terre (*Potato purée*). *See p.* 88.

Carottes à la Vichy

2 *lb. young carrots*	1¾ *pt. water*
3 *oz. butter*	*Parsley*
A pinch bicarbonate of soda	

Scrape the carrots and wash them well. Put them in a pan and cover with 1¾ pints water. Add just a little salt and bicarbonate of soda. Put the pan on a small heat and as soon as the boiling begins, see that the boiling continues to be fast—so that the water evaporates rapidly. When there is hardly any left, add the butter and keep the pan on the stove until the water has all evaporated, then dish up and sprinkle with chopped parsley.

Marmelade de Pruneaux (*Compote of prunes*)

Soak some prunes in water for 6 hours (allow about 1 lb. for four people). Cook them in just sufficient water to cover, adding more if necessary, till they are soft and swollen. Add 3 or 4 oz. sugar. Remove the prunes, take the stones out of the prunes and mash them through a hair sieve. Meanwhile the juice is reducing slowly to a thick syrup. Add a glass of port wine, stirring in well. Serve cold with or without cream.

MENU VI

CRÈME D'ARTICHAUTS
TURBOT NANTUA
PIGEON RÔTI
PETITS POMMES DE TERRE FRITES
CHOUX DE BRUXELLES AU BEURRE
SOUFFLÉ AU CHOCOLAT

Crème d'Artichauts (*Cream of artichoke*)

1 *lb. or more Jerusalem artichokes*	*Few drops tomato ketchup*
3 *or 4 large onions*	3 *peppercorns*
1 *stick celery*	*Tiny shred orange peel*
2 *rashers bacon*	2 *tbsp. roux*
3 *pt. veal stock*	*Grated parmesan*
	1 *tbsp. thickly whipped cream*

Finely chop the peeled artichokes. Peel and slice onions. Dice celery. Simmer for 1¾ hours in stock. Add peppercorns and diced bacon and orange peel. Have ready heated the top container of a double saucepan, add the roux. Strain into this the stock and vegetables, rubbing them through a fine sieve. Continue stirring with a wooden spoon until the soup thickens, and serve with an accompaniment of finely grated parmesan cheese. Add as a garnish whipped cream to which a little tomato ketchup has been added, floated on top on each cupful.

Turbotin à la Nantua (*Turbot Nantua*)

3 *lb. turbot* (*boned*)	½ *lb. fresh shrimps*
½ *pt. cream*	2 *eggs*
2 *shallots*	2 *tomatoes*
1 *carrot*	1 *glass white wine*
½ *lb. spinach*	½ *lemon*

Chop the turbot trimmings, adding to them the shrimps, half the cream, the yolk of 1 egg and the beaten whites of 2 eggs. Spread this paste on the turbot and then pour over it the chopped-up tomato, melted butter and the white wine. Butter a fireproof dish, line with spinach, sprinkle with shreds of carrot and shallots. Lay the turbot on to this, add lemon juice and leave in moderate oven at 300° F. for about 20 minutes. Add the remaining cream to the cooking liquor, seasoned and poured over the fish before putting in the oven.

Pigeon rôti (*Roast pigeon*)

Dress and truss the squabs, place a thin layer of salt pork over the breasts of the birds and tie in place. Roast at 350° F. for 30–45 minutes according to size. Unless the squabs are unusually large it is wisest to allow one per person. Serve on a bed of watercress and pour over it all a gravy made as follows: Pour ½ cupful of water into roasting tin, scrape off all juices and sediment at the bottom of the tin with a fork. Add a little salt, and strain.

Petits pommes de terre frites (*Small new potatoes, fried*)

Choose very small new potatoes, scrub with a stiff brush. Rinse them and dry with a clean cloth. Put ¼ lb. butter into a frying pan and when melted, fry the potatoes slowly for about 20 minutes. Turn them fairly frequently, until they are golden brown all over, but do not burn them.

Choux de Bruxelles au beurre (*Buttered Brussels sprouts*)

Wash 1 quart Brussels sprouts and remove the stems and outer leaves if wilted or imperfect. Cook in briskly boiling salted water for 10–15 minutes—do not cover pan. Drain and re-heat in butter. Season with salt and pepper. Serve garnished with paprika or chopped parsley.

Soufflé au chocolat (*Chocolate soufflé*)

2 *tbsp. butter*	6 *tbsp. sugar*
2 *tbsp. flour*	*Pinch of salt*
¾ *cupful warmed milk*	3 *eggs*
2 *squares of bitter chocolate*	½ *tsp. vanilla extract*
	2 *tbsp. water*

Melt the butter and stir in the flour. Add the warm milk, stir continuously until well blended. Melt the chocolate in a double boiler. Add sugar and water and stir till smooth. Separate the yolks and whites of eggs and beat the yolks thoroughly. Combine both mixtures. Bake in a buttered soufflé case about 20 minutes at 350° F., setting this in a tin of hot water. If a dry soufflé is preferred, bake 5 to 10 minutes longer. Sift with sugar and serve accompanied by whipped or plain cream. *Soufflés must be served at once.*

COLD MEALS AND SUNDAY SUPPERS

> *In a house where there's plenty, supper is soon cooked*
> CERVANTES, *Don Quixote*

For Sunday nights a cold supper is an easy meal to serve. It is also easy to entertain guests at this meal, by having a side table with the food on it, and letting everybody help themselves. Use food that is easily prepared beforehand, with only the garnishes to add. Freshly made salads and hot rolls help to make the meal more appetizing. In some homes cold meat or raised pie, and potatoes baked in their jackets, have been on the Sunday-night menu since great-grandma's day. A cold sweet or fresh fruit and cheese and celery when served enhance a meal.

Begin with a bowl of soup (see pp. 91–94), then choose your first course from the egg or fish dishes on the following pages (or on p. 94). With your cold joint, serve an appetizing salad (see pp. 99–100).

Choose your menu:

SOUP *or an* EGG DISH
FISH *or* MEAT
SWEET *or* CHEESE

If you want a longer meal:

HORS D'ŒUVRES *or* GRAPEFRUIT
SOUP *or* EGG DISH
COLD MEAT
SWEET
SAVOURY
FRUIT

Here are two suggested menus to help you plan:

MENU I

GRAPEFRUIT
LOBSTER MAYONNAISE
PEACHES IN WINE
CREAM CHEESE
COFFEE

Grapefruit

Cut the grapefruit in half, horizontally. Remove seeds. With a knife cut the rim and loosen each section of pulp. Sprinkle with sugar, add a cherry to garnish.

Lobster Mayonnaise

1 *good-sized lobster*	*Some aspic jelly*
1 *lettuce*	1 *endive (if possible)*
Some mayonnaise dressing	3 *hard-boiled eggs*

Remove the flesh from the body and claws of the lobster and cut into pieces. Well wash and dry the lettuce. Cut up and mix it with the lobster and mayonnaise sauce—put a border of chopped aspic on the dish. Heap the mixture in middle of dish and decorate with endive and hard-boiled eggs cut into squares.

Green Salad. *See* SALADE DE LAITUE, p. 99.

Peaches in wine

Peel the peaches, cut into quarters and leave them to soak in a little port wine and sugar—or burgundy and sugar. Prepare this an hour before serving and stand on ice until required.

Cream Cheese

1 pint double cream—2 or 3 days old—place in muslin and tie up. Hang up in a draught to drip until firm. Add chopped chives or a grating of nutmeg.

MENU II

COLD TOMATO SOUP IN CUPS
COLD ROAST MEATS
POTATOES IN JACKETS
GOOSEBERRY MOUSSE

Cold Tomato Soup in cups. *See* p. 89.

Serve cold.

Cold Roast Meats

Serve any cold meats—or sliced ham and tongue.

Potatoes in Jackets

Scrub potatoes and bake for two hours in a slow oven.

Vegetable Salad

Mix chopped celery, apple and beetroot together and dress with mayonnaise.

Gooseberry Mousse

Top and tail 1 lb. gooseberries. Stew them in very little water with 4 oz. demerara sugar, and when cold pass through a hair sieve. Whip 1 pt. cream thick. Add purée of gooseberries to it, also 3 sheets of gelatine melted in a little milk. When nearly set fold in 2 whites of eggs whipped stiffly.

For a Cold Meal, Choose from these Recipes

Cold Devilled Eggs

1 oz. butter	1 tbsp. Worcester sauce
½ tsp. dry mustard	Anchovy paste
2 tbsp. tomato ketchup	Rounds toast
1 tbsp. mushroom ketchup	Eggs, hard-boiled and quartered
Parsley	Watercress

Melt the butter, add the mustard, tomato ketchup, and mushroom ketchup, Worcester sauce, allow to simmer and drop in as many eggs as required. Spread the rounds of toast with anchovy paste, pile on the eggs and pour over the sauce, garnish with parsley and a sprig or two of watercress.

Cold Poached Eggs and Spinach

Eggs	*Béchamel sauce*
Spinach purée	*Chopped parsley*
Croûtons of fried bread	

Poach the eggs, trim them and place them on *croûtons* of fried bread. Pour over them a little Béchamel sauce (see p. 142), sprinkle with chopped parsley and put round them a border of cold spinach purée.

Eggs and Sardines

3 *hard-boiled eggs*	*Strips of toast*
12 *small sardines*	*Olives*
1 *oz. butter*	*Parsley*
A little cream	

Cut up the eggs and pass them through a seive. Bone the sardines, and mix with a lump of butter and cream. Spread on strips of toast and serve, garnished with an olive and finely chopped parsley.

Mock Crab

3 *oz. butter*	*A little vinegar*
2½ *oz. grated cheese*	*Cayenne*
Anchovy essence	*Parsley*

Mix well together and spread on *croûtes*. Garnish with finely chopped parsley.

Fillets of Sole with Horse-radish

Fillets of sole	*Lemon quarters*
Béchamel sauce (p. 142)	*Horse-radish sauce*
Parsley	

Cook the fillets between two buttered plates in a moderate oven. Drain. When cold cover them with Béchamel sauce, sprinkle them with parsley, and garnish with lemon quarters. Serve horse-radish sauce.

Haddock Soufflé

6 oz. dried haddock	Little warm water
1 oz. gelatine	¼ pt. white sauce
¼ pt. cream or evap. milk	¼ pt. aspic
1 hard-boiled egg	Salt, cayenne

Melt the gelatine in warm water. Cook the haddock, remove the skin and bone, and chop finely. Add the white sauce and whipped cream, season. Strain the gelatine and add. Fill some small cases or individual dishes almost full with the mixture. Add a slice of hard-boiled egg and then pour over a little melted aspic jelly (see p. 141). Chill before serving.

Herrings in Wine

½ pt. water	A bayleaf
½ pt. white wine	Herrings
½ pt. white vinegar	Mace
A sliced onion	Peppercorns
2 sliced carrots	Parsley

Put vegetables, water, wine, vinegar and spices into a saucepan and simmer for 10 minutes. Then clean and open as many herrings as required to allow one per person, and let them boil in the liquor for 10 minutes. Remove from heat, and when quite cool serve them garnished with finely chopped parsley and a little liquor and a few peppercorns.

Prawn Salad

Prawns	1 glass claret
2 hard-boiled eggs	1 dsp. wine vinegar
1 large lettuce	1 tsp. chutney or tomato ketchup
Mustard and cress	

Wash, dry and divide lettuce and mix with the mustard and cress; heap in the centre of dish. Cut the eggs lengthways in four and arrange round the dish. Then place the prawns in the centre. Mix the claret, vinegar, chutney or tomato ketchup and pour over the green salad.

Salmon Loaf.

Follow with a main dish from this group:

Beef Loaf

1 *lb. beef*	1 *egg*
1 *onion*	1 *tbsp. chopped pickles*
1 *cupful white breadcrumbs*	*Pepper, salt*
1 *tbsp. chopped parsley*	*A little gravy or milk*

Glaze, aspic jelly

Mince the beef with half the bacon and place in a basin. Mix all other ingredients (finely chopped). Season with salt and pepper and moisten with the beaten egg and a little gravy or milk. Form into oblong loaf. Place in a greased tin, cover with greaseproof paper and bake for 30 minutes. Then lay the rest of the bacon over it and cook until brown and crisp. Allow to cool; glaze, and garnish with aspic jelly.

Aspic Jelly

1 *onion*	$\frac{1}{4}$ *pt. each malt vinegar and*
1 *carrot*	*tarragon vinegar*
1 *bayleaf*	1$\frac{1}{2}$ *pt. water*
2 *cloves*	*Juice of one lemon and rind*
$\frac{1}{4}$ *pt. sherry*	*Small stick of celery*
9 *peppercorns*	*Blade mace*
2 *eggs (whites and shells)*	2$\frac{1}{2}$ *oz. gelatine*

Peel onion, scrape the carrot, and wash the celery; dice and with spices and lemon put into a saucepan with the vinegar and water, and the whisked whites of eggs and broken up shells. Stir over a low heat until the mixture boils and the gelatine is melted. Reduce the heat, then simmer gently for 15 minutes. Strain two or three times until clear. Add sherry. Turn into a jar, when cool cover closely and use as desired.

Chicken and Ham Mould

6 oz. cold chopped chicken   1½ pt. Béchamel sauce

6 oz. cold ham   1 oz. gelatine

1 tsp. each chopped parsley and grated lemon rind

Soak gelatine in a little cold water. Then boil with the white sauce until it is dissolved. Add the ingredients to the sauce, stir well. Turn into moistened mould to set. Serve garnished with lettuce leaves.

Béchamel Sauce

4 oz. butter   4½ level tbsp. flour

1½ pt. milk   Salt, pepper to season

Melt the butter in a double saucepan. Stir in the flour and mix well. Add milk and stir until boiling and for a few minutes after. Season with pepper and salt.

Grouse

Brace grouse   Watercress

Piece toast   Butter

Pluck and draw the grouse. Cut a piece of toast for each grouse to rest on, put the grouse on toast in baking tin, with a little butter, place in a moderate oven, 325° F., and cook for about 35 minutes. Baste well with the butter. Remove from oven, leave to cool, and place the grouse on dish (silver if possible) and serve garnished with watercress.

Cold Pressed Beef

7 lb. salted brisket   6 cloves

2 carrots   1 oz. meat glaze

1 onion   Aspic

1 turnip   Parsley

15 peppercorns   1 tbsp. water (hot)

Put beef, vegetables and spices together into a saucepan and bring to the boil slowly and simmer for 6–7 hours until the meat comes away from the bone and a fork can easily be put through it. When absolutely tender, remove bone and put meat into a cloth and pat into a good shape, press between two plates tied together with string. Before serving, dissolve meat glaze in hot water and brush over the meat. Serve garnished with aspic and parsley.

Mousse of Ham

1 *lb. cooked ham*	*¾ pt. aspic jelly*
½ pt. cream	*Truffles*
Tarragon	*Parsley*

Use a dome-shaped mould, line with a layer of aspic jelly (see p. 141 or use prepared aspic), then take a flat tin a little larger than the mould and line it with aspic jelly; when both are set, decorate with truffles, tarragon and parsley, then run a thin layer of aspic over the decorations. Remove a little fat from the ham, mince it, then pound it on a mortar, pass it through a wire sieve and place in a basin, add the melted aspic jelly and whipped cream. When the mixture begins to set, fill up both moulds with it and leave to cool. When set, turn out the larger tin first, then turn out the other and place it on the first one, put a little aspic round the rim where the two meet and round edge of dish.

(*For another recipe, see p.* 188.)

Paté de Foie Gras

1½ *lb. duck or chicken liver*	*Salt*
2 *oz. butter*	*Pepper*
Chopped onion	*Chopped truffle*
¼ lb. cooked ham	*Dsp. clarified butter*

Sauté the liver with the onion. Add ham, pass all through sieve, season, and add butter. Work into a paste. Add truffle, put into a brown jar. Rub on clarified butter.

Potted Pheasant

1 *pheasant*	4 *oz. butter*
1 *qt. stock*	1 *sprig thyme*
1 *wine glass sherry*	*Salt*
2 *shallots*	*Cayenne*
	Clarified butter

Roast the pheasant and remove the bones. Place in a saucepan with the shallots, stock, wine and seasoning, and boil until it becomes a glaze. Remove all skin and gristle from the pheasant, pound to a paste (in a mortar), add butter and glaze, season and press into pots. Cover with clarified butter.

Rabbit Creamed

1 *rabbit* (*jointed*)	¼ *pt. Béchamel sauce*
2 *oz. butter*	*Pepper*
½ *oz. gelatine*	*Salt*
¼ *pt. cream or evaporated milk*	*Paprika*

Dissolve gelatine in a tbsp. water. Melt the butter. Add rabbit, and simmer together for a few minutes, without browning. Remove from heat, take flesh off bones, pound, and pass through a sieve. Mix gelatine and cream. Add paprika, pepper and salt. Add to rabbit purée. Turn into greased mould and steam for an hour. Turn out and cover with Béchamel sauce and garnish with sliced tomato and cucumber. Chicken or pheasant can be used instead of rabbit.

Raised Pork Pie (cold)

Hot-water crust:

¼ *pt. water*	1 *lb. flour*
4–6 *oz. lard*	½ *tsp. salt*

Boil the water and fat. Sift the flour and salt. Add liquid to flour and mix together with a wooden spoon. Knead together. When the mixture is cool enough to handle, cover and keep in a warm place until required. Mould into the desired shape while still warm and dough is pliable.

¾ *lb. lean pork*	1 *apple*
Salt	*Egg*
Pepper	1 *tsp. gelatine*
Nutmeg	*Mixed herbs*
	⅛ *pt. stock*

Make the pastry and mince the pork. Grease a 5-inch diameter tin—preferably one with a loose base. If this is not available, mould the pastry around a jam jar turned upside down. When the pastry has cooled a little, line the tin or shape by hand. Fill with the meat and seasoning, add herbs and peeled sliced apple. Cover with lid of pastry. Decorate the top with leaves and a rose, a hole in the centre. Bake the rose separately and replace when the pie is ready for serving. If the pie has been moulded by hand, a piece of greaseproof paper in a double band should be pinned firmly round. Brush the top over with egg before cooking. Remove the paper ½ hour before cooking is finished to brown pastry. Bake for 1½ hours, the first 20 minutes at 400° F., then reduce to 310° F., to continue cooking. When the pie is cooked, dissolve the gelatine in the stock and pour into the pie. Replace the rose in the centre and garnish with parsley.

Veal Cake

1 *lb. veal cutlet*	*¼ lb. bacon*
2 *leaves gelatine*	*2 eggs*
½ lemon	*½ pt. stock*
Parsley	*Pepper and salt*
Watercress	*Tomato*

Hard boil the eggs and slice. Chop parsley, grate lemon rind, cut up the veal, rinse a mould with cold water and decorate the bottom and sides with slices of egg and strips of bacon. Chop remaining egg and bacon and mix with the veal; add the chopped parsley, lemon rind and season with pepper and salt. Fill the mould three parts full and add sufficient stock or water to cover it; cover with greased paper and place at 250° F., and bake for 1½ hours; then melt the gelatine and remaining stock in a saucepan, add to mould and leave to cool. Turn out and serve with watercress and sliced tomato.

Apple and Celery Salad

Mix one cup of diced apple with two cups of diced celery. Add mayonnaise and mix. Put on a bed of lettuce. Add chopped nuts just before serving.

Avocado Salad

Cut an avocado in slices or cubes. Marinate, drain, and serve on lettuce leaves with French dressing made with lemon juice.

Macaroni Salad

Cut cold cooked macaroni to desired lengths. Add chopped celery, chopped onion and parsley. Mix with mayonnaise and lemon juice. Chill and serve in lettuce-lined bowl.

Potato Salad. *See p.* 189.

Spaghetti Salad

Make as macaroni salad, above, using spaghetti instead of macaroni.

Tomato and Cucumber Salad

Peel and slice tomatoes and cucumbers. Add some finely chopped parsley and a little chopped onion. Pour French dressing over the salad.

Almond Tartlets

Puff paste	*1 yolk of egg*
2 oz. almonds	*2 whites of eggs*
2 oz. sugar	*Grated rind and juice of lemon*
1 liqueur glass Noyau	*1 tbsp. chopped candied lemon peel*

Make sufficient puff paste to line 8 patty tins and butter them. Prick them and brush over with apricot glaze. Blanch, chop and fry almonds in butter until lightly browned, then pound in a mortar with sugar, add Noyau and egg yolk, stir well, add whites of eggs, lemon juice and grated rind. Mix till creamy. Add peel, and then only three-parts fill patties (to allow for rise in baking). Set them on buttered paper, dust over with sugar and bake in a gentle oven, 250° F., dust lightly with sugar before serving.

Banana Purée

6 ripe bananas	*Juice of lemon*
1 wineglass maraschino	*½ oz. gelatine*
2 gills custard	*1 gill strawberry syrup*
Whipped cream	

Mash the bananas with a silver fork. Flavour with maraschino and lemon juice. Pass through hair sieve into a bowl. Add strawberry syrup. Make 2 gills custard. Blend this with 2 oz. sugar and ½ oz. gelatine, add to bananas. Pour into compote dish and top with whipped cream.

Coffee Creams

1 pt. milk	6 eggs
Coffee to flavour	1 gill cream
	Whipped cream

Flavour the milk with coffee, cool, add the beaten eggs and reheat, but do not boil; strain through a hair sieve, add a gill of cream and then pour into small china moulds and steam until set. Leave to cool, turn out and serve with whipped cream.

Compote of Apricots

1 lb. young apricots	Finely peeled rind and
6 oz. caster sugar	juice of lemon
¾ pt. boiling water	1 sherry glass maraschino
½ tbsp. apricot jam	Whipped cream

Cut the apricots in half, remove stones and peel off skin. Dust with sugar. Then put remaining sugar into a saucepan with the apricot jam, lemon rind and juice. Boil 5 minutes, strain, then return to pan. Add apricots and simmer gently for about 20 minutes. Then allow to cool, add maraschino. Serve on a glass dish with whipped cream.

Fruits with Iced Champagne

Iced champagne   Pineapple   Peaches   Banana   Apricots

Trim the fruit into nice pieces in a china bowl over ice. Make ½ pint apricot syrup, flavour with lemon and a glass of good brandy, and moisten the fruit with this. Turn in with a wooden spoon and fork. Leave to stand. Just before serving pour over iced champagne.

Rhubarb Creams

1 lb. rhubarb	2 gills whipped cream
Syrup	or evaporated milk
Zest of lemon	½ oz. gelatine
	Sherry glass Kirsch

Cut up the rhubarb and simmer with just sufficient syrup flavoured with zest of a lemon to cover it. When soft, strain off juice, add gelatine and dissolve, pass through a sieve. Add juice, add cream and Kirsch, whip all together and fill 1 doz. moistened dariole moulds. Set to chill—when firm, turn out and arrange in a circle on a glass dish and serve.

For the syrup allow 5 oz. sugar, ½ pint water.

Anchovy Puffs

1 *gill aspic jelly (diluted)*	4 *hard-boiled eggs*
12 *fillets of anchovy*	*Mustard and cress*

2 *tbsp. mayonnaise*

Line 12 bouchée moulds with melted aspic jelly about ⅛ inch thick. Make the anchovy cream by pounding together the hard-boiled eggs, anchovy fillets and mayonnaise. Then pass all through a hair sieve. Add 1 gill diluted aspic jelly, and fill the hollows in the lined moulds. Leave to set, then turn out and serve, garnished with mustard and cress.

Canapés of Sardines

12 *sardines*	*Mayonnaise*
12 *pieces fried bread (¼ inch*	*Chopped olive*
thick, length of sandwich)	*Watercress*
Butter	*Beetroot*

Free the sardines from the oil by placing on a long dish and tipping up, and pouring boiling water over them; drain, dry on a clean cloth. Butter each piece of fried bread and lay a sardine on it. Mash with mayonnaise and sprinkle with chopped olive. Arrange on dish. Garnish with watercress and cubes of beetroot.

Cucumber with Shrimps

A good-sized cucumber	*A little mayonnaise*
3 *oz. pounded shrimps*	1 *dsp. cream*
Paprika	*Cress*
1 *oz. butter*	*Salt and pepper*

Cut the cucumber into 2-inch lengths. Peel these very carefully, and with a tube cutter cut out the seeds and form small cases. Pound the shrimps, paprika, butter and seasoning together. Moisten with cream. Fill into cases and serve cold, garnished with green mayonnaise and cress.

Cream of Asparagus

½ *bundle asparagus*	*Mustard and cress*
1 *gill milk*	*Mayonnaise*
1 *egg*	*Butter*

Boil and simmer the heads in milk until tender, then strain and allow them to cool. Cut off the green ends, chop into small pieces, then pass as much of the stalks as you can through a hair sieve, using the milk in which the asparagus was cooked. Make a savoury custard. Butter a mould. Arrange the green tops on the bottom of the mould to form the top when unmoulded. Stir the pulp into the custard. Fill the mould threequarters full, steam gently until set, then cool, and when cold, turn out. Arrange on a flat dish garnished with broken aspic and mustard and cress. Serve with mayonnaise and whipped cream mixed together.

BUFFET SERVICE

Typical buffet settings are those at which the guests help themselves. When possible choose food which does not require a knife.

The sweet may be on the table at the beginning of the meal, and if the table becomes too crowded, move the water and the hot drinks to another surface. It is always wise to decide, when service is completely lacking, what concessions to make to achieve the most peaceful and satisfactory conditions for everyone. Trays or a trolley prepared in the kitchen ready to carry or wheel into the diningroom and placed near the hostess are often a solution. For four or less fill the plates in the kitchen. For a larger number of persons, make attractive platters and casseroles, placing them on the table so that the serving responsibilities can be divided, thus making it easier for the hostess.

For the hot drinks, it is wise to instruct a maid or some other person to keep in frequent touch with the pourers, so that their needs may be anticipated and there is a plentiful supply of hot water and cups, etc.

Buffet luncheons and suppers are found to be easy ways of serving large groups of people. They are characterized by the friendly atmosphere and informality which make an appeal to all ages and income groups.

This type of meal can be either simple or elaborate. Usually a buffet meal is limited to two courses, but fruit or tomato-juice cocktails may be served to the guests if desired before they are brought to the buffet.

A main factor in the success of a buffet meal is the arrangement and attractiveness of the buffet table. Sometimes the arrangement of the variety of foods and the necessary silver and china takes a little extra thought to ensure the food-lovers' interest.

A damask, lace or coloured cloth may be used for the service table, and frequently the floral decoration is replaced by a bowl of fruit, tastefully arranged. Great care is always necessary in the arrangement of contrasting shapes and colours, and the table must not be overcrowded.

The foods must be chosen for their delicious flavours, variation of texture, and palatability. It is frequently found that if too many hot foods are served, too much has been attempted. Therefore choose, whenever possible, foods which are prepared beforehand, with added last-minute crisp garnishes.

Usually for buffet service food is arranged in the order in which it is served. Fish, meat and potatoes, vegetables or salads, desserts, savouries and cheese. Savouries and cheese look well if grouped on a platter or wooden board.

Planning Foods for Buffets

In planning foods for buffets, choose those which are easy to serve. Never serve foods that are too sloppy, or too many foods and salads together on a plate. Individual shells are useful for hot foods. Pay great attention to the garnishing. Provide assorted salads and a good variety of relishes.

Always have a variety of food and keep a reserve to replace the dishes as they are used. Think of colour for salads and their arrangement. Provide a small bowl for the salad dressing, placing it in the centre of a large salad, and arrange the individual salads around it.

Whenever possible for a buffet party, according to season, serve two *pièces de résistance*—in the winter, both hot; in the summer, one cold and one hot. Place these dishes at the end of the table. Keep the 'hot' on an electric hot-plate and in a chafing dish.

All the preparations must be completed before the arrival of the guests, so that the hot dishes may be brought in piping hot and kept so.

The guests may help themselves, but it is often found to be much simpler to ask a friend to preside over a dish.

See that there are hot rolls, dishes of olives, nuts, etc., and a platter of cheese and also a salad.

Remember to provide napkins, glasses, silver and plates.

THE BUFFET TABLE

Probably the best place for a buffet to be set out is in the dining-room (if you have one). Arrange the room so that the table can be pushed up against the wall and so give you more space for guests. Also this makes the seating easy; guests can be seated at small tables (card or other small tables with a cloth or doilies for them). Make sure that everyone finds a seat! Or arrange informal tables and let your guests find their own seats. The tables may be set with flowers, china and silver, pepper and salt as desired. Also be sure to have a few large trays to supplement the tables, and let the 'company' forage for themselves.

For the buffet table—especially when the meal is an evening one—a three- or five-branch candelabrum between the centre piece and serving places at the table-ends is traditional with unfailing grace and charm. Candles may be set at each corner of the buffet table—not close to the edge, but nearer to the centre, and well out of the way.

> *The preparation of meats and bread and drinks, that they may be rightly handled, and in order to this intention, is of exeedingly great moment; howsomever it may seem a mechanical thing and savouring of the kitchen and buttery, yet it is of more consequence than those fables of gold and precious stones and the like.*
>
> **BACON**

L

A BUFFET MEAL FOR FIFTY

SHRIMP COCKTAIL
CREAM OF TOMATO SOUP
VIRGINIA BAKED HAM, MUSTARD SAUCE
VEGETABLE MACÉDOINE
SCALLOPED POTATOES
CHEESE SALAD
LEMON SNOW
LEMON FLUFFY PIE
ASSORTED CHEESE
ASSORTED SANDWICHES (see p. 99)
COFFEE

Wines as chosen
Fruit punch

Shrimp Cocktail

17 *lb. tomatoes* (50 *medium*)	2 *tbs. each, lemon juice,*
2 *lb. shrimps, cut into*	*salt, mustard*
small pieces	1 *tsp. paprika*
1 *qt. celery, diced; or*	*Mayonnaise and chopped*
shredded lettuce	*parsley to garnish*
1 *pt. cucumber*	3 *heads of lettuce*

Scoop out the centre of the tomatoes, fill the shell with the shrimps, celery, cucumber, lemon, salt, paprika and mustard, all mixed together. Garnish with mayonnaise and serve on lettuce leaves.

Cream of Tomato Soup. (*Makes approx.* 3 *gallons.*)

1½ *gal. tomato purée (thin)*	10 *oz. butter or margarine melted*
1 *oz. onion (grated)*	6 *oz. flour*
½ *bay leaf*	2 *oz. salt*
2 *tsp. bicarbonate of soda*	1 *tsp. pepper*
1½ *gal. hot milk*	4 *oz. sugar*

Chopped parsley
1 pt. whipped cream } *to garnish*

Heat the tomato purée, onion and bay leaf to boiling-point; add the bicarbonate of soda. Mix well together. Just before serving make a white sauce with the milk, butter and flour, season with salt, pepper and sugar. Serve in a soup cup garnished with a pinch of chopped parsley and 1 teaspoonful of whipped cream.

Virginia Baked Ham

A 16-*lb. ham—a centre cut,*   2½ *tsp. mustard (dry)*

sliced ½ *inch thick*   ½ *pt. vinegar*

14 *oz. sugar (brown)*   1 *qt. water*

Mix the sugar and mustard together and rub them over the surface of the ham. Place the ham in a baking tin, pour over the vinegar and water. Cover tightly and bake for approximately 2 hours at 300° F.

Mustard Sauce

2 *eggs well beaten*   1 *oz. butter*

2 *tbsp. water*   1 *pt. cream (whipped) or*

4 *tbsp. vinegar*   *evaporated milk*

1 *oz. sugar*
½ *tsp. salt*   } *mix together*
2 *tsp. mustard (dry)*

Put the dry ingredients into a double saucepan; add eggs, water and vinegar. Cook until thick. Add the butter and stir until melted. Cool. When cold, fold in the whipped cream.

Vegetable Macédoine

1½ *lb. each, celery, onions,*   3½ *lb. tomatoes, cooked*

carrots—diced   1 *tbs. salt*

1½ *lb. potatoes, diced*   4 *oz. butter*

2½ *lb. peas, canned or frozen*   1 *oz. flour*

Cook the celery, onion and carrots in just sufficient water to prevent their burning. When partially cooked add the potatoes, peas, tomatoes and salt. When all the vegetables are tender add the butter and flour. Cooking time approximately ¾ hour.

Scalloped Potatoes

11 *lb. peeled potatoes*	6 *oz. breadcrumbs*
2 *oz. salt*	2 *oz. butter*
1 *gal. white sauce*	*Parsley to garnish*

Wash, peel and slice the potatoes, steam them or place in two baking tins. Sprinkle with salt, pour over the white sauce, bake at 350° F., for an hour. Mix together the melted butter and the breadcrumbs and pour over. Return to the oven for a further hour. Just before serving sprinkle with parsley.

Cheese Salad

6 *lb. cream cheese*

3 *lb. tomatoes—raw, peeled and diced*

4 *oz. green peppers chopped (if desired)*

1 *lb. celery, diced; or grated carrot*

2 *oz. salt*

1–1½ *pt. mayonnaise (added to cream cheese)*

8 *oz. diced radishes*

1 *lb. diced cucumber*

Mix well together.

Lemon Snow

½ *lb. cornflour*	2 *qt. boiling water*
1½ *lb. sugar*	16 *whites of eggs*
½ *tsp. salt*	6 *oz. sugar*
2 *tbsp. finely grated lemon rind*	½ *pt. lemon juice*

Mix the cornflour, sugar and salt in a double boiler. Add, stirring the whole time, the boiling water. Cook for about 4 minutes (in the double boiler). Pour on, stirring the whole time, the stiffly beaten whites of eggs and the 6 oz. sugar. Add lemon juice and rind, stir well and pour out into a flat pan (12 × 20 inches). Chill. Cut and serve with soft custard or ice cream.

For the sauce

14 oz. sugar	1 pt. cold milk
2 oz. cornflour	3 qt. hot milk
½ tsp. salt	10 egg yolks

2 tbsp. vanilla essence

Mix the sugar, salt and cornflour together. Blend with the cold milk until smooth (in a double saucepan). Add the hot milk, stirring constantly. Add egg yolks. Blend well. Cook until thickened. Add vanilla. Cool before serving.
Two quarts of ice-cream are required if served with the lemon snow.

Lemon Fluffy Pie for Fifty

1 tsp. salt	20 oz. shortening
20 oz. flour	6 oz. water

Sieve flour, salt; cut and rub in shortening. Add water, stirring constantly. Divide into 8 portions. Roll each out to ⅛-inch thickness. Bake blind at 350° F. (This pastry is best used the same day.) Fill with:

24 egg yolks	4 lb. sugar
½ pt. lemon juice	1 tsp. salt.
3 grated lemon rinds	1 tsp. butter
2 qt. water	½ oz. cornflour in 1½ pt. water

Heat water, sugar, salt and lemon rinds. Add cornflour blended with water. Add slowly, stirring constantly, beaten egg yolks, butter and lemon. When thickened pour into baked pie shells. Top with meringue:

16 whites of eggs stiffly whipped

½ tsp. salt

14 oz. sugar and 2 oz. cornflour mixed

Beat in half the sugar and cornflour, fold the rest in lightly with a metal spoon. Spread on the pies and bake for about 15 minutes at 350° F. (This mixture is enough for the 8 pies.)

Assorted Cheese

Some assorted cheese and cracker biscuits (order 1½ lb.)

10 *bunches of radishes*

2½–3 *lb. of celery, curled*

Coffee

For one cup per head order 1–1¼ lb. coffee.
Allow one roll per head (plus two over).

Fruit Punch

18 *oranges*	4 *lb. sugar*
12 *lemons*	*Water*
4 *grapefruit*	1 *qt. ginger ale*

Extract the fruit juice. Add sugar, stir until dissolved. Add iced water to make 2¾ gallons of liquid. Just before serving add ginger ale.

ASSORTED SANDWICHES FOR FIFTY

Bacon and Tomato Sandwiches

100 *slices of bread*	7 *lb. sliced tomatoes*
4 *lb. bacon sliced and cooked*	½ *pt. mayonnaise*
in rows in oven until brown	2 *heads of lettuce*

Spread half the bread (50 slices) with mayonnaise, place slices of tomato and bacon, and a piece of lettuce on each.

Chicken Sandwiches

100 *slices of bread*	2 *tsp. salt*
3½ *lb. chopped chicken*	4 *oz. diced celery or cucumber*
4 *oz. chopped almonds* (*if desired*)	¼ *qt. vinegar or lemon juice, or mayonnaise*

Mix well and spread on bread.

Cheese Sandwiches

100 *slices of bread*   2 *tsp. salt*
3 *lb. grated cheese*   *Pinch of cayenne*
1 *pt. cream*   *Dash of Worcester sauce*
                4 *oz. butter*

Mix well together and spread on bread.

Ham Sandwiches

100 *slices of bread*   ½ *pt. boiled salad dressing*
4 *lb. ham, boiled and minced* ½ *pt. mayonnaise*
            8 *oz. chopped pickles, or made mustard*

Mix well and spread on bread.
Vary your sandwiches by spreading a blue cheese mixed with cream cheese and adding a few chopped chives and a little French dressing—or mix with the cream cheese a little anchovy essence and mayonnaise or chopped olive in anchovy; sandwich together white and brown bread. If desired cut the sandwiches into different shapes.

Lettuce and watercress may be used to advantage in sandwich filling. Spread both pieces of bread and sandwich together with lettuce in between—use mustard and cress or watercress; or make open sandwiches such as a thin piece of brown bread or half of a bridge roll with a thin slice of smoked salmon, and pipe on small fancy designs with cream cheese or mayonnaise, colouring this if necessary.

For other sandwiches use fillings in above proportions, for example use:—

Salmon.
Grated cheese with tomato sauce.
Chutney and cream cheese.
Cucumber, sliced with cream cheese.
Honey with bananas and chopped nuts.

Of course, the bread may be all white, or all brown or a slice of each.

Family and Miscellaneous Parties

*All happy families resemble one another; every
unhappy family is unhappy in its own way.*
TOLSTOY, *Anna Karenina*

The family is one of Nature's Masterpieces.
GEORGE SANTAYANA, *The Life of Reason*

All happy families resemble one another and at their celebrations nothing is too much trouble to make a party a success. Celebrations throughout the year should be planned with loving care.

The birth of an heir to a great estate means much rejoicing and tradition is still maintained by a dinner to the tenantry, the brewing of ale and the 'putting down' of port to be drunk when the young heir comes of age.

In all families the birth of a child is a specially happy event and there is much festivity.

Monday's child is fair of face,
Tuesday's child is full of grace,
Wednesday's child is full of woe,
Thursday's child has far to go,
Friday's child is loving and giving,
Saturday's child works hard for its living,
And the child that is born on the Sabbath Day,
Is fair and wise and good and gay.

A CHRISTENING PARTY

A christening party may be simple or lavish, but generally the party after a christening is rather quiet. A few very close friends are usually invited to share the 'Christening Caudle' or the glass of 'bubbly'. The party is a tea, either formal or informal, with the christening cake—which is white-iced like a bride's cake. (Sometimes the top tier of the wedding cake is carefully treasured for this occasion.) The initials of the baby and a suitable ornament are placed on the cake.

Serve also a plate or two of dainty sandwiches, and plain, iced sponge cake if there are young children present at this tea party.

The floral decoration on the table may be all white or, if preferred 'blue for a boy' and 'pink for a girl'.

In olden days it was a custom for the sponsors to give the whole twelve Apostle spoons—those in not such good circumstances would give four spoons and poorer people one. But the present-day godfather and godmother give a piece of silver—either a mug, a spoon and fork or whatever they consider useful and ornamental. And it was said in olden days that 'Coral was good to be hanged about children's necks.'

BABY'S FIRST PARTY

A very attractive table may be made with children's plates, a miniature circus, or bunny rabbits. But do remember never to use anything grotesque, for the tiny tot is easily frightened. A queer-looking clown is something amusing to the grown-up but may be terrifying to a child. Do be careful, too, that the sudden pulling of crackers doesn't frighten them.

Serve food which the children can enjoy. Both sandwiches and thin slices of bread and butter, cut into strips, small sponge fingers, tiny pink, white, blue and yellow iced cakes. Perhaps individual jellies or blancmanges, creams, fruit salad, with the fruit cut into very small dice. Serve both milk and fruit juices.

Make the sandwiches for children's parties of both white and brown bread and butter. And, if necessary, mix both white and brown on a plate so that the children eat both.

Use pulped banana, honey, jam, lemon curd, pounded fish, minced chicken, meat or vegetable extract—thinly spread—as fillings.

For the small iced cakes, make of this mixture and ice in different colours:

Fancy Cakes

4 oz. butter	Orange or lemon essence
4 oz. sugar	4 oz. flour
	2 eggs

Cream the butter and sugar. Add eggs gradually to the flour. Beat well, add a few drops of lemon or orange essence. Pour into small well-greased and floured tins. Bake at 400° F. until golden brown. Ice with following icing:

Glacé Icing

¼ lb. sifted icing sugar

4–5 tsp. water or 2 tsp. lemon or orange juice, 2–3 tsp. water

Put the ingredients together in a small saucepan, but do not boil (if boiled, the icing is dull when set). Remove the pan from the heat and beat icing with a wooden spoon. Pour over cake and spread quickly with a warm spoon. Colour if desired.

Fruit Salad
Serve the fruit salad in individual glass bowls. Apples, bananas, pears, peaches, apricots, strawberries, raspberries can be used as desired. See that the sliced and dried fruit is in small pieces.

Jellies and Blancmanges
Make these up in various colours. Children love colour.

CHILDREN'S PARTIES
The toddler's party is the greatest fun, because at this age the children can be so easily amused. Their greatest joy is a colourful table with lots of jelly, sponge cake disguised by different coloured icings and sandwiched together with icing, tea, which is really milk with just a splash of tea; both ice-cream and fruit salad are great favourites; sandwiches—made of both brown and white bread and butter. Chocolate biscuits have thawed many a homesick toddler at his first party.

The elder child's party varies according to age group. This may be a tea party, or an early evening party, and the following could be served:

Cold consommé—tomato juice; creamed chicken and ham *or* eggs and bacon; meringues, ice-cream, birthday cake, fruit salad; bonbons.

Orangeade, lemonade, ginger beer.

Birthday Cake
Make a ribbon sponge cake and ice with the child's favourite coloured icing.

YOUNGER CHILDREN'S PARTIES
Chicken sandwiches, mustard-and-cress sandwiches, jam sandwiches

Birthday cake (or for the very young child—Ribbon Sponge cake)

Jellies, ice-cream, fruit salad, blancmange

Orangeade, lemonade, ginger pop

Bonbons

TEENAGE TO TWENTY

Age? Sixteen. The very flower of Youth.
TERENCE, *Eunuchus*

For the teenage to twenties more planning is necessary. Perhaps one of the simplest forms of entertainment is to roll up the rugs and put on the gramophone or wireless or play some of the games which never fail to please, such as amateur magic, or a treasure hunt. Be sure to have handy a good supply of pencils and a scribbling pad or two, because at this age Consequences and other such games are great favourites.

Arrange a buffet table for refreshments for this type of party (remember the demands of the growing appetite). Have turkey, chicken, cold roast meat, ham, hot sausages, scrambled eggs, hot rolls, etc. Always spread the butter on the bread-stuffs—it is so much easier and more economical. Sandwiches and cake are always popular, chocolate, gingerbread, or a very luscious-looking *gâteau* or two, and ice-cream and fruit salad. Serve as well: hot coffee or tea, sweet cider, fruit squash and ginger pop.

A Teenage Dinner Party

If you are giving a teenage-only dinner party, pay special attention to both food and table setting. Use plenty of colour and your nicest china and silver, and you will have the real party setting.

The teenage group often prefer an evening party—for this a buffet supper will be found to be best.

FRUIT COCKTAIL

CONSOMMÉ

SALMON MOUSSE

GREEN SALAD   NEW POTATOES

CROQUEMBOUCHE

CHEESE

COFFEE

Fruit Cocktail

1 *orange*	*¼ lb. strawberries*
1 *apple*	*¼ lb. grapes*
1 *banana*	*½ teacupful apricot syrup*
3 *cherries*	*Wineglass sherry if desired*

Prepare, skin and arrange all the fruit in goblets. Pour syrup over fruit. Top with cherries and leave to chill. Serve with crushed ice.

Clear Chicken Soup

1 *carcase of chicken*	1 *small carrot*
1 *raw beef bone*	*Salt and pepper to taste*
1 *small onion*	2 *qt. water*

Simmer chicken and beef bone in 2 quarts water. Reduce to 1 quart. Strain and clear. When cool put in refrigerator where it can jelly. Serve either hot or cold.

Salmon Mousse

⅛ pt. aspic jelly (see p. 141)	*Salt*
1 *tin, or* 1 *lb. cooked salmon*	*Paprika*
⅛ pt. whipped cream	*Vinegar*
Worcester sauce	*Cucumber*

Watercress and lettuce

Place mould in refrigerator and chill thoroughly for ½ hour. Remove from refrigerator and line with a layer of aspic jelly and return to refrigerator to set. Mix salmon with whipped cream. Season well with paprika, salt and vinegar and Worcester sauce. Slice the cucumber, dip in aspic and make a design on bottom and sides of mould. Fill up with salmon mixture and chill. Garnish with watercress and lettuce.

Green Salad. *See p.* 94.   **New potatoes.** *See p.* 177.

Croquembouche

3¾ *oz. plain flour*	*Pinch of salt*
1½ *gills water*	3 *oz. butter or margarine*

2 *oz. sugar*

Dry the flour for a few minutes in a warm oven and then sieve with salt two or three times into a piece of kitchen paper. Put the water and butter into a saucepan, bring to boil. Remove from heat, add flour and beat till smooth. Leave to cool. When the mixture is at blood-heat beat in the egg a little at a time. Continue to beat until the mixture looks glossy. Place the mixture in a forcing bag fitted with a plain pin, and shape into small rounds the size of a walnut on to a dry baking sheet. Bake at 400° F., until brown and crisp. When cool, store in an airtight tin until the Croquembouche is required to be completed. Then melt 2 oz. sugar in a little water in a saucepan, boil steadily until the syrup is pale gold. Dip pan in cold water. Using this syrup stick the Croquembouche together. Mount the pastry balls row upon row to form a cone. Garnish with whipped cream and strawberries.

BIRTHDAY PARTIES

One entertainment which the child is always looking forward to is the birthday party.

The birthday celebration for the younger child is always a tea party. For the elders it may be a dinner party instead of a tea party. Remember, simple table decorations are much the best—expensive table decorations are wasted on children. The birthday cake will be the chief attraction and it makes a charming and not over-elaborate scene when the candles at each side are lit and the low floral decorations encircle it. At a dinner party the candles could be lit at the pudding course—and the cake served with ice-cream.

TWENTY-FIRST-BIRTHDAY PARTIES

This celebration can be a cocktail, dinner or buffet type of party, and the table decorations can be in keeping with the festivity. Perhaps it is to be a theatre party—followed by a supper party. Plan the detail so that the whole party goes without a hitch. If you wish to give a large party, buffet service is the simplest and easiest way to entertain your friends (see p. 149).

Here is a suggested dinner-party menu for twelve:

FRUIT COCKTAIL

LOBSTER MOUSSE

CHICKEN FRIED   SAUCE MADÈRE

GREEN PEAS   POTATOES BAKED

MERINGUES AND ICE-CREAM

ASSORTED CHEESE, CELERY, RADISHES

DESSERT

COFFEE

Serve WINE *or* CHAMPAGNE

Fruit Cocktail

Combine fruit juices with one flavour predominating—passion-fruit and pineapple juice with a squeeze of lemon juice, and sweetening added to taste. Serve with the glasses filled three-quarters full.

Lobster Mousse

2 *level tbsp. gelatine*	½ *pt. cream (or evaporated milk)*
¼ *pt. water*	½ *tsp. paprika*
1 *bkcp. cucumber or celery*	*Tomatoes and cucumber sliced*
3 *bkcp. flaked lobster*	*for garnish*
½ *pt. mayonnaise*	*Pinch of salt and pepper*

Dissolve the gelatine in a little warm water (placed in a cup in a basin of boiling water to allow the gelatine to dissolve thoroughly). Add the diced cucumber or celery to the flaked lobster. Stir the gelatine and mayonnaise together. Add the cream; add paprika, salt and pepper; mix with the lobster, etc., turn into a well-moistened mould. Leave to set. Serve garnished with tomato and cucumber sliced, and finely chopped parsley.

Chicken Fried

3 *roasting chickens, jointed*	2 *oz. flour*
1 *egg*	½ *tsp. paprika*
1 *tbsp. water*	*Gravy*
1 *bkcp. breadcrumbs*	½ *lb. mushrooms*
1 *lb. fat*	2 *bananas*

Lettuce

Pre-heat the oven to 350° F. Have the chicken jointed when buying. Heat the fat in a deep saucepan. Toss the chicken pieces in the seasoned flour until well coated. Pile the bread-crumbs on a plate. Beat the egg and water together and dip the chicken pieces into the egg, then into the crumbs, coating them well. When the fat in the pan is boiling at 375° F. (this is when the fat is quite still and a blue haze rises gently), add two or three of the chicken pieces at a time and fry until they are golden-brown all over. When the pieces have all been fried for about

M

five minutes, place them in a baking tin with about ½ pint melted fat and continue cooking them until tender. Baste occasionally. Allow about 1–1½ hours cooking time. Place the pieces on a serving dish. Serve them garnished with fried mushrooms and bananas, and shredded lettuce.

Sauce Madère. (*Makes 2 pt. sauce*)

6 *tbsp. butter*	2 *bay leaves*
8 *level tbsp. flour*	6 *sprigs of parsley*
2 *pt. stock*	⅛ *tsp. pepper*
2 *tsp. each mustard and*	¼ *tsp. salt*
meat extract	¼ *pt. Madeira*

Melt the butter and when sizzling, stir in flour. Blend and cook for two minutes. Add the stock gradually and cook until thick. Add mustard, meat extract, bay leaves, parsley and salt and pepper. Cook four minutes. Remove bay leaves and parsley. Sieve before serving; add the Madeira (if no Madeira is available, use sherry).

Green Peas

6 *lb. unshelled peas (or*	¼ *tsp. salt*
three packets of frozen peas)	2 *oz. butter*
Pinch of sugar	¼ *pt. cream (or evaporated milk)*
Lettuce leaves	*Chopped parsley*

Place peas on lettuce leaves in a double saucepan. Cook them covered until they are tender (about 35 minutes). Add salt, butter, cream, sugar. Just before serving, garnish with parsley.

Potatoes Baked

6 *cups mashed potatoes (about* 12 *medium-sized potatoes cooked and mashed)*	
3 *eggs*	1 *tbsp. chopped parsley*

Separate the yolks and whites of eggs. Beat the yolks and potatoes together. Beat the egg whites until stiff, and fold them lightly into the potato mixture. Drop them from a spoon into even-sized blobs, on to a greased baking sheet. Bake at 350° F., until they are crisp. This takes about 20 minutes.

Meringues. (*This makes* 24)

 3 *whites of eggs* 8 *oz. caster sugar*
 Pinch of salt   1 *pt. whipped cream* (*or evaporated milk*)

Beat the whites of eggs for two minutes with a pinch of salt, then add the sugar gradually, beating continuously, until the mixture is sufficiently stiff to stand alone in peaks. Lightly grease oven trays with butter. Drop the mixture in dessert-spoonfuls from the end of the spoon (using a rotary movement and so rounding them off). Place in a slow oven, 250° F., for 35 minutes. If possible make them the day they are to be used and they will have a lovely squelchy inside when they are put together with the whipped cream.

If they are to be kept, bake for 45 minutes but do not let them brown; remove from oven and press the bottoms gently between finger and thumb to make a hollow. Return to oven and cook for another hour until they are quite dry. Cool well before storing in a tin.

For varied meringues divide mixture and colour as desired before baking.

Buy whatever flavoured ice-cream you wish and serve this with the meringues.

Chocolate Soufflé (*uncooked*)

For each serving desired allow one egg, ¼ pt. cream, ½ tsp. chocolate, a few drops vanilla essence, and one tsp. icing sugar. Separate egg, whisk yolk with chocolate powder till thick, fold in cream and vanilla, whip till thick, fold in stiffly whisked white of egg and sugar. (For large numbers allow two eggs to three servings.)

Assorted Cheese

Have an assortment of cheese with celery and radishes to finish up the meal. Cut the celery into lengths, then split into small pieces. Place in a basin of cold water to soak. It curls when removed and shaken dry.

Using a sharp knife make small incisions all round the bottom edge, then repeat making second incision between first so that cuts meet. Run the knife (with the point downwards) round the inside. The smaller pieces fall out leaving the leaves separated.

HOME PARTIES

When the refreshments come close upon dinner, they must not be substantial, nor must they be too sweet, but they must be dainty and complete.

Choose from these:

Scrambled egg sandwiches
Chicken sandwiches
Savoury creamed chicken sandwiches
Watercress or lettuce brown-bread sandwiches
Cheese and nut sandwiches
Ice-cream, served on glass plates with ice-cream spoons

(If *frappé* cups or glasses are used, it is customary to place each upon a doily-covered plate.)
Serve: coffee, iced coffee, tea, ginger ale, or wine cup.

A *house warming* frequently begins with a cocktail party and then goes on to a buffet type of supper, lasting well into the evening.

Sausages (heat them well, and serve on cocktail sticks), corn knobs and small fish-rolls garnished with watercress are always welcomed
Cocktails
Small sausages, very hot, served on cocktail sticks
Corn knobs
Fish rolls

CARD PARTIES

Cards were at first for benefits designed,
Sent to amuse, not to enslave the mind.
DAVID GANNILL,
Epilogue to Edward Moores Gamester

Bridge and Canasta, or other games of cards, are an entertainment which is both popular and easy. The refreshments may be just drink, coffee, cakes and a few sandwiches. At about 10 o'clock play usually ceases for refreshments. Or you can give your guests drinks alone, or a buffet supper.

TELEVISION PARTIES

To-day in many homes friends come in to view—and there is generally a short interval which allows sufficient time between acts, or in between items on the programmes, to have either a drink, a cup of tea or coffee, and a sandwich. Never have too great a spread as there is not really time.

GARDEN PARTIES

To-day a garden party may be a tea, a reception, or a cocktail party, which is given on the lawn instead of indoors. It is handled in the same way as such an entertainment indoors.

THEATRE SUPPERS

Everybody has his own theatre, in which he is manager, actor, prompter, playwright, sceneshifter, boxkeeper, doorkeeper all in one and audience into the bargain.

J. C. and A. W. HARE, *Guesses at Truth*

It is great fun to give this type of supper party. Set your table before you go out and leave everything ready on your kitchen table so that it is easy to prepare a tempting snack on your return.

You could serve sausages, scrambled eggs and fruit salad, or a rarebit, or if you prefer—a piping-hot bowl of soup, followed by cold meat and salad.

PICNIC MEALS

He who gives a child a treat,
Makes joy-bells ring in Heaven's street.
JOHN MASEFIELD, *The Everlasting Mercy*

Food for packed meals must be easily transportable. Some of the fillings for sandwiches are best when carried in the picnic box, in a little container and spread just before eating.

Never be stingy with greaseproof paper. Always pack each kind of sandwich separately and if packing bread and butter be sure to pack the buttered sides next to each other.

Then, after wrapping well, put into a tin. Never forget to pack the little pokeful of salt. Lettuce leaves or a piece of moist paper are useful in the very hot weather when placed outside the first wrapping paper. Always trim the crusts off the bread.

Rolls split and buttered and then filled with assorted fillings make a change. Use any of the sandwiches suggested in the Buffet service.

Freshly-made toast, split while hot and filled with freshly grilled bacon and dripping and put together again, makes a great change to the bread sandwich. (See SANDWICHES for suggested fillings.) Remember a good slice of cake never comes amiss in a packed meal. Include, whenever possible, some fresh fruit (not strawberries or raspberries as they are apt to go mushy).

Choose foods from BUFFET MEALS (see p. 149); for SANDWICHES, see p. 99; for CAKES, see p. 101.

A 'WELCOME HOME' OR A 'BON VOYAGE' LUNCHEON

> *'Tis here they say the journey ends*
> *And little doubt it must be so*
> *But, as I tell my bestest friends,*
> *   I hate to go.*
>
> EDEN PHILLPOTS,
> *Lament*

Choose gay decorations for your table for this luncheon and a simple menu, and allow plenty of time for your guests to linger over their coffee. It may be some time before they will be able to meet again and there is much to discuss on such occasions, just as when giving a 'Welcome Home' luncheon time must be allowed for your guests to chat together.

Choose your menu from LUNCHEONS (pp. 81–91).

Weddings

and

Anniversaries

A good husband makes a good wife.
ROBERT BURTON, *Anatomy of Melancholy*

I . . . chose my wife, as she did her wedding-gown, not for a fine glossy surface, but such qualities as would wear well.

OLIVER GOLDSMITH,
The Vicar of Wakefield

There are many feasts and festivities, but of them all, engagement-parties and weddings are those which mark the most joyous events in our lives.

ANNOUNCING AN ENGAGEMENT

Generally an engagement is announced by notes or telephone calls from the bride to her closest friends. Then follows the announcement in the newspapers. Or perhaps a more personal way is to make an announcement at a dinner or luncheon or small cocktail-party, given by the bride's parents.

With the announcement of an engagement there follows for the engaged couple a round of festivities. These may be parties of any type—sometimes the guests bring small gifts to start the home (kitchen gadgets and equipment are useful) or for the trousseau.

When sending out an invitation for such a party, the hostess either writes or tells her guests on the telephone the types of small gift to bring. On the card is also written 'to meet ——' (the name of the bride).

A very pretty table decoration for such an occasion is two candles with a heart-shaped mass of red roses surrounding the base of each.

It is great fun to plan such a party, be it a luncheon, tea, dinner or buffet meal, and to carry out an attractive colour-scheme in food and table decorations, and so make the meal both effective and appetizing.

A BRIDESMAIDS' LUNCHEON

A happy bridesmaid makes a happy bride.
TENNYSON, *The Bridesmaid*

A few days before the wedding the bride can give an informal brides-maids' luncheon (just as the groom gives his last 'stag party'). The bride-to-be herself presides at one end of the table with the maid-of-honour or chief bridesmaid at the other. Often it is at this luncheon that the bride gives her gifts to the bridesmaids. These are usually 'something small and important-looking'.

The table decorations for the bridesmaids' luncheons take their tone from the wedding to come. Both floral decorations and colour schemes for such an occasion may be simple or very decorative according to taste.

This menu can easily be varied if desired by substituting some other main dish.

SALMON BOILED WITH HOLLANDAISE SAUCE

GREEN PEAS   CUCUMBER SLICED

NEW POTATOES

CHICKEN MOUSSE

FRUIT FLAN

Salmon (Boiled).

4 *lb. salmon*   ¼ *pt. any Sauterne*

1 *qt. court bouillon (see p.* 131)   *Parsley or watercress*

Wipe the fish with a damp cloth, tie in a piece of muslin, place in a large, wide fish kettle. Pour *court bouillon* and wine over (the liquid should cover the entire fish). Bring quickly to boiling-point. Reduce heat. Cover and simmer gently for 30 minutes or until the fish flakes when tested with a fork. Carefully remove fish from liquid and from muslin, arrange on a pre-heated dish, garnish with parsley and watercress and serve piping hot with—*Hollandaise Sauce*

2 *egg yolks*   ¼ *pt. boiling water*

4 *tsp. lemon juice*   ¼ *tsp. salt*

4 *oz. butter*   *Pinch of cayenne*

Break egg yolks into top section of double boiler; beat lightly, add lemon juice, beat again. In separate bowl cream butter with wooden spoon; add to egg mixture, blend well. Insert top section double boiler into lower section, half filled with boiling water. Place on heat, cook until butter melts and mixture thickens, stirring constantly. Add salt and cayenne, stir gently. Add boiling water very slowly. Continue to stir until very smooth. Serve immediately.

New Potatoes

New potatoes	Sprig of mint
Salt	Chopped parsley
Boiling water	Small knob of butter

Have the potatoes as much the same size as possible. Scrape and wash, then drain them carefully. Drop them into boiling water, add mint, cook uncovered until they are tender. Drain, add butter and chopped parsley. Shake well together.

Green Peas

Green peas	Sugar	
Salt	Mint	Butter

Wash, then shell green peas. Cook them uncovered in a very small quantity of boiling water. Add salt, sugar and mint. Cook till just tender. Drain. Add butter and serve piping hot.

Cucumber Sliced

Cucumber   Pinch of salt   Vinegar

Peel and slice the cucumber very thinly, add salt. Leave for ½ hour, then drain off salt. Cover with vinegar and serve in a small dish.

Chicken Mousse

1 pt. aspic jelly (made with chicken stock)	½ gill aspic jelly
½ lb. cooked chicken (no bones or skin)	½ oz. gelatine
1 tcp. rich white sauce	1 gill cream
Slices tomato, cucumber, pimento, truffle	1–2 tbsp. sherry

Line a cake-tin or charlotte mould with aspic jelly and leave to set. Decorate with sliced tomato or pimento on bottom. Cover carefully with a little cold aspic. When set add further aspic to the depth of about 1 inch. Leave to set. Mince and pound chicken with sauce. Season well—add sherry and the gelatine, dissolved in ½ pint aspic jelly. Whip the cream until thick and then fold in the chicken mixture. Pour into the prepared tin. Leave in a cool place until firm when touched. Unmould, serve garnished, with the chopped aspic, lettuce and—

Tomato and Cucumber Aspic Jelly

1 *pt. stock* (*chicken, veal*	1 *oz. gelatine*
2 *tomatoes*	½ *gill sherry*
½ *cucumber, sliced*	1 *white of egg*

Dissolve gelatine into even-flavoured stock. Add sherry and the egg-white whipped to a froth. Put into pan, bring to the boil and whisk briskly until nearly boiling. Remove whisk and allow to boil, and the jelly will rise to top of pan. Remove from heat. Repeat this procedure 3 times. Leave pan uncovered away from heat. Strain through a jelly cloth. Line a mould with aspic, put slices of tomato and slices of cucumber round. When set fill with remaining jelly. When this has set, unmould and serve garnished with lettuce leaves or mustard and cress.

Fruit Flan

½ *lb. puff pastry*   1 *tbsp. jam*
Stewed fruit (*cherries, strawberries, grapes, raspberries*)

Roll out the pastry into a rectangle ¼ inch thick, fold into two, lengthways, and cut a piece 1 inch wide. Open out the pastry. Roll the centre piece and trimming very thinly, place on a wet baking sheet. Brush over with egg white and lay the fruit on top. Decorate and neaten the edge, prick in the middle and bake at 400° F., for about 20 minutes. Cool. Melt the jam in a little water, strain and then boil until thick. Brush the centre of flan with jam glaze and arrange the fruit in rows. Brush with glaze again. Serve ice-cream with this if desired.

THE WEDDING BREAKFAST

To the church in the morning, and there saw a wedding in the church, which I have not seen for many a day: and the young people so merry with one another!

SAMUEL PEPYS, *Diary*, 25th Dec. 1660

It is said that sometimes wedding breakfasts are rather dull affairs, or that they are stiff and formal. So if you are catering for a wedding, plan the food carefully, be it a small 'sit down' wedding breakfast or one with a buffet service.

THE BRIDE'S TABLE AND WEDDING BREAKFAST

Bride cakes are said to have originated from an old Roman custom where marriage was solemnly conducted in the presence of the witnesses, a cake of wheat or barley being eaten at that time. At one period it is said the bride had the cake of wheat thrown upon her head as she left the church. Later the wheat disappeared and was replaced by bride cakes. Still later the one cake which we know to-day with all its elaborations became the vogue. The old custom of passing slices of cake through the wedding ring is no longer fashionable.

White is the colour. White satin ribbons can span the table from the Bride's Cake to the edge of a buffet wedding-breakfast table. Gardenias, lilies of the valley, white roses, all make delightful floral decorations. They can be banked round the bridal cake.

If the bridal table is a 'set table' the main concern is for the table with the actual wedding party, which will, of course, include the bride and her groom, the maids of honour, or bridesmaids, best man and ushers. The parents of the happy couple usually sit at another table with the clergyman and his wife (if present), and a few of the nearest relations or close family friends. Should there be ample space sometimes a horseshoe-shaped table is set, but the one long table-setting, of course, depends upon space and the numbers who are to partake of the wedding feast.

For weddings large or small the buffet table is a practical and popular method of service. With rich linen and an array of shining silver, the deep satiny green of the foliage, and the gardenias and perhaps smilax, lilies of the valley and white roses, a very simple but beautiful effect can be obtained.

When there is a separate table for the wedding party, the cake usually occupies a prominent place. The cake is cut by the bride (sometimes by her and the groom when a sword is used or there is difficulty in getting the first slice out).

The first slice is shared by both bride and groom. Then the other guests are served. At some weddings small boxes of cake are placed by the door for a 'taste' for those unable to come, or to be sent off to absent friends.

Champagne is the general wedding beverage. The time to pour is as soon as the guests begin to arrive, or at the beginning of the first course, so that a toast to the bride and bridegroom may be given. It is frequently proposed by the best man or some near male relative or friend.

When a buffet table is used there should be, where possible, one hot and one cold main dish (unless it is a buffet tea party), and salad, rolls, sandwiches and ices. Consommé can be served from one end of the table, and tea, coffee and chocolate from the other.

Give me champagne and fill it to the brim.
LORD CHESTERFIELD

Bride's Cake

1 *lb. fresh butter*	½ *lb. glacé cherries*
1 *lb. sugar*	2 *oz. ground almonds*
3 *tsp. coffee essence*	2 *oz. shredded blanched almonds*
The grated rind of a lemon	2 *heaped tsp. cocoa*
1 *lb. eggs in shell* (8 *eggs*)	½ *tsp. powdered cinnamon*
1 *lb. sultanas*	½ *tsp. ground ginger*
2 *lb. currants*	½ *gill brandy*
¼ *lb. raisins*	1–4 *tbsp. sherry*
½ *lb. candied peel*	1½ *lb. flour*

A large pinch of salt

Clean and stew the currants and sultanas. Remove the sugar from the peel, shred and cut the peel finely. Stone the raisins and slice coarsely. Blanch, shred and dry the almonds. Roll the sugar heavily on a pastry-board with the rolling pin to remove the lumps. Mix all fruits together, except the glacé cherries, and warm slightly. Sieve the flour, salt, cocoa, spice, beat the eggs. Cream the butter thoroughly, add the sugar and cream again, adding the coffee essence. Add the well-beaten eggs by degrees with plenty of beating between each addition. Mix in a third of the sieved flour lightly. Mix in the fruit, add cherries, moistening with spirit and lastly gradually add the remaining sifted flour. Put the mixture into an 11-inch cake dish which has been previously lined with six thicknesses of newspaper, then an inner layer of ungreased kitchen paper. Place the cake in a very moderate oven and bake for about 5 hours. It is best to make the cake 2–3 months before required for use. When cool wrap in 3 thicknesses of greaseproof paper and store in an air-tight tin.

Three coatings of royal icing will be required; allow each coat a week to dry.

Royal Icing

3 *whites of eggs*

A few drops of blue colouring

½ *tsp. diluted acetic acid*

About 1 lb. finely sieved icing sugar

Slightly beat the egg whites, and add the icing sugar, a little at a time, beating it in rapidly until about half has been added. A few drops of vanilla essence will help to counteract the flavour of the acid.

Add the blue and acetic acid and beat well for some minutes. Beat in the remaining sugar gradually until a smooth, pliable icing is obtained. The amount of sugar required might be varied—according to the size of the whites of eggs. The icing first is spread over with a rounded or palette knife, frequently dipped into boiling water; the second coating may be plastered over the cake; it may be 'roughened up' with a fork instead of elaborate piping if preferred.

WEDDING ANNIVERSARIES

> *It was their Silver Wedding*
> *Such lots of silver presents*
> *Quite a show.*
>
> HECTOR HUGH MUNRO

Wedding anniversaries have been celebrated since the early days of Christianity. While to-day the twenty-fifth and fiftieth anniversaries seem to be great occasions, long ago celebrations took place more frequently. It would be possible to have a special dinner party for any of these dates with, of course, the special banquets on the twenty-fifth and succeeding anniversaries.

1st year, known as the Cotton Wedding.
2nd   „   „   „   „ Paper   „
3rd   „   „   „   „ Leather   „
5th   „   „   „   „ Wooden   „
10th „   „   „   „ Tin   „
12th „   „   „   „ Silk   „
15th „   „   „   „ Crystal   „
20th „   „   „   „ China   „
25th „   „   „   „ Silver   „
30th „   „   „   „ Pearl   „
40th „   „   „   „ Ruby   „
50th „   „   „   „ Golden   „
60th „   „   „   „ Diamond   „

The menu chosen for these special dinner-parties—when there is little domestic help—should, when possible, be easy to dish up and serve. Otherwise the hostess is apt, in her rush, to see 'things are right'—and so miss part of the party, and be so harassed that she does not enjoy it.

For the early anniversaries, plan a suitable table decoration with matching table linen. When the Silver Wedding party comes round, try to get a grey cloth and white flowers, or perhaps the same floral decoration as at the original wedding breakfast. Perhaps you may be having a luncheon, dinner or buffet meal for this celebration. Choose your menu and whatever it is, plan carefully.

For a Golden Wedding breakfast, either choose a spotlessly white cloth, draped as in days of old (fifty years ago it was fashionable to have draped buffet and dining tables for weddings), with a floral decoration of those times—such as red roses and lilies of the valley with smilax trailing along the table amongst the drapery, which could be yellow chiffon—or use a foundation cloth of striped damask and napkins to match, china banded with gold, or yellow china with an important golden centre piece.

The true essentials of a feast
are only fun and feed.
O. W. HOLMES

Festive Days and Meals

Hogmanay, like all festivals, being but a bank from which we can only draw what we put in.

J. M. BARRIE

The New Year, like an infant heir to the whole world, was waited for with welcomes, presents and rejoicings.

CHARLES DICKENS

NEW YEAR'S EVE AND DAY

Throughout the year, there is hardly a month which has not, or may not be made to have, a characteristic holiday which gives an opportunity for planning a dinner or some other celebration.

As the old year comes to a close the fun and nonsense of New Year's Eve provides a perfect setting for a buffet supper, and this colourful party, with Christmas red still much in evidence, is cheery and bright in the dark short days. But it is possible to ring changes of colour. Choose your table colour-scheme, be it silver with silver candlesticks and deep blue china, or snow-white with green leaves and seasonable flowers. Plan the party with special 'Hogmanay' foods, and if it is to end in the early hours of the morning—which is the usual time for this party—you could serve brawn and eggs and beer and coffee. Just before your guests depart, serve a bowl of piping hot soup.

In Scotland, New Year's Eve and New Year's Day are known as the 'Daft Days' and in every household someone is waiting to receive the visitors, and from most households somebody is out 'first footing'. The first person to cross any threshold after midnight is known as the 'first foot'. He must never enter the door empty-handed; so nearly everyone carries round cake, wine, whisky and a kettleful of hot punch. It is always said that it is much luckier to have a man as 'first foot' than a woman. He must not be fair-haired—the darker the better—nor must he have flat feet. He must enter the door without knocking and go straight to the fire before speaking.

It is a yearly custom in London for the Scots people to meet in St. Paul's Churchyard to see the New Year in, and to sing 'Auld Lang Syne'. There is a gathering too in Trafalgar Square to see the 'old out and the new in'. In the northern counties and in all families who hail from the north, wherever they may be, the New Year customs are clearly observed. Their houses will be tidy and the ashes cleaned out of the fire and the hearth clean—and the 'steaming' hot punch and drop of Scotch will be awaiting, and shortbread, mince pies and plum cake. For your New Year's party serve:

COLD AND HOT HORS D'ŒUVRES

CHICKEN SOUP

HAM MOUSSE   HAM AND EGGS DICED   LOBSTER STEWED

SHRIMPS CREAMED   OYSTER CASSEROLE

ASSORTED COLD MEATS

AUBERGINES STUFFED

CREAMED CORN, GREEN PEAS, POTATO SALAD

PEACHES JELLIED, ZABAGLIONE, MINCE PIES, SHORTCAKE

COFFEE

PUNCH

FOR THE COLD HORS D'ŒUVRES (*See also pp.* 56–59.)

Almonds. Salted; or other nuts placed in small dishes.

Cabbage. Finely shredded raw cabbage-heart with dressing. Red cabbage pickled, finely chopped.

Camembert. Remove the skin and work the soft centre until like butter. Add seasoning and pepper and salt to taste. Form this into small balls; roll in fine browned crumbs.

Caviare and Smoked Salmon. Make the thin slices of smoked salmon into cornucopias; fasten these with a tooth-pick, then fill with caviare; add a squeezing of lemon juice.

Celery. Cut the stalks up into neat even-sized pieces; fill them with:
    (1) Finely minced ham and cream cheese.
    (2) Grated cheese mixed with a little butter and Worcester sauce.
    (3) Cream cheese garnished with paprika.
    (4) Mango chutney and cream cheese.
    (5) Tomato pulp garnished with chopped chives.
    (6) Split the celery; place in cold water; leave an hour; remove; dry on cloth, and the celery will curl up.

Liver Pâté. Cut into neat thin strips and place on toast fingers; garnish with finely chopped parsley.

Olives. Ripe and green olives stuffed with pimento.

Salami. Spread very thin slices of salami with mustard. Add a little finely chopped watercress. Roll up and fasten with a tooth-pick.

Sausages. Small cocktail sausages may be served hot or cold.

Sandwiches. Make your sandwiches and cut them into very small-sized fingers and diamonds.

Sweet-Corn Fritters. *See p.* 215.

Cheese. May be served on a large platter with other small savouries, garnished with mustard and cress. Cut into neat cubes on tooth-picks or, if preferred, stick the tooth-picks into a grapefruit or orange forming a pattern.

HOT HORS D'ŒUVRES

Chicken Liver Broiled

Cut the livers into suitably small-sized pieces to run on to tooth-picks. Broil in butter. When done sprinkle with onion juice and season lightly with salt and pepper.

Bacon

Remove rind and cut rashers into small pieces; then fry lightly and serve on tooth-picks.

Cheese Dreams

Cut wedges of cheese; place them between three slices of bread (cut thin), cut into small triangles and broil lightly.

Corn Knobs

Take a tin of sweet corn and turn into saucepan. Bring to boil. Add blended cornflour and milk to thicken (to fairly stiff consistency), allow to cool, divide into very small balls or rolls. Roll in fine browned crumbs; drop into deep fat to brown lightly. Drain and serve piping-hot on tooth-picks.

Chicken Soup. *See p.* 206.

Ham Mousse. (*For another recipe, see p. 143.*)

½ lb. finely chopped ham	½ tsp. dry mustard
4 tbsp. horse-radish sauce	1 tbsp. gelatine
2 tbsp. mayonnaise	¼ pt. cold water

¼ pt. heavy cream or evaporated milk

Dissolve gelatine in cold water. Heat for ten minutes, add to cream and mayonnaise, beat well together. Add remaining ingredients. Mix all together and turn into moistened mould. When set, unmould and serve garnished with cress and lettuce heart.

Eggs and Diced Ham

Eggs	Sherry
Ham	Breadcrumbs

White sauce

Hard-boil the eggs; dice the ham; pour on a cream sauce seasoned with sherry to taste. Add breadcrumbs to stiffen and bake in 300° F., for 30 minutes.

Lobster Stewed

1–2 bkcp. cooked (or tinned) lobster

1½ pt. milk	4 oz. butter

½ pt. celery stock or cream of celery soup

Salt and pepper

Heat the lobster and milk, butter and stock together for 5 minutes. (If soup is used, reduce milk to 1 pint.) Season with salt and pepper. Serve garnished with finely chopped parsley on toast or cracker biscuits.

Shrimps Creamed

2 tbsp. butter	2 tbsp. tomato ketchup
½ grated shallot	1 bkcp. cold boiled rice
¼ pt. cream or evaporated milk	½ pt. cleaned shrimps (canned may be used)

Heat the butter and onion together. When very hot, add the cold boiled rice. Stir until the mixture boils, then leave on a reduced heat to simmer for about 10 minutes. Then add the ketchup (to serve 5 to 6 people increase rice and cream). Add the shrimps. This can be made in the morning and reheated for a Sunday or other supper dish. If desired save a few shrimps for garnish.

Oyster Casserole

Spaghetti or boiled rice	*Butter*
Oysters	*Paprika*
Ketchup	*Parsley finely chopped*
Green pepper	

Take an oval-shaped oven-dish. Well grease with butter and spread with the spaghetti or boiled rice. Dot with butter, over this put a layer of oysters, season with ketchup, paprika, parsley and green pepper and cover with white sauce. Repeat the layers until dish is full. Bake at 300° F., for 40 minutes.

White Sauce

To each ½ pint oyster liquor allow ½ pint milk and 2 tablespoonsful each butter and flour.

Potato Salad

Cook the potatoes until just done; then slice while hot, into a salad bowl, add mayonnaise, toss them gently and garnish with chopped chives and parsley.

Aubergines Stuffed

Allow ½ per person

3 *aubergines* (*large*)	3 *bkcp. soft breadcrumbs*
2 *tbsp. lard*	(*soaked and squeezed dry*)
3 *shallots sliced*	3 *chopped green peppers*
1 *lb. fresh minced pork*	*or*
Salt and pepper	¼ *lb. mushrooms* (*sliced*)

Cut open the aubergines and boil 20 minutes. When very soft scoop out the inside. Heat lard in the frying pan, add shallots and lightly brown. Add aubergine pulp and pork. Cook for about 10 minutes, stirring well, then add the bread and green peppers. Fry a further 10–15 minutes, add mushrooms. Fill the skins. Sprinkle with grated cheese, then place in buttered casserole and bake 20 minutes.

Green Salad

Choose heart of lettuce leaves, peeled and sliced tomatoes, dressed with French dressing (see p. 208).

Mixed Vegetable Salad

Wash, peel and grate beetroot, carrot, turnip; shred cabbage heart, arrange on platter. Sprinkle with French dressing, garnish with chopped parsley.

Creamed Corn

Open the tin and turn corn into pan. Heat. Serve hot or cold.

Green Peas

Use frozen peas; their colour is effective.

Peaches Jellied

Peaches   *Red-currant jelly*

Skin the peaches by dropping them in hot water, so that the skins drop off easily; arrange them in dish, melt a little red-currant jelly; pour this over the peaches.

Zabaglione

3 *eggs*   1 *tbsp. lemon juice*

¼ *lb. sugar*   *Rum or Marsala to taste*

Pinch of salt

Beat 1 whole egg and 2 egg yolks together. Add rum and sugar, put in the top of a double boiler. Stirring constantly, cook until thickened; remove from heat, add lemon juice and the stiffly whisked whites of eggs. Pour into glasses, serve very hot or serve cold in a glass dish lined with sponge fingers.

Mince Pies or Individual Pies

Line a pie plate or patty tin with puff pastry, fill with mince-meat, add a little brandy; cover the pie with an upper crust and bake at 450° F., for about 20–25 minutes for a large pie, or 10–15 minutes for small pies.

Shortbread

4 oz. icing sugar	½ lb. butter
1 tsp. vanilla	1 lb. sifted plain flour

¼ tsp. each, salt and baking powder

Sift flour, salt, baking powder together. Cream the sugar and butter until well blended, sprinkling over vanilla. Add flour, etc., gradually to the cream, rubbing in with the finger-tips. Roll out the dough to thickness ⅓ inch, and cut into 2 cakes.

> Now the New Year reviving old Desires,
> The thoughtful Soul to Solitude retires.
>
> EDWARD FITZGERALD

NEW YEAR'S DAY DINNER

HORS D'ŒUVRES
FISH SOUFFLÉ, HOLLANDAISE SAUCE
ROAST TURKEY
or
ROAST GOOSE
POTATOES BAKED   LETTUCE SALAD   CELERY
MINCE PIE;   CHARLOTTE RUSSE
CHEESE STRAWS
DESSERT
CAFÉ NOIR

Hors d'Œuvres. See p. 56.

Fish Soufflé

2 soles—about 1½ lb. each	4 eggs
½ pt. milk	2 tbsp. dry breadcrumbs
4 oz. flour	2 tbsp. butter
½ tsp. sugar	⅛ tsp. thyme
1 oz. butter	Salt and pepper

Clean and steam the fish until it flakes easily. Remove, take out bones. Remove skin and flake fish with a fork, then chop small. Prepare the soufflé mixture: melt the butter in a saucepan over a low flame. Gradually stir in the flour, heat 2 minutes stirring constantly; slowly add milk; blend until smooth; cook 5 minutes while stirring. Remove from heat. Cool. Meanwhile separate the yolks of egg from the whites. Add egg yolks and chopped fish to mixture in saucepan. Season with salt, pepper and thyme. Beat whites until stiff and fold into the mixture with a spoon (silver). Butter a soufflé case with ½ tsp. butter. Spread breadcrumbs over the bottom. Pour fish mixture into the case, place in shallow pan of boiling water. Bake in pre-heated oven 375° F., for 30 minutes. Serve piping hot with Hollandaise sauce.

Hollandaise Sauce. *See p.* 176. **Roast Turkey.** *See p.* 221. **Roast Goose.** *See p.* 210.

Baked Potatoes

Select smooth, medium or large potatoes. Wash, using vegetable brush, and dry, oil skins. Bake 40 minutes at 300° F. or at 425° F. for about 20–25 minutes. Serve at once. Break the skins to let steam escape before serving.

Lettuce Salad. *See p.* 99. **Celery. Mince Pies.** *See p.* 190. **Charlotte Russe.** *See p.* 89.

Cheese Straws

2 oz. butter	2 oz. grated parmesan cheese
3 oz. flour	Cayenne pepper and salt
1 egg yolk	

Rub butter and flour, add cheese and seasoning, mix with yolk of egg, if necessary add another egg yolk. Roll out and cut into fingers about ¼ inch wide and 2 inches long. Lay on a greased baking sheet. Stamp out some rounds with a cutter the size of an egg cup. Make them into rings by stamping out the centre. Lay on greased baking sheet. Bake till pale fawn at 350° F. Serve them with a bundle of straws in each ring.

TWELFTH NIGHT (January 5th—Epiphany)

Now, now the mirth comes
With cake full of plums,
Where the beane's king of sports here
Besides we must know, the pea also
Must revell, as queen in courts here.

ROBERT HERRICK, *Hesperides*

Twelfth day, old Christmas day, the feast of the Magi, has always an appeal for a party. It is the last opportunity of merrymaking at the close of 'yuletime'.

There are various superstitions and peasant beliefs which centre around the twelve days between Christmas and Epiphany. It is claimed that anything done in the twelve days' period foretells the luck in the next twelve months. Mince pies and plum puddings should be eaten on each of the twelve days to ensure good luck and riches.

At Twelfth Night parties the Twelfth cake is most important. It is usually a white iced cake with some kind of fancy decoration on top. Inside are tokens—a bean, a pea, a clove, and whoever gets one of these in his or her piece of cake has to assume for the rest of the evening a special role: the bean, the King of Beans; the pea, the Queen of Peas; the clove, the knave, In the north a dish of lobscouse, which is made of beef, potatoes and onions all fried together, was eaten and a drink called 'ponsondie', which is very like lamb's-wool, was drunk.

ST. VALENTINE'S DAY (February 14th)

Called on in the morning by Mr. Moore, whose voice my wife hearing in my dressing chamber with me, got herself ready, and came down and challenged him for her valentine.

SAMUEL PEPYS, *Diary, Feb. 14th, 1660*

St. Valentine, one of the best-loved saints in the Christian calendar, gave his name to this day. In days of old this was a very sentimental day. Valentine cards were sent—sometimes they had charming lace borders, and flowers such as roses, forget-me-nots, lilies of the valley and pansies, with messages such as 'Be mine' or 'I love you'.

Choose old-fashioned paper and lace valentines for your invitations. You could write this particular invitation in a sentimental frame with flower decoration:

'*Come—meet your fate at my sweetheart*
supper on St. Valentine's at 8 o'clock.'

Here are some suggestions:

Cut your sandwiches into heart-shapes and garnish them with radish roses. You can spread them with red-currant jelly and cream cheese, or the usual fillings (see p. 99).

Make a selection of small cakes in heart-shaped moulds. Cover them with different coloured icings.

Choose for buffet meals, from the menus of New Year's Eve and other festive days, whichever dish appeals to you.

SHROVE TUESDAY

Pancakes are eat by greedy gut
and Wobs and Madge run for the slut.

ROBIN'S ALMANACK

This day, just before Lent, may occur on any Tuesday between the 2nd February and the 8th March. In Scotland it is known as Fastern's E'en. There is much dancing and feasting on this day prior to the Lenten fasts.

For pancakes:

2 *tsp. flour*	*Pinch of salt*
4 *egg yolks*	2 *egg whites*

Few drops orange-flower water

Mix flour and salt. Beat egg yolks and whites. Add orange-flower water, then stir into flour. Leave this to stand an hour. Pour batter into jug. Butter a small omelette pan, put in a small quantity of the batter and cook for one or two minutes, then turn and cook the other side. Turn on to a piece of sugared paper. Roll up the pancake and sift sugar over. Add a squeeze of lemon juice and put on a hot dish.

ST. DAVID'S DAY (March 1st)

St. David's Day put oats and barley in this day.
JOHN RAY

St. David or Dewi, the patron saint of Wales, founded many monasteries in the southern part of Wales. It is said that as he preached with a white dove on his shoulder to a vast assembly in Cardiganshire, the ground rose under him until it became a mountain. He died on March 1st at St. David's.

See that you serve leeks to-day, in honour of Wales. The Welsh Guards always wear a leek in their caps on this day.

ST. PATRICK'S DAY (March 17th)

On favoured Erin's crest be seen
The plant she loves of emerald green.
SIR WALTER SCOTT

When St. Patrick preached the Gospel to the pagan Irish (about the year 432) he illustrated the doctrine of the Trinity by showing them a trefoil, or three-leaved grass with one stalk—the shamrock, which has from time immemorial been worn upon this Saint's anniversary to commemorate the event. The Irish people look upon the shamrock as their sacred plant, and it was with this holy herb that St. Patrick drove all the snakes from the land.

For a party on this day, decorate your table with a green cloth, or mats and matching table napkins, or if preferred, have white linen, and a bowl of shamrock and if you serve soup, see that it is green in colour. Put a green maraschino cherry in the grapefruit. Have a shamrock salad, and this menu:

GREEN PEA SOUP

GRILLED SOLE   GREEN SAUCE

CHICKEN À LA PATRICK

SALAD

GOOSEBERRY FOOL

Green Pea Soup

2 pt. peas	1 qt. stock
Sprig of mint	1 tsp. sugar
A grated onion	1 gill cream
1 oz. butter	Pepper and salt

Fry the peas with mint, onion and butter. Add seasoning and simmer with stock. When tender, rub through a sieve, then add sugar and cream. Re-heat but do not boil. Serve garnished with chopped mint.

Grilled Sole

Clean, skin and trim the fish, remove gills and fins. Make slashes across the girth on both sides. Rub a little flour and chopped onion all over the fish, then dip it in seasoned flour and grill. Place on a hot dish, sprinkle well with lemon juice and garnish well with finely chopped parsley, and serve with melted butter.

Green Sauce

½ cupful melted butter	⅛ tsp. salt
1 tbsp. flour	3 tbsp. freshly chopped parsley
2 tbsp. milk	½ tsp. freshly chopped chives

Place in a double boiler and cook until smooth.

Chicken à la Patrick

1 tbsp. sherry	1 egg yolk
1 cupful diced cooked chicken	3 tbsp. butter
½ cupful diced sauté mushrooms	3 tbsp. flour
¼ cupful diced canned pimento	1½ cups chicken stock

Pepper and salt

Melt 3 tablespoonsful butter or chicken fat, stir in and blend 3 tablespoonsful flour, add slowly 1½ cupfuls chicken stock. When smooth and boiling, add the chicken, mushrooms and pimento, reduce heat and add a lightly beaten egg yolk. Season with salt and pepper, and a tablespoonful of sherry. Add a few drops of green colouring to make the sauce green.

Salad. Place lettuce leaves on individual plates in the form of shamrock. *See p. 99.*

Gooseberry Fool

Stew a quart of gooseberries, hulled and wiped previously, adding about ½ lb. loaf sugar, 1 gill water and the juice of a lemon. When the fruit is tender, rub through a fine hair sieve. When the pulp is cold, add to it a pint of cream or custard. Serve in a shallow dish or in custard glasses if desired; fold through the stiffly whisked white of 2 eggs just before serving.

MOTHERING SUNDAY (The Fourth Sunday in Lent)

> *I'll to thee a simmer bring*
> *'gainst thou go a-mothering*
> *So that, when she blesses thee*
> *Half that blessing thou'll give me.*
>
> ROBERT HERRICK

Ornamental rich cakes baked at Christmas-time are eaten this Sunday, and in most Lancashire towns it is known as 'Simnel Sunday'. A writer in the *Gentleman's Magazine* (1867) informs us: 'from time beyond memory thousands of persons come from all parts to that town (Bury) to eat simnels. Formerly nearly every shop was open, with all the public houses—quite in defiance of all law respecting the closing during Service.'

It is an old custom to bake a simnel cake and send it away to a son or daughter to be eaten this day. In some families where the children are scattered over the commonwealth and elsewhere, these cakes are baked soon after Christmas and sent off on their long journey, so as to keep at home and afar this traditional eating of simnel.

Simnel Cake

4 oz. butter	3 oz. each of peel and sultanas
Grated rinds of ½ lemon,	10 oz. currants
½ orange	½ tsp. mixed spice
4 oz. sugar	Small tbsp. rum
3 eggs	⅛ pt. milk
6 oz. flour	

Cream butter and orange and lemon rind. Add sugar, and cream again. Beat in the well-whisked eggs. Caramelize a little sugar and dissolve in milk. Add to make the cake a good colour. Add a third of the flour, then the fruit and the remaining flour and spice sifted together. Turn the mixture into a 6½-inch tin previously lined with double paper. Bake at 350° F., for about 2 hours. Next day cut the cake transversely and cut up one-third of the almond icing. Roll the rest into a round the size of the cake and place between the two portions of the cake. Form the icing, cut up into a ring round the top of the cake. Mark with fork and brush with beaten egg. Brown gently under a hot grill and bake at 400° F. When cool and dry, dust the centre with icing sugar or put a layer of glacé icing in centre hollow. Decorate as desired with small coloured eggs.

For the Almond Icing

½ lb. ground almonds	2 or 3 drops almond essence
½ lb. caster sugar	1 tsp. lemon juice
1 egg	Small tbsp. sherry

Pound together the almonds and sugar. Add essence, egg, lemon juice and sherry. Whisk well together.

GOOD FRIDAY

One a penny, two a penny Hot Cross buns
If you have no daughters
Give them to your sons.
One a penny, two a penny Hot Cross buns.

For centuries past hot cross buns have been eaten hot for breakfast. They were known as 'cross buns' because of the sign of the cross on them.

Hot Cross Buns

½ lb. flour	⅛ pt. lukewarm water
⅛ tsp. salt	1 oz. sugar
1½ oz. margarine	2 oz. currants
1 egg	1 oz. sugar
½ oz. yeast	½ tsp. spice

Sift flour and salt and spice. Cut and rub in fat. Make a well in centre and add the egg. Add yeast, sugar and water. Knead well. Then put to rise. When risen to twice the original bulk use as desired. Turn dough on to board, knead in fruit and sugar. Divide into 8 pieces. Shape into buns. Knead down firmly. Mark with a cross. Cup dough with the hands to form a ball. Place on greased tray and put to prove (to rise). When doubled in bulk, bake at 400° F.

EASTER SUNDAY

> 'Twas Easter Sunday. The full blossomed trees
> Filled all the air with fragrance and with joy.
>
> LONGFELLOW

Pace-egging is a custom on this day—hard-boiled eggs which have been gaily decorated or dyed are eaten. In some families the children write their names with the point of a candle, then roll each egg up in onion skin or coloured fabric, boil and dye them. While the eggs are boiling the dyes colour them. In the northern counties they are rolled up and down grass banks.

AN EASTER-DAY LUNCHEON

SHRIMP COCKTAIL

LAMB CHOPS AND MINT SAUCE

NEW POTATOES   GREEN PEAS

GOOSEBERRY PUDDING

Shrimp Cocktail.

1 *lb. shrimps (unshelled)*	1 *clove garlic*
½ *pt. olive oil*	2 *bay leaves*
¼ *pt. lemon juice*	½ *tsp. salt*
½ *onion sliced*	⅛ *tsp. pepper*

Chives and watercress

Shell the shrimps—remove black vein which runs down the centre-back. Blend the olive oil, lemon juice and salt and pepper. When smooth, add onion, garlic and bay leaves. Place shrimps in a bowl, pour sauce over the shrimps, cover. Chill 2 hours; serve on small individual plates, or in cocktail glasses garnished with chives and watercress.

Lamb Chops

Order the chops to be cut in uniform thickness, about 1½ to 2 inches, with the fell (paper-like tissue) and chine bone at the end removed. Place them on a grill tray under a moderate heat with the fat rim up and allow them to brown, this will take about 10 minutes. Then lay the chops flat and brown on both sides, turning them once only—do not pierce the surface but stick fork into fat rim. (To test, stick narrow blade of a small knife close to the bone.) Reduce heat if necessary—the cooking time will be about 20–25 minutes. When done, the chops should be golden brown and juicy. To serve, place the chops on a well-heated dish, sprinkle with pepper and salt and place a knob of butter on dish—turn the chops on both sides in the hot butter. Drain any excess fat from the grill pan, add 2 tablespoonsful hot water, just sufficient to loosen the brown essence at the bottom, bring to boil and pour over the chops. Garnish with parsley and serve immediately on very hot plates, as lamb fat cools and congeals quickly. Serve with mint sauce.

Mint Sauce

4 *tbsp. freshly cut mint leaves*   2 *tbsp. caster sugar*
½ *cup strained lemon juice or equal parts of vinegar and water*

Wash mint, drain, dry between folds of a cloth. Cut leaves off the stems, then cut fine with scissors. Put the leaves in a sauceboat, add sugar and lemon juice, mix, stand in a cool place for at least an hour before serving.

New Potatoes. *See p.* 116.   **Green Peas.** *See p.* 83.

Gooseberry Pudding

¼ *lb. beef suet*   1¼ *pt. gooseberries*
½ *lb. flour*   2 *oz. moist sugar*
½ *tsp. baking powder*   *Cold water*

Top and tail gooseberries, chop suet finely, adding a little flour. Sift remaining flour and salt into a basin, add a pinch of salt, the suet and baking powder. Moisten with cold water to form a stiff paste. Roll out the paste on a floured board and line with it a greased quart-sized pudding basin. Fill it with gooseberries. Add the sugar, and about 2 tablespoonsful cold water. Trim off the edges of the paste and roll it out with the remainder to a round. Cover with this, having previously wetted the edges round the rim of the basin. Press the edges well together and trim neatly. Dip a pudding cloth into boiling water, and sprinkle one side with flour. Tie this (the floured side down) over the basin, allowing for the pudding to swell. Place in a saucepan containing boiling water. Cook this for about 2 hours. To serve, remove the cloth, turn the pudding out on to a hot dish, dust with caster sugar and serve with cream.

THE FEAST OF WEEKS (Pentecost)

A MENU OF TRADITIONAL JEWISH RECIPES

TOMATO SOUP AND EINLAUF

GEFILLTE FISH

APPLE STRUDEL

CHEESE KREPLECH

Tomato Soup and Einlauf

3 *oz. sago*	3 *pt. water*
1 *lb. pot-herbs*	*Salt and pepper*
	2 *lb. tomatoes*

Soak the sago in ½ pint of water. Cut up the pot-herbs and put them with the tomatoes in a large casserole with 2½ pints water and seasoning. Bring to the boil. Add the sago and stir well. Put in the oven and cook slowly for 1½ hours. Remove from oven and put on hot-plate burner. Drop the *Einlauf* into the soup from the end of a spoon. Cook for 3 minutes, and then serve. The *Einlauf* is made by mixing 1 egg, 3 tablespoonsful flour, ¼ cup water and a pinch of salt into a smooth paste.

Gefillte Fish

1 *large haddock*	1 *tbsp. breadcrumbs*
5 *medium-sized onions*	1 *onion*
Parsley	1 *small carrot*
2 *eggs*	1 *tbsp. flour*
Salt and pepper	*Milk*

Cut the haddock into thick slices. Leaving the skin and backbone as they are, scoop out a hole in each slice. Chop the fish which you remove on a board with the five onions and parsley until they are very fine. Mix with the eggs, breadcrumbs and salt and pepper. Put this mixture back into the holes in the fish. Place the fish in a casserole, with cold water to cover, adding onion, parsley, carrot and seasoning. Bake at 350° F., for an hour. Mix the flour to a smooth batter with some milk. Add to this a cupful of hot liquid in which the fish has cooked. Stir well. Pour back into casserole and cook for 5 minutes more. Should be served hot.

Apple Strudel

½ *lb. flour*	1½ *lb. apples*
¼ *oz. yeast*	*Cinnamon*
1 *tsp. sugar*	3 *oz. stoned raisins*
5 *oz. warm water*	3 *oz. currants*
	Oil

Warm the flour. Mix together yeast and sugar, and add warm water. Pour this into the middle of the flour and let stand 10 minutes. Mix into a dough. Knead well and leave for an hour, to rise. Knead again lightly. Roll it out very thinly. Lift the paste on to a cloth. Pull it out gently to the thinness of a wafer. For the filling, chop the apples and mix with cinnamon, raisins, currants and enough oil so that the mixture will spread over the dough. After spreading the filling, hold the cloth by one end, roll the *Strudel* and tip on to a greased baking tin. Bake for 40 minutes at 350° F., when it should be brown, basting now and then with oil.

Cheese Kreplech

1 *egg*		1 *egg*
1 *tbsp. water*		1 *oz. sugar*
Pinch of salt	For filling	¼ *tsp. cinnamon*
Flour		*Grated peel of* 1 *lemon*
½ *oz. butter*		*Pinch of salt*

Beat an egg with a tablespoonful of water, add salt, and sufficient flour to make a stiff dough. Mix slowly, stirring always in the same direction. Turn out on to a board, knead well and roll out very thinly. Cut into 3-inch squares.

For the filling, melt the butter, beat an egg, mix sugar, cinnamon, lemon peel and salt with the egg, add butter and mix well. Dab beaten egg on edges of the squares of dough. Put some of the filling in the middle of each square, and fold over, pressing the edges to form triangles. Drop into boiling milk. When the *Kreplech* are done, they will rise to the top of the milk. Serve with melted butter.

WHITSUN

> *It hath been sung at festivals,*
> *On ember eves and holy ales.*
> SHAKESPEARE, *Pericles*

Ale was a drink prevalent in olden times. It became part of the name of various festivals: leet-ale—lamb-ale—bride-ale (Bridal)— and Whitsun-ale. Much dancing and festivity took place at such times.

This ale was a very strong brew and profits from the sale of it at Whitsun went to the funds for church repairs.

WHIT SUNDAY

BUTTERED EGGS WITH ASPARAGUS
ROAST STUFFED SHOULDER OF VEAL
NEW POTATOES   FRENCH BEANS
STRAWBERRY FRITTERS
CREAM CHEESE

Buttered Eggs with Asparagus

Melt in a frying pan over a low heat 3 tablespoonsful butter, 3 tablespoonsful cream, or top of the milk. Cook for a few minutes. Beat and pour into the pan 6 eggs, 3 tablespoonsful cream, add pepper and salt to season. When the eggs begin to thicken, break up with a fork. Serve on hot toast, lightly buttered, garnished with hot asparagus tips.

Roast Stuffed Veal

Order a piece of shoulder of veal as large as desired, entirely boned, sewed on two sides and left open on the third side for stuffing (for 6 people—allow 3 lb.). Stuff and roast in a slow oven, 300° F. Allow 30 minutes per lb. Sprinkle the tin with salt and pepper, and place the roast in it, then sprinkle the veal with salt and pepper. As veal is lean, cover the top of the roast with slices of suet or bacon. Secure with toothpicks or, if preferred, spread with fat. Do not baste or sear, as strong heat dries the surface of veal—the roast when finished should be light brown, done through and juicy. If the roast is not brown 20 minutes before cooking, raise oven temperature. Lift from the tin to a hot dish and make the gravy, with half milk and half water.

For Stuffing. (*For 4–5 lb. meat.*)

2½ pt. breadcrumbs	3 tbsp. milk
1½ tsp. salt	5 tbsp. fat
Pepper to taste	4 tbsp. finely grated lemon peel
2 tsp. poultry seasoning	6 tbsp. minced celery (if desired)

Melt fat and put 1 oz. onion and celery in it. Mix other ingredients together and add. Stir carefully until it looks steamy. Then add milk. Fill pocket with stuffing. Sew or 'shut' with skewer at end.

New Potatoes. See p. 116.

French Beans

String and shred the beans lengthwise. Drop them into a small quantity of boiling water (1½ teaspoonsful salt to 1 quart water). Cook, uncovered if you wish to preserve the colour, for about 25 minutes. Drain and serve tossed in butter.

Strawberry Fritters

4 oz. caster sugar	3 oz. flour
4 yolks of eggs	1 oz. cornflour
3 whites of eggs	A few drops of vanilla essence
1 whole egg	1 tbsp. icing sugar
½ lb. small ripe strawberries	Clarified butter for deep frying

Cream the sugar with the egg yolks, whisk the whites to a stiff froth. Flavour with vanilla essence and gradually incorporate with the above, adding the sifted flour and cornflour. Put the mixture into a forcing bag with a plain tube, and force out small round heaps (brioche shapes) on to a buttered baking sheet. Bake at 350° F. for 15–20 minutes. Remove them carefully from the sheet, scoop out the centre of each and fill it with picked strawberries sweetened with icing sugar, and place each two together with batter or egg. Dip in beaten egg and plunge into hot clarified butter, fry for a few minutes. Take up, drain well, and sprinkle over with vanilla sugar. Dish up and serve hot.

Cream Cheese. *See* p. 138.

MIDSUMMER'S DAY (June 24th)

Our maid Betty tells me, if I go backwards without speaking a word, into the garden on Midsummer Eve, and gather a rose and keep it in a clean sheet of paper, without looking at it, until Christmas day, it will be as fresh as in June: and if I then stick it in my bosom, he that is to be my husband will come and take it out.

CONNOISSEUR DURY, *Book of Days*

Perhaps you live in the country and can listen to the nightingale on a summer night as you look up to the sky at dusk, or perhaps you live in one of London's old-fashioned squares where the trees were neatly lopped this spring, and from the fresh young leaves there's renewed bird-song at eventide wafting forth. Perhaps you've only a busy London street and not a sign of a tree from your flat window, but your joy is your window-box. Wherever you are there's no reason why you cannot enjoy a midsummer-night's supper. Make your table gay, and the warm air perfumed, by using night-scented stocks for your floral decoration, or if you prefer it, those old-fashioned, deep-red roses, and have in the room tobacco flowers.

A MIDSUMMER'S MEAL

WATER-MELON WITH SHERRY DRESSING

CHICKEN SOUP

SALMON LOAF WITH FROZEN HORSE-RADISH SAUCE

NEW POTATOES STEAMED: GREEN CORN BOILED

ASPARAGUS SALAD

STRAWBERRY SHORTCAKE

ASSORTED CHEESE

Water-Melon with Sherry Dressing

Remove the seeds, cut centre of the water melon into small balls. Chill well for an hour in a refrigerator. Serve in stemmed glasses or on crisp lettuce leaves, dressed with:

¼ lb. sugar	2 tbsp. sloe gin
¼ pt. sherry	Few grains salt

Mix the ingredients in order given. Leave until sugar is dissolved.

Chicken Soup

4 cups chicken stock	2 sticks celery
2 oz. butter	1 tbsp. flour
2 sliced carrots and onions	½ bkcp. soft breadcrumbs
1 pt. milk	Salt, pepper

Cook the vegetables, finely cut, in 3 tablespoonsful butter for 2 or 3 minutes; add stock and breadcrumbs, boil for 10 minutes and strain. Blend milk with remaining butter and flour, cook together and add to stock. Season with salt and pepper. When a richer soup is desired use one cup each of milk and cream in place of all milk. Serve with melba toast.

Salmon Loaf

1 *tin salmon*	1½ *tbsp. melted butter*
½ *tbsp. salt*	6 *tbsp. milk*
1 *tbsp. flour*	3 *tbsp. vinegar*
1 *tsp. mustard*	¾ *tbsp. granulated gelatine*
1 *egg*	2 *tbsp. cold water*

A few grains cayenne

Remove salmon from can and rinse thoroughly with hot water, then flake. Mix together salt, flour, mustard, cayenne; add egg, slightly beaten, butter, milk and vinegar. Cook over hot water until mixture thickens, stirring constantly at first, then occasionally. Then add gelatine soaked in cold water. Strain the mixture and add to fish. Turn into mould, chill and remove from mould. Arrange on lettuce leaves.

Frozen Horse-radish Sauce

1 *tbsp. butter*	6 *oz. heavy cream*
1 *tbsp. flour*	½ *tsp. salt*
¼ *pt. milk*	*Few grains pepper*
½ *pt. chicken stock*	2 *tbsp. vinegar*

¼ *lb. grated horse-radish root*

Melt butter, add flour and, while stirring constantly, gradually pour on milk and chicken stock. Cool, freeze, and add cream beaten until stiff, salt, pepper, vinegar and grated horse-radish root. Continue freezing until consistency of very thick cream.

New Potatoes Steamed

Choose potatoes of uniform size. Wash and peel or scrape. Cover them with cold water and soak 10 minutes. Cook in boiling salted water uncovered until soft, drain, remove to vegetable dish, pour over melted butter and sprinkle with finely chopped parsley.

Green Corn Boiled

Remove husks and silk from corn, cook for 10 minutes in equal parts boiling water and milk (this keeps the corn white). Serve in folded napkin.

Asparagus Salad

Asparagus *Lemon* *French dressing*

Chill stalks of cooked asparagus and then marinate with a French dressing. Remove thick slice from both ends of a lemon. Cut into ½-inch slices and remove pulp to leave rings, then carefully place three or four stalks of asparagus into each ring. Arrange on lettuce leaves.

French Dressing

2 tbsp. vinegar *4 tbsp. olive oil*

Salt and pepper to taste

Mix thoroughly and pour on salad before serving. This dressing may be varied according to taste by adding French mustard, lemon juice, chopped garlic or fine herbs.

Strawberry Shortcake

1 lb. flour *¼ lb. butter*

4 tsp. baking powder *1 egg*

1 tbsp. sugar *1 tbsp. milk*

½ tsp. salt *Strawberries*

Sift flour, salt, baking powder; cut and rub in the butter with the finger tips. Add sugar. Beat egg until it is very light, then add milk, then combine with flour, mix. Toss on to floured board, divide into two parts, pat, roll out and line flan rings.

When cooked, split and remove soft part, spread with butter. Sprinkle strawberries with sugar, warm slightly and crush and put between and on top of the shortcakes. Cover with whipped cream, sweeten and flavour. Garnish with whole berries.

MICHAELMAS DAY (September 29th)

And when the tenants come to pay their quarter's rent
They bring some fowl at Midsummer, a dish of fish in Lent,
At Christmas a capon, at Michaelmas a goose,
And somewhat else at New-Year's tide, for fear their lease fly
    loose.

GASCOIGNE—1575

It is said that Queen Elizabeth was eating her Michaelmas goose when she received the joyous news of the defeat of the Armada. Very often a goose was presented to the landlord by his tenant to 'ease' their relationships. September 29th is the day chosen for the election of the Governors of cities and civil Guardians of the Peace. The 'Michaelmas goose' is usually eaten at the feasts held on that day.

Decorate your table with Michaelmas daisies. There are many blooms among the dwarf varieties which lend themselves to table decorations. See, too, that you have some really rosy-cheeked apples among your dessert fruits. They are a glorious sight with the varied purple clusters of flowers.

This dinner can easily be varied if desired:

HORS D'ŒUVRES

FILLETS OF SOLE WITH MUSHROOM SAUCE

ROAST GOOSE, GIBLET GRAVY   APPLE SAUCE

RICED POTATOES   GLAZED ONIONS

CHIFFONADE SALAD

COFFEE ICE-CREAM

ASSORTED CHEESE   CRACKERS

CAFÉ NOIR

Hors d'Œuvres
Choose your selection from pp. 56–61.

Fillets of Sole with Mushroom Sauce

8 *fillets sole*	2 *tbsp. butter*
¼ *pt. white wine*	3 *tbsp. flour*
½ *lb. mushrooms peeled*	¼ *pt. thick cream*
2 *slices onion*	*Flour*
Bit of bay leaf	*Fat*
1 *pt. cold water*	5 *slices carrot*
Sprig parsley	10 *peppercorns*

Salt, pepper, cayenne

Put the fillets into a shallow dish. Sprinkle with salt and pepper. Add wine and cover, leave 1 hour. Drain and dip each fillet separately in heavy cream, then in flour. Fry in deep fat and drain. Remove to hot serving dish, cover with mushrooms browned in butter, then cover with sauce.

Mushroom Sauce

Put the skin and bones of the fish into saucepan, add carrot, onion, parsley, bay leaf and peppercorns, cover with cold water, bring to boiling-point and continue boiling until stock is reduced to ½ pint, then strain. Melt 2 tablespoonsful butter, add flour, pour on gradually fish stock, cream and slightly beaten egg yolk; season with salt, pepper and cayenne.

Roast Goose

Goose	*Salt*
Dripping	*Pepper*
Watercress	*Cranberries*

Sage

Take the plucked and drawn goose, wash well with cold water, wipe. Stuff, sprinkle with sage, and truss. Sprinkle with salt and pepper and put breast-down on the rack in dripping tin. Place at 400° F., and roast for two hours. Baste every 15 minutes. Then place on back for last 15 minutes cooking time. Remove to hot platter, garnish with watercress and a few fresh red cranberries.

Stuffing

Put eight medium-sized potatoes through a mincer, add ½ pint cream, 2 oz. butter, season with salt and pepper, 2 large chopped parboiled onions and sage. Add 3 well-beaten eggs. Mix well together.

Giblet Gravy

Cook the giblets (heart, liver and gizzard) until tender. Drain the stock and finely chop the giblets. Melt 3 tablespoonsful butter and cook until brown. Add 3 tablespoonsful flour. Continue browning; then, while stirring, gradually pour on the stock (there should be about ¾ pint stock); add 2 tablespoonsful Madeira wine and season with salt and pepper.

Apple Sauce

Apples	*Squeeze lemon juice*
1 *to* 2 *tbsp. butter*	*Cinnamon if desired*
	Sugar

Wash apples and cut into quarters. Place in a saucepan and partly cover them with water (old apples need more than new ones). Stew until tender, then pass through a sieve. Return apple pulp to pan, add sugar to taste, and cinnamon. Reheat, add butter and serve.

Riced Potatoes.

8 *medium-sized boiled potatoes*   *Salt and pepper*

Put potatoes through ricer or sieve, season with pepper and salt, heap on dish.

Glazed Onions

Peel small onions, cook in boiling salted water until tender; drain and sauté in butter, to which is added a small quantity of sugar, until delicately browned.

Chiffonade Salad

Few sticks celery	*Few grapes*
1 *green pepper*	*Heart of lettuce*
	4 *tomatoes*

Boil the green pepper for 2 minutes, cool, remove seeds and shred finely, using scissors. Blanch and peel tomatoes, cut into quarters. Clean celery and cut in ¼-inch slices. Remove skin and pips of grapes, wash the lettuce and arrange in salad bowl among peppers and tomatoes in sections alternately, then place cut celery and cover with sections of grape.

Over this pour French dressing:

¼ tsp. salt	3 drops onion juice
⅛ tsp. pepper	4 tbsp. olive oil
Pinch of sugar	2 tbsp. lemon juice or vinegar

Mix in order given, stir until well blended.

Coffee Ice-cream

1 pt. milk	1 egg
¼ pt. ground coffee	½ tsp. salt
10 oz. sugar	1 qt. thin cream
1 tbsp. flour	1 tbsp. vanilla

Scald milk with coffee. Mix sugar, flour, salt, and add egg slightly beaten. Then gradually pour on hot mixture. Cook over hot water for 20 minutes. Stir occasionally. Cool; add cream and flavouring. Strain through double thickness of cheese cloth and freeze.

Café Noir. *See pp.* 69 and 156.

HALLOWE'EN (October 31st)

> The auld guidwife's well-hoondit nuts,
> are round and round divided,
> And mony lads and lasses fates,
> are there that night decided.
> Some kindly, couthie, side by side,
> and burn together trimly;
> And lump out—owre the chimly.
> Fu' high that night.
>
> R. BURNS

It is believed that on Hallowe'en divination attains its highest power, and the gift asserted by Glendower of calling the spirits from the vasty deep is available to all who choose to make use of the privileges of this occasion.

In the United Kingdom nuts and apples are consumed in great numbers. This night is known as 'nutcrack night' in the north, where nuts are not only eaten but put on to the bars of the fire. If young women want to know if their lovers are faithful they put three nuts upon the bars of the grate, naming the nuts after the lovers. If a nut cracks or jumps the lover will prove unfaithful; if it begins to blaze or burn, he has a regard for the person making the trial. If the nuts named after the girl and her lover burn together they will be married.

Apples are hung up on a stick horizontally by a string from the ceiling—putting a candle on one end and an apple on the other— the stick is twisted and the merry-makers leap and snatch at the apples with their teeth (no use of hands allowed)! Or apples are floated in a tub of water and heads are ducked in lightly to get the apples out.

GUY FAWKES' DAY (November 5th)

Please to remember,
The Fifth of November,
Gunpowder treason and plot;
I know no reason
Why gunpowder treason
Should ever be forgot.

On this day many children love to have a party with fireworks and a bonfire, sometimes roasting unpeeled potatoes and chestnuts (which they eat with relish!) in the hot embers at Guy Fawkes' feet as he burns. If you are having a children's party, see the suggestions on p. 163.

THANKSGIVING DAY (November 25th)

Our rural ancestors, with little blest,
Patient of labour when the end was rest,
Indulged the day that housed their annual grain
With feasts, and off'rings, and a thankful strain.
POPE, *Imitations of Horace*

On November 27th, in 1621, the Pilgrims had their first Thanksgiving dinner—to commemorate the plenteous harvest after a year of very great hardships in the Massachusetts Colony. The settlers celebrated with feastings and psalms, and military drill by a few well-trained soldiers of Miles Standish. Four men were delegated by Governor Bradford to go out and search for game to grace the Colonists' boards, and the wild turkeys with which they returned were very joyfully received by the thrifty housewives, who dressed and roasted the birds with the skill for which the seventeenth-century housewives were famed. Pies, cakes, goodies, vegetables, were all added to the fare on this great day.

Until 1680 Thanksgiving was celebrated somewhat irregularly in Massachusetts. From then onwards it was established as the annual festival in the colony. It was almost two hundred years later, during Abraham Lincoln's administration, by yearly proclamation of both the President and the State Governors that the day became a national holiday.

For your party decorations have cut-outs of autumn leaves, pumpkins, ears of corn, turkeys; and don't forget to scoop out a pumpkin and fill it with creamed corn to suggest the gift from the Indians to the white man's first Thanksgiving feast.

The menu on this day should be of the traditional fare, which has delighted generations of *Thanksgiving feasters*.

MULLIGATAWNY SOUP

ROAST TURKEY   NEW ENGLAND STUFFING   SAUSAGE AND

CHESTNUT STUFFING

CRANBERRY JELLY   CORN FRITTERS

CREAMED BAKED ONIONS

COLE SLAW

PUMPKIN PIE

Mulligatawny Soup

1 *diced onion*	½ *cup diced cooking apples*
2 *oz. butter*	2½ *pt. chicken broth*
1 *tbsp. flour*	½ *cup boiled rice*
1½ *tbsp. curry powder*	½ *cup diced chicken*

4 *oz. hot cream*

Brown the diced onion in the butter. Add flour and curry powder. Cook 5 minutes, then add the chicken broth. Let simmer ½ hour. Add apples, rice and chicken. Boil gently for 15 minutes. Add the hot cream, and serve at once.

Roast Turkey (*See p. 221.*)

New England Stuffing

12 *slices bread, ½ inch thick*	1 *egg*
Stock or water to moisten	*Salt and pepper*
2-*inch cube fat salt pork, chopped fine*	*Sage*

Take crusts off bread. Toast, then chop it, and moisten with stock. Add pork, beaten egg and seasoning.

Sausage and Chestnut Stuffing

1 *small onion, chopped*	*Salt and pepper*
2 *tbsp. butter*	*Pinch of thyme*
½ *lb. sausage meat*	2 *tsp. chopped parsley*
4 *doz. chestnuts*	1 *cup breadcrumbs*

Cook onion in butter for 3 minutes. Add sausage meat and cook 5 minutes. Boil chestnuts and mash half of them. Add mashed chestnuts and all other ingredients to the onion and sausage meat. When thoroughly mixed, add the whole chestnuts.

Cranberry Jelly

1 *lb. cranberries*	8 *oz. boiling water*
14 *oz. sugar*	

Remove stems from cranberries and wash in cold water. Put in saucepan. Add boiling water, heat quickly to boiling-point, then boil gently for about 20 minutes or until berries are soft. Remove from stove and force through a sieve. Add sugar to strained berries. Heat slowly to boiling-point, then let boil for exactly 4 minutes. Turn into moulds or glasses and let stand until firm.

Corn Fritters

4 *oz. flour*	2 *oz. milk*
1 *tsp. baking powder*	½ *tbsp. melted butter*
Salt and pepper	1 *cup tinned sweet corn, well*
1 *egg*	*drained*

Mix dry ingredients. Beat egg, and add milk gradually; then add melted butter and corn. Sift in dry ingredients and when smoothly mixed, drop by spoonfuls and fry in deep fat. Drain on paper.

Creamed Baked Onions

Large onions

Salt and pepper

Powdered cloves

Brown sugar

Cream sauce

Cut onions in half, crosswise. Boil 15 minutes and drain, keeping water for sauce. Put onions, cut side up, on large baking tin. Sprinkle each with salt, pepper, cloves and a little brown sugar. Make sauce by adding to 8 oz. of the onion water 1 tablespoonful each of blended butter and flour, with a little cream. Pour sauce gently over the onions. Bake 40 minutes in a slow oven.

Cole Slaw

3 cups finely shredded cabbage

2 tbsp. sugar

4 oz. cream, sweet or sour

2 tbsp. vinegar

Mix together sugar, cream and vinegar. Pour over shredded cabbage and toss together lightly.

Pumpkin Pie

1¼ cups cooked and
strained pumpkin

½ cup sugar

2 tbsp. butter

2 tbsp. black treacle

1 tsp. ginger

1 tsp. cinnamon

Pinch of salt

2 eggs

1¼ cups scalded milk

Pastry for one pie-crust

Line a pie plate with short crust. Add to pumpkin the following ingredients: sugar, butter, treacle, ginger, cinnamon and salt. Add egg yolks slightly beaten. Add milk and mix thoroughly. Fold in stiffly beaten egg whites. Pour on to pie crust and bake in a hot oven for the first 15 minutes, then in moderate oven until filling is firm.

ST. ANDREW'S DAY (November 30th)

We find the following directions for Haggis Royal in the Minutes of Sederum of the Cleikum Club.

MEG DODS

St. Andrew's Day or Andermas is a Scottish national day. In olden days, soup, minced collops, sheep's head, haggis and other national dishes, such as solan goose, Tup's Head and trotters, haunch of venison, buttered partans (crabs), plum damas pie (prune), black cock and ptarmigan would have been eaten. To-day for this festive day you could serve:

COCK-A-LEEKIE SOUP

TAY OR TWEED SALMON

HAGGIS ROYAL

MINCE PIE

Cock-a-leekie Soup

A fowl	*12 large leeks*
1 qt. beef or veal stock	*12 prunes (if desired)*

Pepper and salt

Remove roots and part of head of leeks, cut into pieces about one inch long, split if desired, and wash well in two or three waters; if strong blanch for a few minutes in boiling water. Place in a large saucepan with the trussed fowl, cover with stock, add pepper and salt. Simmer for three hours, keeping well skimmed. Half an hour before serving add prunes, remove fowl and cut in pieces. Place in a tureen and pour over broth.

Tay or Tweed Salmon (*See p.* 176.)

Haggis Royal

3 *lb. mutton, chopped*	*A little chopped parsley*
1 *lb. suet, chopped*	*Grated lemon rind*
A little beef marrow	*Cayenne pepper*
Breadcrumbs (crumb of	4 *yolks of eggs*
loaf) or oatmeal	½ *pt. red wine*
3 *anchovies*	*A veal caudle*

Put mutton, suet, marrow and breadcrumbs in mixing bowl, add the anchovies, parsley, lemon rind and seasoning. Beat yolks of eggs lightly, add to wine. Blend all ingredients well together and put them neatly into the veal caudle. Bake in a deep dish in a hot oven. Turn out and serve with venison sauce:

1 *glass red wine*   1 *lb. red currant jelly*

Melt the jelly in a glass of warmed wine and serve.

Mince Pie (*See p.* 190.)

CHRISTMAS FESTIVITIES

Twas the Night before Christmas, when all through the house
Not a creature was stirring, not even a mouse.

CLEMENT CLARKE MOORE

On Christmas Eve get ready for your Christmas Day meals; do as much of the preparation as possible. While you are cooking, remember to make some 'whigs'; these are traditional Christmas Eve fare. Also, do not forget to make some gingerbread men, and a tiny gingerbread house, if you have young folk to your yuletide party.

Christmas Day is an outstanding celebration of the year, so let us first consider 'Christmas dinner'. Red and white are the predominant colours for this day. A snow-white damask cloth and the red berries, so typical of the season, make an appropriate background. A miniature Santa Claus may appear with his reindeer, pulling a sledge laden with tiny parcels—small gifts for those around the table.

Silver and gilded candles, a metallic Christmas tree, or trees of appropriate size, perhaps with one larger one, gaily lighted with red, blue and yellow lights—or a small tree composed entirely of small, coloured lustre balls—are most effective. A piece of mirror with tufts of cotton wool, dusted with frost, can also be used to good effect. For a more formal table a bowl of holly and mistletoe, surrounded with decorative crackers and two or four candlesticks (on silver or Sheffield plate)—each with a red candle, or alternating red and white candles—enhances many a Christmas dinner-table.

In some families Christmas recipes are handed down from mother to daughter—strict family secrets.

Make your table specially gay for the yuletide festivities. Have bonbon dishes on the table with stuffed olives, muscatels, salted almonds, and one or two with chocolates and assorted candies.

"Oh, a wonderful pudding." Bob Cratchit said, and calmly, too,
that he regarded it as the greatest success achieved by Mrs.
Cratchit since their marriage . . . then Bob proposed a Merry
Christmas to us all, my dears, God bless us, which all the family
re-echoed, "God bless us" everyone said, Tiny Tim last of all.

DICKENS, *Christmas Carol*

CHRISTMAS DINNER

MOCK TURTLE SOUP

HALIBUT TIMBALES	SHRIMP SAUCE
ROAST TURKEY	CHESTNUT STUFFING

BROWN GRAVY   CRANBERRY SAUCE   BREAD SAUCE

MASHED POTATOES   BRUSSELS SPROUTS

GRAPE SALAD

PLUM PUDDING	BRANDY SAUCE
STILTON CHEESE	CELERY

DESSERT

CAFÉ NOIR

Mock Turtle Soup

1 *calf's head*	1 *bkcp. calf's head meat*
4 *cloves*	1 *pt. brown stock*
10 *peppercorns*	4 *oz. butter*
1 *tsp. allspice berries*	4 *oz. flour*
2 *sprigs thyme*	½ *pt. stewed strained tomatoes*
2 *sprigs parsley*	*Juice ½ lemon*
½ *onion sliced*	¼ *cup Madeira wine*
6 *slices carrot*	*Salt and pepper*
2 *stalks celery*	3 *qts. boiling water*

Clean, wash and soak the calf's head for 1 hour in sufficient
water to cover, then place in saucepan, cover with boiling
water, add vegetables and seasonings. Place over a low heat
and simmer until tender. Remove head and boil stock. Reduce
to 1 quart, strain and cool. Melt and brown butter slightly, add

flour, stir until well browned, then gradually pour on the brown stock. Add calf's head stock and tomatoes. Dice calf's face meat and add with the lemon juice, simmer for about 10 minutes. Add royal custard cut into dice, season with salt and pepper, add wine.

Royal Custard

3 *egg yolks*	*¼ pt. calf's head stock*
1 *egg*	*⅛ tsp. salt*
Smallest pinch cayenne	

Beat the egg lightly, add head stock and seasonings, pour into small buttered tin mould (to depth ½ inch). Place the mould in a pan in hot water. Place in oven at 375° F. Bake until firm, cool, remove from mould and cut into ½-inch cubes.

Halibut Timbales

1 *lb. raw halibut*	*¼ tsp. pepper*
1 *cup soft breadcrumbs*	*Few grains cayenne*
½ pt. cream or evaporated milk	*Few drops onion juice*
1 *tsp. salt*	4 *whites of eggs*

Wipe fish with damp cloth, remove skin and bones. There should be 1 lb. raw halibut; chop very finely, then rub through a sieve. Place the crumbs and cream in a saucepan, cook until a smooth paste, then gradually add the fish and seasonings. Beat the whites of eggs until stiff and dry, cut and fold into mixture. Turn into slightly buttered, individual moulds set in a baking tin of hot water, cover with buttered paper and bake at 325°F. for about 20 minutes until firm. Remove from moulds to hot serving-dish and pour on the shrimp sauce.

Shrimp Sauce

3 *oz. butter*	*½ tsp. salt*
3 *tbsp. flour*	*⅛ tsp. pepper*
¾ pt. boiling milk	2 *tbsp. anchovy sauce*
½ lb. shrimps (shelled)	

Melt only half the butter, add flour, and gradually, stirring constantly, the milk. Bring to the boil, reduce and simmer for 5 minutes. Add seasoning to the shrimps which have been broken into pieces. Add the remaining butter just before serving, stirring it in.

Roast Turkey

Turkey*	Salt
¼ lb. flour	¼ lb. butter

Fat bacon

Dress, clean, stuff and truss turkey. Rub over with salt, also rub inside cavity; cover with layers of fat bacon, and then a piece of well-greased greaseproof paper. Place in dripping tin (preferably on a rack). Cream butter and flour and spread breast, legs and wings, dredge the bottom of the tin with a little flour. Place in a hot oven, 300° F.; when the surface is browned reduce heat; baste well every 20 minutes.

Stuffing

3½ bkcp. stale white breadcrumbs

½ pt. boiling water	1 tsp. each thyme and parsley
¼ lb. butter or suet	¼ lb. finely chopped celery
1 tsp. salt	⅛ tsp. pepper

Pour the water over the bread and leave for 15 minutes. Put in cheese cloth, press out all water possible, add butter and seasonings and celery.

Chestnut Stuffing

½ tbsp. chopped shallot	3 oz. soft breadcrumbs
3 tbsp. butter	2 doz. whole boiled chestnuts
¼ lb. sausage meat	½ lb. chestnut purée

12 mushrooms peeled and chopped ½ tbsp. finely chopped parsley

* Allow ¾ to 1 lb. turkey per person and allow 25 minutes per pound for a 12 lb. bird and 20 minutes per pound for a larger bird.
If desired the crop may be filled with one kind of stuffing and the body with another.

Cook the shallot and butter together for 5 minutes. Add sausage meat, mushrooms and chestnut purée. Cover for 7 minutes. Add parsley, again bring to boiling-point, add the breadcrumbs and the chestnuts. Cool before using for stuffing.

Brown Gravy

Pour liquid in tin in which the turkey has been roasted. From liquid remove 4 tablespoonsful fat, return to roasting tin and brown with 4 tablespoonsful flour. Pour on gradually, while stirring constantly, 1 pint stock in which the giblets, neck, and tips of wings have been cooked. Cook 5 minutes. Season with salt and pepper. Strain and serve.

Cranberry Sauce

1 *qt. cranberries*	1 *lb. sugar*
1 *pt. boiling water*	$\frac{1}{8}$ *tsp. salt*

Wash and pick over the cranberries. Boil the water, sugar and salt together for 5 minutes. Add the cranberries, and cook uncovered without stirring until transparent, about 5 minutes. A rapid cooking is usually sufficient. Skim and cool.

Bread Sauce

$\frac{3}{4}$ *pt. milk*	2 *tbsp. butter*
$\frac{1}{2}$ *onion*	1 *bkcp. soft breadcrumbs*
2 *cloves*	$\frac{1}{3}$ *tsp. salt*
A *tiny clove mace*	$\frac{1}{6}$ *tsp. pepper*

Stick the cloves into the onion, place in saucepan with milk, bring to the boil, add mace and breadcrumbs, cover and keep thoroughly hot without boiling for 15 minutes. Remove onion, cloves and mace, add butter, pepper and salt, beat thoroughly and serve.

Mashed Potatoes

For 12 servings allow 12 medium size potatoes

4 *pt. boiling water*	2 *tbsp. salt*
1 *bkcp milk or cream*	4 *oz. butter*

Remove any sprouts or eyes and peel, soak in cold water for about 30 minutes. Drain and cook uncovered in 4 pints boiling water. Add 2 teaspoonsful salt. When they are done, drain well. Mash with a fork and add 4 oz. butter, 2 teaspoonsful salt, breakfastcupful hot milk or cream. Beat until creamy and keep hot over panful of boiling water. If desired brown lightly under grill.

Brussels Sprouts

Allow 6 lb. sprouts for 12 servings   *6 oz. butter*

Water   *Salt*

Pull off any wilted outer leaves, cut off stems, then cut a cross-wise gash in the stem. Soak the sprouts for at least 10 minutes in cold salted water. Drain and drop into rapidly boiling water (with 1½ teaspoonsful salt to each quart water), cook uncovered until just tender. Drain and serve with a little melted butter. Allow ½ tablespoonful butter to each pound sprouts.

Grape Salad

Remove the skins from some green grapes and cut in halves lengthwise and remove seeds. Add an equal quantity of walnuts and celery finely chopped, moisten with French dressing (p. 208), and fill into small nests made of lettuce leaves. Garnish with cranberries.

Christmas Pudding

½ *lb. stale breadcrumbs*	¼ *lb. grated carrot*
½ *pt. scalded milk*	½ *lb. grated suet*
6 *oz. brown sugar*	¼ *pt. brandy*
5 *eggs*	½ *grated nutmeg*
½ *lb. raisins (seeded, cut*	¾ *tsp. cinnamon*
small and well floured)	⅓ *tsp. cloves*
6 *oz. currants*	½ *tsp. finely grated lemon peel*
4 *oz. chopped walnuts*	⅓ *tsp. mace*
2 *oz. sultanas*	1½ *tsp. salt*
¼ *lb. chopped citron*	

Soak the breadcrumbs in milk for an hour, add sugar, beaten egg yolk, raisins, currants, sultanas, lemon peel, walnuts, citron;

add the suet and beat up by hand, using a wooden spoon. Add brandy, spices and salt; add the stiffly whisked whites of eggs. Turn into a buttered bowl-shaped mould. Steam 6 hours. Unmould and serve garnished with a sprig of holly, surrounded with burning brandy. Some people add a tablespoonful or two of stout when mixing to give the pudding a richer colour.

Brandy Sauce

¼ lb. butter	Few grains salt
½ lb. icing sugar	½ cup thick cream (evaporated
Whites of 2 eggs	milk beaten stiff)

2 tbsp. brandy

Cream the butter, add the sugar gradually and continue beating. Put over hot water, add stiffly beaten whites of eggs and beat until well blended. Cool. Add brandy, salt and cream.

Almonds to Salt

¼ lb. almonds	1½ tbsp. butter
Salt	1½ tbsp. lard

Blanch almonds, dry on a clean cloth. Put butter and lard in a saucepan and, when melted and well heated, add almonds, fry until delicately browned, stirring constantly so that the almonds brown evenly. Remove with small skimmer, drain on brown paper and sprinkle with salt.

It was always said of him that he knew how to keep Christmas well.
CHARLES DICKENS

Wines and Wine Glasses

*And Noah he often said to his wife when he
  sat down to dine,
"I don't care where the water goes if it
  doesn't get into the wine."*

G. K. CHESTERTON

Je ne connais rien de sérieux, ici bas, que la culture de la vigne.

VOLTAIRE

Wine and food are good partners. Wine not only aids the digestion but helps to enhance an insipid dish and, of course, a glass of champagne ensures a party's success.

Wines can be classified in three groups:

BEVERAGE WINES, which when taken in moderation are healthful and stimulating. They may be black, green, golden, pink, red or white. Among this group are Bordeaux, Burgundies, Moselles, the Rhine wines and Sauternes.

FORTIFIED WINES, to which brandy has been added. These include Australian, Madeira, Marsala, Port, Sherry and the South African dessert wines.

SPARKLING WINES. Among these are Champagne, Saumur and Sparkling Moselle.

In the kitchen, for culinary purposes, wine may be blended with, and cooked with, the ingredients of a dish, or added at the last moment. Sometimes food is 'marinated' in wine, or wine may be added to a jelly or cold sweet to give added flavour. With Christmas pudding, and mince pies, the spirit is ignited and the dish served alight.

Correct methods of keeping wine are an important factor in the final bouquet, and may make or mar the success of a whole evening. A dark, dry cellar is the ideal resting place, without heat or vibration, and having a temperature of about 55 degrees. Many people wonder why bottles are kept lying on their sides: this keeps the corks damp. If they get dry they shrink.

Bottles should be brought up from the cellar several hours before use. Some wines are served at room temperature, while others are slightly warmed, as will be seen from this list:

WINES SERVED AT SPECIAL TEMPERATURES

Burgundy . . .	70° F.	Claret . . .	60° F.
Burgundy, Sparkling .	Cold.	Claret, White . .	50° F.
Burgundy, White . .	45° F.	Chablis . . .	45° F.

WINES SERVED AT SPECIAL TEMPERATURES—*continued*

Champagne. .	. 35° F.	Rhine .	. .	. Cold.
Graves .	. . Cold.	Sauterne	.	. 50° F.
Madeira	. . 60° F.	Sherry .	. .	. 40° F.
Marsala	. . 40° F.			

When wine is served, a little is poured into the host's glass; he sips this (this is a relic of the olden days, to prove there was no poison in the drink). The bottle is then passed clockwise around the table, but never to the right as it is said to be unlucky to drink wine from a bottle that has been circulated anti-clockwise. Wine and coffee are always served on the right, while food is served on the left. Never shake the bottle—especially if it is an old one—lest you disturb the lees. Always try to serve the right wine; the wrong wine can completely ruin a meal.

Before deciding upon the wine when planning a menu, the different courses and food must be taken into consideration:

As an apéritif	Sherry, Marsala, Madeira, French *vin tonique*—such as Dubonnet
With:	
Caviare	Vodka or Champagne
Oysters	Chablis, Champagne, or a special White Burgundy
Hors d'œuvres	Chablis, Champagne or any Sherry
Caviare and smoked salmon	Champagne, Hock, Moselle
Soup	Dry or medium Sherry, Marsala or Madeira
Fish soups	Hock, Moselle or Sherry
Lobster and shell-fish	Hock, Chablis, Champagne if no red wine is to follow, or White Burgundy
Fish	Rhine Wines, Sauterne, White Wine
Entrées	
Removes	
Roasts	Burgundy, Claret
Venison and hare	
Entremets	Champagne
Cheese	Port, Brown Sherry, Burgundy

Dessert	Claret, Port, Madeira, Brown Sherry, Chateau d'Yquem
Coffee	Liqueurs, Cognac

SHERRY is decanted and served at room temperature in a glass smaller than a wineglass. It is often served instead of a cocktail and is enjoyable with soup, even if half a glass only is served and this is added to the soup. Sherry is also served as a mid-way drink, or at any other time when it is desired to extend hospitality.

RED WINE means *Red Bordeaux* or *Claret, Burgundy, Chianti* and similar wines which are partners with roasts of beef, and venison, but not with fish or with chicken. These wines are best served at room temperature in their own bottle, in a straw container with a handle, which holds the bottle on its side with least disturbance and ensures full flavour. Due to their low alcoholic content they spoil very readily when opened and exposed to air. If they are decanted, this needs special care. The *Claret* glass is easily recognized by the more bulky-shaped glass on the taller stem, not so broad as a champagne glass. *Burgundy* is served at room temperature and in the same sort of glass as claret, though it is a fuller-bodied and stronger wine. It is a good partner with duck and all game.

WHITE WINE is served chilled and kept in its own bottle, wrapped in a napkin. If desired, it may be served throughout the entire meal. The 'extra dry' is best with oysters and fish, the slightly less dry goes well with fowl or entrées, while the sweeter white wines are served with the sweet or dessert course, if champagne is not being drunk throughout the meal. Glasses for white wine have a smaller and more contracted bowl than claret glasses. *Rhine Wines* have their own specially long-stemmed glasses, either crystal or coloured, to ensure that the wine is kept cool.

CHAMPAGNE is distinctly a wine for more formal occasions. Should it be served throughout a meal, *dry* champagne is preferable to *sweet*. If sweet is to be served just before dessert, it must be well chilled, and it is not served or uncorked until just before the course. Like all the white wines, champagne remains in the bottle, which is wrapped in a napkin. Champagne glasses should be of thin crystal. They may be of the saucer type or have hollow stems. When champagne is served at a reception or large party, it usually passes amongst the guests in small narrow-topped glasses or flaring-topped tumblers, which are less liable to upset. (These can be obtained from caterers.)

When the dessert plates are all on the table, the PORT is served. It is put on the table before the host, and then handed round— clockwise—by the butler or parlourmaid.

At a formal dinner, LIQUEURS, such as *Cognac, Crème de Menthe, Kümmel, Benedictine, Chartreuse,* follow; and the servant asks which one is preferred. Liqueurs are served in the smallest of the range of table glasses. They are of varied design, and may be the tiniest tumblers on a stem, or miniature-sized wine-glasses. Liqueurs usually accompany the coffee after dinner, with cigars and cigarettes.

BRANDY glasses are crystal clear, with a bulbous exaggerated bowl, into which as a liqueur only a small amount of brandy is poured. Then the hands cup the bowl of the glass (to warm it slightly), and through this the perfect bouquet is enjoyed while it is shaken round before being drunk. Some people to-day enjoy drinking a brandy and soda before a meal as an alternative to other short drinks.

WINE GLASSES

CHAMPAGNE. Holds 6½ oz. Saucer-shaped glass, with or without hollow stem.

CLARET. Holds 8–9½ oz. Stemmed tulip-shaped glass.

COCKTAIL. Holds 3½–5 oz. Stemmed cup-shaped glass.

HIGHBALL. Holds 12–14 oz. A tall tumbler.

ICED TEA. Holds 12–14 oz. Often interchangeable with a highball glass.

JUICE. Holds 5 oz. A small tumbler for fruit juices.

LIQUEUR. Holds 2½ oz. A stemmed glass.

OLD-FASHIONED COCKTAIL. Holds 7½ oz. A flaring tumbler.

PUNCH. A small glass cup with a handle.

SAUTERNE. Holds 5 oz. A tulip-shaped stemmed glass.

SHERBET. Similar to and often interchangeable with the champagne glass.

SHERRY. Holds 4 oz. A flaring glass on a stem.

RHINE WINE. Holds 7 oz. A stemmed glass tapering towards the top.

WATER. A tumbler holding 11 oz.

> *Give me a bowl of wine.*
> *In this I bury all unkindness.*
> *Julius Caesar,* iv, 3.

Appendix
French and Other Foreign Terms

Elphinston: What, have you not read it through? . . .
Johnson: No, Sir, do you read books through?

DR. JOHNSON,
Letter to Joshua Reynolds

APPENDIX

FRENCH AND OTHER FOREIGN TERMS

These terms may be useful when you dine out.

Abaisse. Dough crust/paste. Thinly rolled-out paste.

Abat-faim. Literally 'hunger reducer', such as a substantial joint of roast beef. Hence the meaning *pièce de résistance*—something to cut at and come again.

Abats. Liver, lights or offal.

Abattis. The head, neck, liver, comb, kernels and wings of a bird—giblets.

Able. A fish of the salmon type, but smaller. Found on the Swedish coast.

Ablette (Ablet). Bleak; a very small, sweet fresh-water fish, chiefly caught in the Seine; somewhat like our whitebait.

Ablette de Mer. White fish.

Abondance. Watered wine. Abundance.

Abricota, Abricotine. Two names of a popular liqueur made with fresh or dried apricots, sugar and brandy, or a cheaper spirit.

Abricote. Crystallized apricots, or bonbon, masked with apricot marmalade.

Abusseau. A small fish, one of the Athenines; a kind of smelt common on the Atlantic seaboard of France, from la Baule to Arcachon.

Accola. (*Ital.*) A marinaded fish, similar to tunny fish.

Accolade. 'A brace'—as of pheasants, partridges, etc. These are sometimes served two together, or *en accolade*.

Acéphale. Fish-like—oysters, mussels, cockles, scallops, limpets, periwinkles, etc. Literal meaning—'without heads'.

Aceto Dolce. (*Ital.*) Sour and sweet. An Italian pickle.

Ache. Smallage; a kind of parsley.

Achillée. Milfoil.

Acquacedrata. (*Ital.*) Water sweetened with sugar and flavoured with lemon, rather resembling lemonade.

Âcre. Sharp, piquant.

Adragante (Gomme A.). Gum Tragacanth. Principal ingredient used for gum paste.

Affrité. Ready to fry.

Africaine (à l'). African style.

Agneau. Lamb.

Agras. A sweet soft drink made with unfermented grape juice, sugar, crushed almonds and water. It is essential to serve it really well chilled.

Agriote. Wild cherry.

Aide de cuisine. Assistant cook.

Aigre au Cédrat. Orangeade, flavoured with the juice of mulberries, sweetened, with lemon juice added. This drink was a favourite of Cardinal Richelieu.

Aigre-Douce Sauce. (*Agro-dolce—Ital.*) A sharp sweet sauce made with vinegar, sugar, pine kernels, almonds, chocolate and small currants. Served hot.

Aigrette. A French term much used in ornamental confectionery; it signifies, literally, 'a bunch or group'.

Ail. Garlic.
Une gousse d'ail. A clove of garlic.

Aileron. Small wing of birds; fin of some fish. Sometimes used to garnish dishes, or served as a ragout.

Aillade. A piece of bread that has been rubbed with garlic.

Aine. Top of sirloin.

Aiou. A 'provincial' sauce made with olive oil, egg yolks, and garlic. In Provence this name is given to any dish served with garlic sauce.

Airelle Myrtille. Huckleberry, whortleberry. There are two sorts. The first originates in America and is eaten freshly picked with savoury milk, or if preferred, a cream sauce. The other, a kind of whortleberry, is smaller, a dark blue in colour, used for seasoning certain dishes, and some wine merchants use it to colour wine. Hence its French name *teint-vin.*

Aiselle. A species of beetroot, used both in salads and as a vegetable.

Ajolio. (*Sp.*) Sauce made of oil and garlic. See **Ayoli** (under Menu terms).

Ajoutées. Mixed or added to. Used to denote small garnishes or small side-dishes, served as a vegetable course.

Alliance (à la Ste.). Name of a garnish consisting of braised carrots, artichoke bottoms and small onions.

Allumette. Match, strip.

Almacciva. (*Ital.*) An Italian sweet dish, similar to semolina pudding.

Alose. Shad.

Alouette (or **Mauviette**). Lark.

Alphabétique. Paste letters used in soups, etc.

Alphénic. White barley sugar, or sugar candy.

Alvéole. Wax cell of honeycomb.

Amalgamer. To amalgamate—to mix substances together.

Amande. Almond.
Pâte d'Amande. Almond paste. A mixture of pounded almonds and sugar and whites of eggs or water, made into a paste and used for cake coverings, etc.

Amandes Douchées. Shelled almonds.

— Pralinées. Burnt almonds.

— Salées. Salted almonds.

Amarante. Amaranth, a kind of spinach.

Ambigu. A convenient French name for a repast of one course. A buffet lunch or ball supper. A meal where both meat and sweets are served at the same time.

Ambroisie. A cold drink. Milk with vanilla or Kirchwasser flavouring.

Ameaux. A kind of puff paste and egg.

Amer, Amère. Bitter.

Américaine (à l'). Applied to game served with a sauce of which black-currant jelly forms a principal ingredient.

Amidon. Starch. A white farinaceous substance, obtained by a peculiar process from flour or potatoes. It is slightly soluble in cold water, but quickly melts in boiling water, and through cooling it becomes a mass similar to jelly. It is then called *Empois* in French, or stiffened starch.

Amiral (à l'). Admiral style. Name of a garnish.

Amourettes. Spinal marrow cut in strips and crumbed. Lamb's fry.

Amphitryon. Host.

Amylacé. Starchy.

Ananas. Pineapple.

Andouille. Literally meaning 'a hog's pudding'. A variety of French sausage meat made of pork and chitterlings.

Ânesse (Lait d'). Ass's milk.

Angloise. A kind of plum tart.

Angobert. A large cooking pear.

Animelles. Lamb's fry.

Api. See **Pomme d'Api.**

Apostelkuchen. (*Ger.*) A German savoury cake eaten with cheese.

Appareils. Culinary term denoting mixture; preparation for an event.

Appétissant. Appetizing—something to whet the appetite. An hors d'œuvre consisting of stuffed Spanish olives, dressed on *croûtons* of French bread.

Apprète. A sippet or narrow slice of bread.

Apprêté. Prepared, cooked, dressed.

Argenteuil. Name of a district in France celebrated for asparagus: *Asperges d'Argenteuil.*

Ariese. A town in France celebrated for its sausages, *Saucissons d'Ariesi.*

Ariston. (*Greek.*) A kind of milk bread like rusks.

Armagnac. A brandy from the district of that name.

Arroche. Spinach.

Assaisonner. To season and flavour.

Assiette. Plate. Also a French term for hors d'œuvres.

Assiettes montées. Raised dishes.

Assorti. Assorted, as *Gâteaux assortis.*

Assyrien. Assyrian style.

Athérine. Sand smelt. A species of fish similar to smelts distinguishable by the absence of cucumber smell, which is so peculiar to the latter.

au, aux. With. See Menu terms, p. 48.

Auberge. An inn.

Aubergiste. Inn-keeper. Hotel-keeper.
    à l'—. Inn-keeper's style.

Auflauf. (*Ger.*) Soufflé or puff-omelette, or baked soufflé pudding.

Aveline. Filbert.

Avi. The burnt part of the loaf. Sometimes spelt *havi.*
    Un pain qui a reçu l'avi. A loaf that has been burnt.

Avoine. Oats.

Crème d'—. Cream of oats used for puddings and soups.

Azy. Rennet: made from skimmed milk and vinegar.

Azyme. Unleavened bread.

Babeurre. Buttermilk.

Balantier. Wild pomegranate.

Bandes. This term is used in French cooking for styles of paste used for various purposes, such as lattice work on tarts.

— **des cervelas.** Strings of sausages.

— **du tour.** These are the long pieces of paste which are used to surround the others and keep them together.

Baraquille. This is the name of a savoury French pastry which is filled with minced partridge, chicken, veal, sweetbread, truffles and mushrooms, and seasoned according to taste.

Barbarie (à la). A mode of dressing meat, game and poultry.

Barbe-de-bouc. A plant resembling the salsify. It is boiled in seasoned water or stock, or baked.

Barbe-de-capucin. Monk's beard. The French name for a kind of blanched chicory.

Barbe-de-Jupiter. House leek.

Barcelonnettes. A sort of French iced cake, surmounted with comfits.

Barque. A piece of pastry formed in the shape of a ship.

Bassin. (Ger. *Becken*—from which we get 'beaker'; Ital. *Bacino*.) Basin. Many varieties and sizes of basins are used for culinary purposes.

Batterie de cuisine. A complete set of cooking utensils.

Baveux. The French term for slimy—commonly used to signify a partially cooked omelette, as *omelette baveuse*.

Béatilles. Delicate luxuries, such as sweetbreads, cocks' combs, Strasbourg fat livers and viands of that description. *Une assiette de Béatilles* means a plate of dainty choice food.

Bécasseau. Sandpiper.

Bécassine. Snipe.

Berlingot. The French name for a sort of American caramel. A kind of barley sugar.

Beurré. A pear having a soft and melting flesh.

Bigarade. The name for the Seville or bitter orange.

Bigarré. A term signifying 'parti-coloured'.

Bigarreau. White-heart cherry.

Biscotin. A small crisp biscuit of various kinds, usually served with ices, creams, wine, coffee or chocolate.

Blanc. White. This term is used in French cooking to denote meats that are served *au blanc*, that is, with white sauce.

Bonbons. Sugar confectionery. A French term for sweetmeats generally, or other kinds of delicacy. It is merely the repetition of the word *bon*—good. It answers to our child's term, 'goody-goodies'.

Bonne Bouche. The literal translation of this term is 'a good mouth' or a titbit.

Bonnet de Turquie. A piece of pastry made to resemble a Turk's cap.

Bordures. (Ger. *Ränder;* Ital. and Sp. *Bordos.*) Borders. Pretty dishes suitable for moulding fruit and jellies and for filling the centre with different entremets.

Bouchère (à la). Butcher's style.

Bouilli. 'Boiled', as *bœuf bouilli*—beef boiled.

Bouilloire. Boiler, kettle.

Bouillon. Broth. This term has been very much adopted in recent years as a generic term for concentrated and other beef essences.

— **de Bœuf.** Beef broth not clarified.

— **de Mouton.** Mutton broth.

— **aux Œufs.** Beef broth with beaten egg, served in cups.

— **en Tasses.** Beef broth in cups.

— **de Veau.** Veal broth.

— **de Volaille.** Chicken broth.

— **de Volaille à l'Orge.** Chicken broth thickened with pearl barley.

Boules de Berlin. Doughnuts.

Boulettes. Little balls of chopped meat or breadcrumbs, chiefly used for garnishing.

Bouquet garni. A bunch of sweet herbs.

Bourguignon. A French term which is applied to several dishes prepared with red wine, as *Bœuf Bourguignon*—beef with Burgundy.

Brasillé. 'Toasted quickly'—as of a slice of bread.

Brésoille. An entrée consisting of several kinds of meat. Also ragout of veal.

Brife. A large portion of bread.

Brignole. A species of dark red cooking plums from Brignoles, a district in France.

Brin. Sprig.

Briscotine. The name of a light entrée of forcemeat etc.

Broc. Wine pitcher.

Brocard. Young roebuck.

Broché. Trussed and skewered ready for roasting.

Brochet. Pike. Seasonable October to January. A fish found in almost all waters, much liked on account of its delicate flavour.

Brochette. Skewer; spit.

Brötchen. (*Ger.*) 'Little bread'—hence *Brötchen* comes to signify 'sandwich'.

Brouet. Broth liquor.

— **d'Andouille.** Tripe liquor.

Brouillé. Scrambled, mixed, beaten up. Usually applied to eggs.

Brouissin. A mixture of soft cheese with vinegar, pepper and salt.

Brut. Unsweetened, natural, raw.

Bruxellois (-e) (au). Brussels style.

Choux de Bruxelles Cantabres. Braised brussels sprouts with slices of ham and Basque sausages.

Choux de Bruxelles à la Maître d'Hôtel. Boiled with parsley butter or parsley sauce.

Choux de Bruxelles Sautés. Brussels sprouts, boiled, drained and then tossed in fresh butter.

Bruyère (Coq de). Heath cock, grouse.

Bucarde, Boucarde, Bucardier. Cockle.

Buccin. A type of mollusc. Whelk.

Cabrillons. Small cheeses made from goats' milk in Lyons and Auvergne. They are not much known in this country.

Cabus. Broccoli.

Caen. A town in France, famous for its tripe, and other delicacies (*À la mode de Caen*).

Café au lait. Coffee with milk.

— **double.** Coffee of double strength.

— **frappé.** Iced coffee.

— **glacé.** Iced coffee.

— **noir.** Black coffee.

— **turc.** Turkish coffee.

— **vierge.** An infusion of whole coffee beans.

Cafetière. Coffee pot.

Caillebotte. Curds.

Cailleteau. Young quail.

Caillot-rosat. A kind of pear with a rose flavour.

Caisse. Case (Ramekin case), etc.

Canard Sauvage. Wild duck.

Cane. Hen duck.

Caneton Rôti. Roast Duckling.

Canneberge. Cranberry.

Capucin (Barbe-de-). Chicory.

Capucine. Indian cress, nasturtium.

Carafe. Decanter.

Carbonado. An ancient dish prepared from a fowl or joint of veal or mutton roasted, carved, and cut across and across; the pieces were then basted with butter, sprinkled with breadcrumbs and grilled.

Carbonnade. Stewed or braised meat.

Carcasse. The body of an animal: the bones and skeleton of poultry or game.

Cardamine. Wild cress or bittercress.

Carême. Lent.

Carême. A celebrated chef born in Paris in 1784, died in 1833. The author of several culinary works. Chef to the Prince Regent, George IV of England, and the Emperor Alexander I of Russia.

Caret. Green turtle.

Cari. Curry.

Carmin. Carmine, crimson. Red colouring used in confectionery.

Carte du Jour (la). Bill of fare for the day—a list of daily dishes with the prices attached to each dish.

Cartouche. Cartridge, a culinary term meaning a circular piece of greased paper used for covering meat, etc., during the process of cooking.

Carvi. Caraway seed.

Casse. Case, pan.
     — *à rôti.* Dripping pan.

Cendre. Ashes or embers.
     Cuit sous la —. Cooked under the ashes.

Cerise. Cherry.

Cervelas. Saveloys, of which the English name is a composition.

Chair. Flesh.
     — *blanc.* White meat.
     — *noir.* Dark meat.
     — *à saucisse.* Sausage meat.

Chapelure. Rasped bread crust.

Chaponneau. Young capon.

Charbonné. Burnt.

Charcuterie. This word means badly carved, but in a culinary sense, it denotes pork, prepared in any fashion. Black pudding, pigs' feet truffled, smoked pigs' ears, navy sausages, saveloys, pigs' liver, are all items of *charcuterie.*

Charcutier. Pork butcher, *chair cuite.* A purveyor of cooked and dressed meats.

Charponnière. A special type of stewpan.

Châtaigne. Chestnut used for stuffing and sweet dishes.

Chateaubriand. The name of Viscount Françoise Auguste, a great French gourmand born in 1768 and died in 1848. A favourite dish of double fillet steak is called after him.

Chaudeau. A sweet sauce served with puddings, etc.

Chaud-froid. Literally hot-cold; applied to certain methods of preparing birds, served cold, usually garnished with savoury jelly and truffles after being masked with cold sauce.

Chaudron. Calf's chitterlings.

Chaufferette. Chafing dish.

Chaussons. French pastries answering in many particulars to English puffs. They are described as a sort of pastry made of a round of paste folded across the middle filled with apple or other marmalade compote— and served cold.

Chevesne, Chervaine, Chevenne. Chub.

Cheveux d'Ange. A sweetmeat prepared from young carrots.

Chevreuse. Small gooseberry tartlets.

Chiche. Chick-pea.

Chopine. Half-bottle.

Choucroute. The French term for the German *Sauerkraut.*

Chou-fleur. Cauliflower.

Cimier. Saddle; haunch (generally of venison).

Ciseler. To make an incision in the under skin of a fish so that when grilled it will not crack.

Citronelle. Balm mint.

Citrouille. A kind of vegetable marrow.

Civet or **Civette.** A brown stew of hare, venison.

Clou de Girofle. Clove.

Clouté. Studded. To insert nail-shaped pieces of truffle, bacon or tongue into fowl, poulards, cushions of veal and sweetbreads. The holes to receive them are made by using a skewer.

Clupe. A genus of fishes, of which the herring is the type. Also included: anchovy, sardine, brisling, pilchard, shad, etc.

Cochevis. The cropped or crested lark.

Cochon de Lait. Sucking pig.

Cochonnaille. Hog's or pig's pudding.

Cocotte. Small earthenware pans in individual or large sizes. Cooking vessel. *Cocotte de Volaille, Poulet en Cocotte, Œufs en Cocotte.*

Coing. Quince—a fruit used for both marmalade and compote.

Coingvarde. A liqueur distilled from quinces; also the name of a marmalade which is made from quinces and grapefruit.

Colin. Whiting, pollock.

Collet. Scrag-end of the neck of mutton or veal.

Colombe. Pigeon, dove.

Coloquinte. Colocynth, a bitter cucumber.

Compiègne. A light yeast cake with crystallized fruit.

Compote de Pigeon. Pigeon stew.

Concasser. To pound, to crush.

Condé (à la). Name for a purée of red haricot beans, and a dish made of apricots and rice.

Contiser. To insert small pieces or strips of truffle, bacon, ham, etc., into fillets of fish, poultry, etc., into holes which were previously made by the point of a skewer. Sometimes when small scallops of truffles, smoked tongue, etc., are inlaid, or used as a garnish in fillets, they are said to be *contisés.* See **Clouté.**

Contrefilet. Fillet of beef, slices of boned sirloin.

Copeaux. Shavings.
　Pommes en —. Potato shavings.

Coq. Cock.

— de Bruyère. Woodcock, but also the French equivalent for grouse.

— Noir. Black game.

Coquille. Scallop shell.

Coquilles, En. Made-up dishes.

Corbeille. Basket.

Corette. Jew's Mallow (an Egyptian herb).

Corme. Shad apple. Service-berry.

Cornichon. Gherkin.

Coryphène. Blue fish—the *dorade* (q.v.) belongs to the Genus Coryphaena, which includes mackerel.

Cosaques. The term applied to what are more familiarly known as crackers.

Côtelettes. Cutlets, literally 'little ribs'.

Côtes de Bœuf. Ribs of beef.

Cougloff. (Ger. *Kugelhopf.*) A German cake—a kind of rich dough or yeast cake, with currants and raisins.

Coulis. A liquid seasoning used for brown and white stews. Also the name of filtered soups, purées and certain creams.

Coullis. A smooth sauce, very highly but delicately flavoured—used for soups and entrées.

Coupe. Cup, drinking vessel.
— *à légumes.* Vegetable cutter.
— *à pâte.* Pastry cutter.
— *St Jacques*—A fruit salad served in glass cups with vanilla ice cream on top.

Courge, Courgeon. Squash.

Courlis, Corlis, Corlieu. Curlew.

Couronne. Crown.
en — To dish up in the form of a crown.

Craquelin. Cracknel.

Crème. Cream.
— **d'Orge.** Finely ground barley—a white soup made from barley.
— **de Riz.** Finely ground rice—a white soup made of powdered rice.

Crémeux. Creamy.

Créole. The name given to certain dishes of which rice forms a part—also to sweets masked with chocolate.

Crêpes. French pancakes.

Cresson de Fontaine. Watercress.

Crêtes. Giblets of poultry and game.
— **de Coq.** Cocks' combs.

Crever. To burst or crack, generally used for rice.

Crevette. Shrimp, prawn.

Croquant. Crisp. Crackling.

Croquantes. A transparent mixture of fruits and boiled sugar.

Croquembouches. Large set pieces for suppers and dinners such as iced cakes, nougat, fruits covered with boiled sugar, to give them a brilliant appearance.

Croquer. To crunch.

Croquignole. A kind of fondant (*petit-four*).

Croûte. Crust; a thick piece of fried bread upon which entrées, etc., are served.
— **au pot.** Beef broth—a favourite soup of France.

Croûtons. Thin slices of bread cut into shapes and used for garnishing dishes.

Cru. Raw or uncooked.

Cuillère de cuisine. Wooden spoon.

Cuisine. Kitchen.
Chef de — is the head-cook and his assistants are *Aides de cuisine*.
Faire la —. To cook, or to dress victuals.

Cuisinier. A cook who prepares, cooks and dresses food.

Cuisse. Leg.
— *de volaille*. Leg of chicken or fowl.

Cuisson. A method of slowly cooking meat. It is finished off by cooking in its own juice, generally whilst in an oven.

Cuissot. Haunch; *Cuissot de Veau, Cuissot de Cochon*, etc.

Cuit. Cooked.

Culinaire. This term is applied to anything in connection with the art of cooking and with the kitchen. A good cook is called *un artiste culinaire*.

Culotte. Rump, aitchbone of beef.

Curcuma. Turmeric.

Daal. (*Hind.*) Split pulse, such as grain, lentils or haricot beans from which numerous dishes are made, one of these being a famous curry.

Darne. A slice of certain fish, such as *Darne de Saumon*—slice of salmon.

Daube. A powerful seasoning of meat, as beef *à la Daube* or *en Daube*. Name applied to meats or poultry braised.

Daubière. An oval-shaped stew-pan in which meats or birds are braised, stewed or daubed.

Daurade. A sea fish about 18 inches long, sometimes called sea bream (*brème de mer*). Mostly baked or cooked in tomato or white caper sauce. It is also fried, but must not be confounded with Dorade.

Dégraisser. To take off grease from soups, etc.

Déjeuner. Lunch. *Petit déjeuner*. Breakfast.
— *à la Fourchette*. A meat breakfast or luncheon.
— *de Noce*. Wedding breakfast.

Demi-deuil (en). A culinary expression which means half-mourning. When white meats such as fowl, veal, sweetbreads are larded with truffles they are called *en demi-deuil*.

Demi-glace. The name of a brown sauce of rather thinner consistency than ordinary sauce. Also the name of a cream ice which is very popular in Paris.

Demi-tasse. Half a cup. A current expression used for a small cup of black coffee or bouillon.

Dent-de-lion. Dandelion.

Dépecer, *Découper*. To carve, to cut into pieces.

Dés. Dice.
en —. Cut into shapes.

Dessécher. To stir a purée pulp or paste with a wooden spoon whilst it is heating until it loosens from the pan.

Diablé. (From *diable*—devil.) Devilled.

Diablotins. The literal meaning of this term is little imps—which French cooks apply to sweetmeats of various kinds.

Diavolini. Italian name for small devilled rice or farina cakes fried.

Dîner. Dinner.

— Mi-carême. Lenten dinner.

Dolmas. A Turkish dish of chopped meat wrapped in fig leaves and stewed.

Dorade. Dorado, dolphin.

Doré. Brushed over with beaten egg-yolk.

Dormant or **Surtout de Table.** Decorative objects which remain on the table to the end of the meal.

Dorure. Yolks of egg beaten, used for brushing over pastry.

Doucette. Corn salad.

Douilles mobiles. Movable tubes, adjusted on forcing or savoy bags used for the purpose of filling and decorating.

Doux (–ce). Sweet.

Dragées. The name for certain coated sweetmeats such as sugar plums. Also small lentiform pieces of plain chocolate.

Dressé or **Garni.** Dressed or garnished.

Duglère. A famous French chef who invented the method of serving sole dressed with tomato flavour blended with Béchamel and fish essence, finished off with fresh butter and chopped parsley.

Eau. Water.

— de Fleur d'Oranges. Orange flower water.

— de Vie. Spirits of wine, old brandy, etc.

— de Vie Prunelle. Sloe gin.

Ébarber. To remove the exterior parts of a piece of meat or fish.

Ébullition. Boiling-point.

 Chauffer à l'—. Heat to boiling-point.

Écarlate (à l'). Signifying a mode of cooking by which the red colour, as of meat, is preserved.

Échalote. Shallot.

Échauder. To steep in boiling water. This is often done with fowl or game, as it will facilitate the removing of the feathers or hair.

Échaudes. Cakes resembling Simnel cake.

Éclanche. Shoulder of mutton.

Écossaise (à l'). Scotch style.

Écumé. Skimmed.

 Écumoire. Skimming ladle or perforated spoon.

Écuyer. Equerry. A title which was given to cooks in olden days.

Ekneck Kataif. A Turkish meal porridge.

Émincé. Finely shredded or sliced.

Émonder. To blanch, e.g. to steep almonds in boiling water so that they may be peeled.

Empois. Starch paste.

en. In, denoting 'served in' as *en Casserole*—in a pipkin.

— **Brochette.** To place pieces of meat, fish or vegetables on a long metal skewer and grill them.

— **Croûte.** Encrusted. Wrapped or enclosed in paste prior to cooking.

— **Papillote.** Fish, meat or birds which are wrapped in greased paper in which they are cooked and sent to table.

— **Tasse.** Served in cups—this is chiefly applied to clear soups.

Entrecôtes. Rib steaks cut from between the ribs. They are declared by epicures to be second only to fillet steaks.

Épice. Spice, seasoning, aromatic plants and their seeds.

Érable. Maple tree.
　　Sirop d'—. Maple syrup.
　　Sucre d'—. Maple sugar.

Escargots. Edible snails.

Espagnole. *Sauce à l'Espagnole*, Spanish sauce. A rich brown sauce—the foundation of nearly all brown sauces.

Estomac. Stomach.
　　Estomacs de Poulet. Breast of chicken.

Estouffade. This expression is used to signify the slow cooking of meats with very little liquid in a covered stew pan, braised, stewed or steamed.

Estragon. Tarragon.

Esturgeons. Sturgeons.

Étamine. Tammy cloth, coarse muslin.

Extra-fin. Of the best quality. Denoting the quality of articles also *sur-fin*, *très fin*, *fin*, etc.

Faïence. Earthenware crockery.

Faire revenir. A term frequently used in French cookery books—it means to partly fry meat or vegetables—being tossed, slightly browned, without cooking.

Faire suer. To cook meat in its own juices (those which ooze from it), without liquor in a covered stew pan.

Faisans. Cock pheasants, *faisanes*—hen pheasants, and *faisandeaux*—young pheasants.

Faisan Piqué. Larded pheasant.

Farce. Forcemeat or stuffing.

Farine. Flour.

Fariné. Dredged or powdered with flour.

Faubonne. A vegetable purée soup which is seasoned with savoury herbs.

Faux, Fausse. Mock, false, as *Fausse Tortue*—Mock Turtle.

Fécule de pommes de terre. Potato flour.
— **de riz.** Rice flour.

Fendre. To split, as *fendre un poulet pour griller*—to split a chicken for broiling.

Fenouillette. A little russet apple with a flavour of fennel; also the name of a liqueur made from fennel seed which at one time was offered after wine at French tables.

Feuillage. Leaves.

Feuillé. With a leaf garnishing.

Feuilletage. Puff paste said to be so called after one Feuillet—a chef to the house of Condé.

Fèves d'Espagne. Scarlet runners, string beans.
— **des Marais.** Broad beans.

Figaro. The name of a cold sauce and mixture of mayonnaise and tomato.

Filet de Bœuf. Fillet of beef.
— *de Chevreuil.* Fillet of venison or roebuck.
— *en Chevreuil.* Mutton cooked and served in imitation of venison.
— *de Veau.* Fillet of veal.

Financière. A ragout of truffles, cocks' combs, etc., used as a garnish.

Flamand. Flemish. This is the name also given to a very rich cake.

Flamande (à la). Flemish style.

Flamber. To singe poultry or game.

Flan. A custard tart or an open fruit tart.

Flanc, Flanchet. Flank of beef or cod fish.

Flancs. Name of side dishes served at a big dinner.

Flétan. Halibut and similar fish.

Fleurons. Little half-moons of baked puff-paste which are used for garnishing.

Foie de Veau. Calf's liver.

Fonce. Strong gravy, meat stock, bottomed as in a mould with a paste lining.

Fond. Strong gravy, meat stock. Bottom, as in *fond d'artichaut*.

Fondant. Melting. A kind of icing, French dessert bonbons.
Faire un —. To make a hollow or well, as in the flour in the bowl or on the table.

Fondu. Melted.

Fondue. A preparation of melted cheese originally made in Switzerland—a cheese savoury.

Fontaine. Fountain.

Fouetté. Whipped with the whisk.

Fourchette. Fork.

Fourré. Coated with sugar, cream, etc. Also applied to stuffed birds.

Fraise. Strawberry, also the mesentery of a calf or lamb.

Fraiser la pâte. To plait, to make rough, to ruffle pastry.

Framboise. Raspberry.

Française (à la). This is, generally speaking, applied to a number of dishes of French origin.

Francatu. A russet apple.

Frappé. Iced.

Fressure. Haslet or lights, e.g. *fressure d'agneau*—lamb's lights.

Friand. An epicure—a dainty person.

Friandises. Name given to small dessert dainties, *petits fours*, etc.

Fricandeau. Braised cushion of fillet of veal.

Fricandelles. Small thin braised steaks of veal.

Fricassée. Fricassee. A white stew of veal or rabbit.

Frisé. Curled, as *chou frisé*—curled Savoy cabbage.

Frit or **Frite.** Fried. Anything dipped in frying batter and fried in fat.

Friture. This word has two significations—it applies to the fat which may be oil, or to lard or dripping in which articles are fried. It is applied to anything that has been fried—such as egged and crumbed fish, fried potatoes, croquettes, or rissoles.

Froid. Cold.
  Service —. Cold service.

Fromage. Cheese.

— **Blanc.** A soft white cheese made of soured milk, eaten with salt and pepper.

— **Cochon.** Brawn.

— **à la Crème.** Cream cheese—also known as *Colur à la Crème*—eaten with sifted sugar.

— **Glacé.** An ancient expression for an ice-cream or frozen pudding in the form of a cheese.

Fromageon. A white cheese which is made in the South of France from sheep's milk.

Fumé. Smoked—smoked bacon, fish, ham and sausages.

Fumet. The flavour or essence of game, fish or any other highly-flavoured concentrated substance which is used to impart a specially rich flavour to certain dishes or sauces.

Galantine de Dinde. Boned turkey or turkey galantine.

Galette. A kind of pastry—a light, round, flat-shaped breakfast roll.

Galimafrée. A kind of ragout, made of cold meat.

Galoni. The Spanish term for small cakes generally used for garnishing entremets. They should be light and cut in fanciful shapes so as to have the appearance of lace when set round as a garnish.

Garbure. A kind of maigre broth which was originally made of cabbage and bacon—to-day it is made of bread and vegetables.

Garçon. Waiter.
  Premier —. Head waiter.
  — *de salle*. Restaurant waiter.

Gardon. Roach.

Gargotage. Badly dressed victuals.
  Gargote. Common or cheap restaurant.

Gargotier. A bad cook, a keeper of a common cook shop.

Gastronome. A caterer; a hotel or restaurant keeper.

Gastronomie. Gastronomy.

Gaufre. Wafer, waffle; a light biscuit.

Genièvre. Juniper-berry.

Génoise. Genoese style.

Gervais. A sweet French cream cheese.

Gibelotte. A ragout generally prepared from rabbits.

Girofle. Clove.

Gitana (à la). Gipsy fashion.

Glace. Ice. This term is also applied to concentrated stock, i.e. meat glaze.
— **de Sucre.** Icing sugar; mixed with egg white and called 'Royal Icing' (*Glace Royale*).
— **de Viande.** Meat extract or glaze. Stock or gravy reduced to the thickness of jelly, used for glazing cooked meats, etc. to improve their appearance. Well made glaze adheres firmly to meats; it is also used for strengthening soups.

Glacé. Frozen, iced.

Godard. The name given to an entrée of chicken by the inventor— Benjamin Godard, the celebrated French composer.

Godiveau. Rich veal force-meat—quenelles—used mostly for garnish.

Gourmet. An epicure, a judge of good living; one who values and enjoys good eating; a connoisseur of wines.

Goût. Taste or savour. Relish as perceived by the tongue. The sense of tasting.

Goûter Fin. Afternoon meal; a meat tea. To taste; to relish.

Goyave. Guava.

Graisse. Fat suet, grease.

Granite. Granolata. A kind of half-frozen lemon or other fruit water-ice— served in glasses.

Grenade. Pomegranate.

Grenadier. The pomegranate-tree.

Grenadine. A grenadine syrup—the syrup made from the juice of the pomegranate and sugar.

Grenadins. A small kind of fricandeaux—slices of veal (heart-shaped) larded and then braised.

Grenouille. Edible frog.

Grianneau. A young goose.

Griblette. Collop of grilled pork.

Grillade. Broiled meat.

Grillé. Grilled.

Griotte. A dark red cherry, known as an Armenian cherry, used for preserves.

Grive. Fieldfare.

Groseilles vertes. Gooseberries.

Gruau. Gruel, oatmeal—water gruel.

R

Haché. Chopped up into small pieces—from which we derive our 'hash', minced meat.

Hacher menu. To mince meat finely.

Hachis. Hash—hashed meat. This is a method of saving cooked meat, such as *salmi de gibier*.

Hareng. Herring.

— Fumé. Bloater.

— Mariné. Pickled herring.

Harenguets. Sprats.

Haricot. Haricot beans. Also applied to a thick stew.

Hâtelette or **Hâtelle.** Small pieces of meat roasted on a skewer.

Hâtereau. Sliced pig's liver which is wrapped in pig's caul and then cooked on skewers.

Hâtiveaux. Early peas. This name is also used for other early fruits.

Haut goût. Fine taste; strong seasoning; high flavour. In Scotland this term is used for bad or tainted.

Hirondelle. Swallow.

Homard. Lobster.

Hongroise. Hungarian.

Huîtres frites. Fried oysters.

Hure. Boar or pig's head. Also the head and shoulders of some large fish.

— de Sanglier. Wild boar's head.

Indienne (à l'). Indian style—generally applied to dishes containing curry or chutney or both, accompanied with a dish of boiled rice.

Irlandaise (à l'). Irish style. This dish usually contains potatoes in some form. Also used when a garnish of potatoes surrounds a dish.

Jambonneau. A very small ham.

Jarret. Shin, knuckle.

— de Veau. Knuckle of veal.

Jaune-manger. Literally 'yellow food', as contrasted with *blanc-manger* (white food), from which it differs little except in colour.

Jetée. A throw.
Filer du sucre à la —. To spin sugar by throwing.

Jets d'houblon. Hop sprouts.

Jus. Gravy of meat. Meal served with its own gravy is said to be served *au jus. Jus lié* is thickened gravy.

Kaffeeklatsch. (*Ger.*) Coffee gossip. Coffee chocolates flavoured with vanilla, beaten egg and cream; wafers and cakes—provided for guests on special occasions.

Kagne. A sort of vermicelli.

Kaiserfleisch. (*Ger.*) Smoked sucking pig.

Klösse. (*Ger.*) Small dumplings usually served in soups.

Knickebein. (*Ger.*) The literal translation of this work is 'weak-kneed person'. It has been given to a pick-me-up made of egg, brandy and curaçao.

Knödel. (*Ger.*) A Bavarian name for a kind of small dumpling.

Krapfen. (*Ger.*) Fritters.

Kraplen. (*Ger.*) Tasty German cakes.

Kufte. (*Tur.*) A dish made up of meat in hard cakes shaped like small rolls and served with brown butter sauce.

Ladog. The name of a herring found in Lake Ladoga in Russia.

Laitance. The soft roe of a fish, of herring, carp or mackerel—which is considered a delicacy.

Lait sucré. Sugared milk.

Langouste. Crayfish.

Langues-de-chat. Very small tea or dessert biscuits—literally 'cat's tongues'—also fine wafers of chocolates.

Languier. Smoked hog's or pig's tongue.

Lapereau. Young rabbit.

Lapin. Rabbit.

Laurier. Bay leaf.

Lavat. A lake trout which abounds in certain Swiss lakes, also Austrian and Bavarian Lakes.

Lax. (*Norwegian.*) (Ger. *Lachs.*) Smoked salmon which is preserved in oil.

Lazagnes. (*Ital.*) Thin strips of noodle paste.

Levain. Leaven ferment; dough or batter prepared with yeast before mixing with the rest of the flour.
Pain sans —. Unleavened bread.

Levraut. Leveret. A young hare.

Levure. Yeast.

Lit. Bed. Thin slices of meat or vegetables spread in layers for culinary purposes.

Lorgnette. Fried onion rings. This name is also used for small dessert biscuits and candied fruits.

Lotte. Burbot, eel-pout.

Lucine. Clam.

Lucines Papillons. Soft clams.

Macéré. Steeped, macerated, soused.

Mâche. Lamb's lettuce, corn- or field-salad.

Macoquer or **Calebasse.** Fruit of the Calabash tree (*calebassier*) grown in America—resembles a melon.

Macque (Pain de la). French pastry something like cream puffs.

Macreuse. Widgeon; a black water-fowl of the wild duck tribe.

Madeleine. A particular kind of small cake, well known throughout France.

Madère. Madeira wine.

Maïs. Maize or Indian corn.

Maitrank. (*Ger.*) A May drink—a beverage originally consumed in Germany, made of Hock and other white wine.

Malart or **Malard.** Mallard, the common wild drake.

Mandarine. Mandarin orange.

Mange-tout. The name of a variety of sweet peas, wax, and butter beans of which the pod is also eaten.

Mangle. The fruit of the mangrove.

Manié. Kneaded—mixed with the hands.

Mansard. Woodpigeon. Ring dove.

Marabout. A large coffee pot.

Marbré. Marbled. Word used in connection with certain cakes and gelatine dishes.

Marcassin. Grice: a wild boar under a year old, usually cooked whole.

Marennes. Place on the South-western coast of ·France—whence come the famous Marennes oysters.

Margot. Magpie.

Mariné. Pickled, cured.

Marinière (à la). Mariner style.

Marjolaine. Marjoram.

Mark or **Marquer.** To prepare meats, etc., for roasting, braising, stewing.

Marrons. Large chestnuts.

— Glacés. Candied or crystallized chestnuts.

Martin sec. A winter pea much used for cooking.

Matelote. A rich brown freshwater-fish stew with wine and herbs—usually prepared with eel, carp, tench or pike.

Maton. A local French name for curdled milk.

Mauve. Gull.

Mauviette. Common name for a fatted lark (*alouette*).

Médaillon. Medallion. Name applied to round fillets; meat preparation, etc., in a round form.

Médiants. Name given to four different kinds of dried dessert fruit; almonds, filberts, figs, and dried Malaga grapes.

Mélange. Mixture.

Mélangé. Mixed.

Mélanie. A colouring matter.

Mêlé. Mixed.

Melettes. Sprats.

Mélisse. Balm mint.

— Eau de. A liqueur made in Roumania, from *Melissa officinalis*.

Menthe. Mint.

   Crème de —. A liqueur of peppermint flavour.

Meringue. Light pastry made of whites of eggs and sugar, filled with custard, cream or ice-cream.

Meringué. Frosted.

Merise. Wild cherry; Kirschwasser is made of this fruit.

Merle. Black-bird.

Merluche. Haddock—this term is also applied to hake—also cod, haddock and hake when dried.

Merville. The name applied to a kind of small cake.

Méteil. Maslin. A mixture composed of two-thirds wheat to one-third rye flour.

Mets. The meal or dish.

— de Farine. Farinaceous foods.

Miche. A loaf.

— de pain. Loaf of bread.

Mie de pain—soft bread; crumb (of a loaf).

Miel. Honey.

Miette. Crumb of bread.

Mignon. Name applied to small portions—fillets—*filet mignon*, etc.

Mignonette pepper. Coarsely ground white pepper corns which are like mignonette seed.

Mignonne. A kind of peach—a variety of pear.

Mignot. A cheese made in Normandy.

Mijoter. To cook slowly (to simmer).

Minute (à la). A name for dishes hurriedly prepared—omelettes and grills come under this heading.

Mirabeau. A rich sauce, and a garnish of anchovies and olives named after the French Revolutionist son of the Marquis de Mirabeau.

Mirabelle. A kind of small yellow plum of quince flavour.

Mirliton. A kind of French pastry; tartlets with a basis of puff pastry filled with a custard mixture.

Miroton. A kind of made-up dish.

Mitonner. To steep and allow to boil a certain time.

Mode (à la). This word is understood to signify 'in the French style'.

Moelle de bœuf. Beef marrow—the fatty substance in the hollow part of bones.

Moka. Mocha. A coffee of fine quality. *Crème de Moka*—a liquid with coffee flavour.

Mollet. Soft.

Œufs Mollets. Lightly boiled eggs.

Mont d'Or. The name of an excellent Swiss white wine—also a French cheese.

— Frigoul. A soup, in which semolina is the chief ingredient.

Montmorency. A bitter cherry.

Montpellier. A savoury herb butter—a French city renowned for its many culinary specialities.

Mortifié. A term applied to meat and game—well hung.

Morue. Cod.

Moscovien. Muscovite, Moscow style.

Mote or **Moti.** Name of an Indian fish curry.

Mouille-bouche. Bergamot pear.

Mouiller. To add broth, or water or other suitable liquid during the cooking of meats.

Mouillette. Toast dipped in liquid.

Moule. Mould—also mussel.

Mousse. A light ice-cream.

Mousse frappé. A dish prepared with whipped cream and flavouring—unstirred.

Moussé. Whisked, whipped.

Mousseux. Frothy; sparkling (of wine).

Mousseron. A kind of white mushroom chiefly used for ragouts.

Mufle de Bœuf. Ox cheek.

Mûre. Mulberry.

— de Ronce; — Sauvage. Blackberry.

Muscade (Noix). Nutmeg.

Muscadelle. Musk pear.

Muscat. Muscadine—a white grape (Muscadine grape); musk pear.

Myrtille. Bilberry. A fruit used for compotes, syrups and sweet sauces.

Napolitane (à la). Naples or Neapolitan style, often applied to dishes, notably a tricoloured ice cream which is made in brick form.

Nappe. Table cloth.

Napper. To cover lightly, mask or coat with sauce or jelly; to dip in fondant.

Naturel (au). Uncooked or boiled in water; plain or simple, plainly cooked and quickly prepared.

Navette. Wild turnip.

Nèfle. Medlar.

Neige. Snow; the white of egg beaten to a stiff froth.

Nids. Nests.

— d'Hirondelle de Chine. Chinese birds' nests.

Noce. Wedding.

Déjeuner de —. Wedding breakfast.

Gâteau de —. Wedding cake.

Noisette. Hazel nut, also the name for the small round pieces of lean meat such as lamb or mutton cutlets with the bone removed. *Noisette* in cookery also means nut, or kernel, or part from the middle, hence slice from the centre—noisette of beef—tenderloin.

Noix. Walnut.

— de Brésil. Brazil nuts.

— de Coco. Coconut.

— Muscade. Nutmeg.

— de Veau. Cushion, or kernel of veal.

Nonnat. A small fish similar to whitebait.

Nonnettes. Small anis-flavoured cakes.

Nonpareils. The coloured sweets commonly known in this country as 'hundreds and thousands'.

Nouilles. Noodles, a very useful paste preparation consisting of a stiff dough made with flour and eggs rolled out very thinly, cut into thin strips and boiled. Served as a garnish or fried, also served as a sweet or savoury.

Nourrir. To enrich by adding cream, butter, oil, etc., to other ingredients.

Noyau. The stone of a fruit. *Eau de*—or *Crème de*—. Noyau (a liqueur flavoured with peach or nectarine kernels).

Œuf. Egg.
    Blanc d'—. White of egg.
    Jaune d'—. Yolk of egg.
    Œufs Brouillés. Scrambled eggs.
    Œufs à la Coque. Boiled eggs.
    Œufs Durs. Hard-boiled eggs.
    Œufs Farcis. Stuffed eggs.
    Œufs Frits. Fried eggs.
    Œufs Mollets. Soft-boiled eggs.
    Œufs Pochés. Poached eggs.

Oie. Goose.

Oignon. Onion.
    — *Soupe à l'.* Onion soup.

Oiseau. Bird.

Oison. Gosling—young goose.

Okroshka. (*Russ.*) A Russian national soup.

Ombre. Grayling.

Orangeat. Candied orange peel.

Orge. Barley.

Orgeat. Barley water or almond milk.

Origan. Wild marjoram.

Os de moelle. Marrow bone.

Oseille. Sorrel—a sour plant of green colour used for soups and stews, and sometimes served as a vegetable.

Oublie. A thin pastry—a dessert biscuit.

Outarde. Bustard.

Paillasse. A grill effected over hot cinders.

Paille. Straw-coloured.
    Paillettes or *pailles.* Straws.

Pain. Bread, but also applied to small shapes of forcemeat.
    — *Bis.* Brown bread.
    — *d'Épice.* A kind of gingerbread.
    — *Fourré.* Small rolls filled as sandwiches.
    — *de Ménage.* Home-made bread.
    — *Mollet.* Light bread.

Pain. *Noir.* Bread made of a mixture of wheat, rye, buckwheat.
— *Rassis.* Stale bread.
— *Rôti.* Toast.
— *de Seigle.* Rye bread.
— *de Volaille.* Small moulds of finely pounded chicken, purée or farci.

Palais de Bœuf. Ox palate.

Pamplemousse. Grapefruit.

Panaché. Mixed with two or more kinds of vegetables, fruits, etc.; also used for sweet creams.

Panais. Parsnip.

Pancalier. A kind of spring cabbage.

Pané. Breaded, crumbed, dipped or rolled in breadcrumbs.

Panure. Breadcrumbs grated or bread raspings.

Panurette. A preparation of grated rusks used for crumbing—for coating inside moulds or decoration used in place of lobster coral.

Parfait. Perfect. A kind of light, rich ice cream—or a soufflé type of fish, fowl or game which is enriched with the essence of its chief ingredient.

Parfait Amour. A French liqueur flavoured with grated citron peel.

Parisienne. Parisian style—dressed in an elaborate style—principally applied to meat dishes.

Passer. A word much used in cookery—to pass sauce, soup, vegetable or meat, or to run it through a tammy cloth, sieve or strainer. This word also has the same meaning in culinary language as *faire revenir*—to fry slightly in butter or a quick fat, so as to form a crusty surface to meat or vegetables which are to be finished by some other process of cooking —stewing or braising.

Passoire. Colander; strainer.

Pastèque. A water-melon.

Pastillage. Gum paste for ornamental confectionery—*pièce montée*, etc.

Pâte à Croissant. Rolls.
— *à Feuilletage.* Puff paste.
— *à Fonces.* Ordinary crust.
— *à Frire.* Frying batter.
— *à Nouilles.* Noodle paste.
— *à Patés.* Patties paste.
— *à Ravioles.* Ravioli paste.
— *à Roll.* Tea rolls.
— *à Savarin.* Savarin paste. Used for Baba Savarin.
— *Croquante.* Crisp almond and sugar paste.
— *d'Amandes.* Almond paste.
— *d'Anchois.* Anchovy paste.
— *Feuilletée.* Puff paste.
— *Frisée.* Short crust paste.
— *Sucrée.* Sugar paste.

Pâté. A pie, pasty, savoury meat pasty or raised pie.
— *de Bifteck.* Beef steak pie.
— *de Foie-gras.* A delicacy prepared from the livers of fat geese.
— *de Périgord.* A French pie which derives its name from Périgueux—a place which is very celebrated for its truffles.

Pâtisser. To make pastry.

Pâtisserie. Pastry—a pastry-cook's business. The word is also used to denote a paste made of flour, salt, fat and water, used to cover pies, etc.; also means all kinds of fancy tartlets.

Pâtissier. Pastry cook.

Pâtisson. A kind of squash.

Pattes d'Ours. Bear's paws.

Paupiettes. Slices of meat rolled with forcemeat.

Pavot. Poppy.

Paysanne (à la). Peasant's fashion—prepared in a homely way.

Périgord or **Périgueuse (à la).** Périgord style, applied to dishes wherein a truffle sauce, or garnish consisting of truffles has been used.

Perles de Nizam; Perles du Japon. A special large kind of barley.

Persil. Parsley.

Petit-lait. Whey.

— **Pain.** Bread roll.

— **Salé.** Bacon, lean salt pork.

Petite Marmite. A French soup; beef and chicken broth.

Petite-oie, pieds de Porc. Pettitoes, pigs' trotters.

Petits Fours. The generic name for all kinds of very small fairy cakes— usually highly decorated with fairy icing.

— **Pains Fourrés.** Small rolls scooped out and stuffed with various savoury purées which are served as savoury or side dishes.

— **Pois au Beurre.** Green peas done in butter.

— **Pois Verts.** Small green peas.

— **Pots de Crème Chocolat.** Small pots of chocolate cream.

— **Pots de Crème Vanille.** Small pots of vanilla cream.

— **Vol-au-Vent aux Huîtres.** Oysters in patty cases.

Pets de Nonne. Ancient name for Queen Fritters—or small *beignets soufflés.*

Picholine. A green olive, prepared to be eaten raw as hors d'œuvres.

Pièce de Résistance. The principal joint or other important dish of a dinner.

Pièces montées. Centre pieces; set or mounted pieces.

Pieds d'Agneau (*de Porc; de Mouton*). Lambs' (pigs', sheep's) feet or trotters.

— *de Veau.* Calves' feet.

Pigeonneau. Squab.

— **au Cresson.** Squabs with watercress.

Pimprenelle. Salad burnet; a herbaceous plant.

Pincer. To pinch—to decorate or ornament with paste before it is baked.

Pinson de Neige. Snowbird.

Piqué. Larded—to insert narrow strips of fat bacon, truffles, tongue, into lean meat, poultry, game or fish.

Piquer. To lard.

Pissenlit. Dandelion.

Pluche. A garniture for soups.

Plume. A bunch—as in plume of grapes.

Pocher. To poach.

Poêle. A frying pan.

Poêler. A mode of braising meat, etc., using a fire-proof earthenware dish.

Poêlon. Small skillet.

Point (à). Cooked to a turn.

Points d'Asperges. Tips or points of small green asparagus.

Poire. Pear.

Poireau. Leek.

Poissonnière. Fish kettle, fish pan.

Poivre. Pepper.

Pollo con Arroz. (*Sp.*) A Spanish dish of chicken and rice.

Pomme. Apple.
> *Beignets de Pommes.* Apple fritters.
> *Tarte aux Pommes.* Apple tart.

— **d'Amour.** Tomato.

— **d'Api.** A small red and white dessert apple.

— **Bonne Femme.** Baked apple.

— **Cannelle.** Custard apple.

— **en Rôle.** Apple dumpling.

— **Sauvage.** Crab apple.

Pommes meringues. Meringue apples.

Portugaise (à la). Portuguese style, usually some dish of which tomatoes form a part.

Potage. A term generally applied to soups.

Potiron. Pumpkin.

Potpourri. A stew of various kinds of meats and spices—a favourite Spanish dish.

Pré-salé. Mutton raised on the salt marshes of France—the word means 'salt-field' and the sheep to which this refers are mostly bred in the Ardennes and in the Brittany district called Dol—the flesh is moderately fat and darker than that of the ordinary animal; the name is also applied to prime Southdown mutton.

Pressoir. An appliance for pressing apples, grapes, etc.

Présure. Rennet.

Primeur. This implies edibles forced in order to be enjoyed out of their otherwise usual season—tomatoes, beans, peas, strawberries, hastening their growth under glass—etc.

Provençale (à la). Of or belonging to Provence. Generally applied to certain French dishes and usually implies that garlic or onion and olive oil are used in their preparation.

Prune. Plum.

Pruneau. Dried plum.

Prunelle. Sloe, wild plum.

Puits d'Amour. French pastry made of puff paste.

Punch à la Romaine. A kind of soft white ice usually served in goblets, it is made of lemon juice, water, white of egg, sugar, rum.

Purée. A smooth pulp, mashed vegetables, thick soup. This name is also given to meat, or fish, which is cooked, pounded in a mortar, and passed through a sieve.

— **de Légumes.** Vegetable purée.

— **de Pois.** Pea soup.

— **de Pommes de Terre.** Potato purée, mashed potatoes.

Quartier d'Agneau. A quarter of lamb.

— **de Derrière.** Hind-quarter.

— **de Devant.** Fore-quarter.

Queux. Name given to cooks during the Middle Ages.

Râble. Back—used only to designate the back or loin of a rabbit or hare.

Racines. Root vegetables usually served as a garnish.

Rafraîchir. To refresh; to cool.
  Glace à —. Ice to put into drink.

Raie. A flat sea-fish, in season October to April.

Raifort. Horse-radish.

Raisin. Grapes.

Raisins de Corinthe. Dried currants.

Rambour. A large early sour baking-apple.

Ramequin. Ramekin—cheese fritter, savouries or small entrées, served in ramekin cases.

Ramereau. Young wild wood-pigeon.

Ramier. Wild wood-pigeon.

Râper. To shred or grate.

Raton. A kind of cheesecake.

Ratonnet. Small skewers of meat generally of mutton.

Ravioles or **Ravioli.** Very small squares or rounds of noodle paste, usually enclosing a preparation of spinach, cheese, and minced meat, served with a sauce and sprinkled with Parmesan. Also used as soup garniture or as a savoury.

Réchaud. Warming dish, chafing dish.

Réchauffé. Warmed again—the name is applied to various hot dishes made up of cold cooked meat and other things.

Recherché. Exquisite; dainty.

Recrépi. Crimped; a term applied to fish, salmon, cod or turbot.

Réduire. To boil down—to reduce; to boil gradually to reduce to desired consistency.

Réforme (à la). A garniture consisting of finely cut strips of cooked carrots, ham, truffles and hard-boiled-egg white. Also the name given to a brown sauce containing above items as garniture.

Refroidi. Cooled; chilled.

Régal. Banquet; feast.

Réglisse. Liquorice.

Reine-Claude. Greengage.

Reinette. Russet apple.

Relevé. The remove; a course of a dinner, consisting of large joints of meat, four-footed game, and sometimes joints of fish.

Remouillage. Second stock.

Remoulade. A cold sauce, flavoured with savoury herbs and mustard, used as a salad dressing.

Renversé. Turned out on a dish. Also applied to a caramel custard, called *crème renversé*.

Repassé. Strained repeatedly.

Restaurant. A high-class eating-house—originally the name given to a soup invented in 1557 by a Frenchman named Palissy. In 1765 a tavern was opened in Paris under the title Restaurant.

Réveillon. Name given to a gastronomic festivity which takes place in France at Christmas Eve.

Revenir (faire). To fry lightly or brown without cooking.

Rhum. Rum.

Ris d'Agneau. Lamb's sweetbread.

— de Veau Piqué. Larded sweetbreads.

Ris Pisi Fan. (*Ital.*) Soup made of rice and green peas.

Riz. Rice.

Rob. (*Arabic*) Inspissated fruit juice which is of the consistency of honey.

Robe de Chambre (en). In dressing gown—paper cases which are filled with ice-cream. Potatoes cooked and served in their jackets.

Robert. The name of a brown spicy sauce, which is usually served with pork and other meats which are hard on digestion. It was named after a restaurant keeper in Paris in 1789.

Robine. A kind of pear, also known as *Royale, Muscat d'Août*.

Rocambole. A plant of the *allium* tribe (*Allium scorodoprasum*), closely allied to garlic, which is less pungent than the ordinary Spanish shallot.

Rognon. Kidney.

— de veau. Calf's kidney.

— de mouton. Sheep's kidney.

Rognon de Coq. Cock's kernels.

Rognures. Remnants; parings; trimmings.

Romaine. Cos lettuce.

Romaine (à la). Roman style.

Romarin. Rosemary, a herb from a pungent and fragrant plant.

Rompre. To break—to work the dough or paste two or three times.

Roquefort. A blue French cheese made with sheep's milk—which comes from the district of Roquefort. It should be well aged, crumbly and creamy.

Rôtissoire. Roasting pan.

Rousselet. Russet pear.

Roussi. An ancient term for 'roux'—applied also to brown flour turned into roux.

Rubané. Ribbon-like; decorated with ribbons.

Sabayon. A kind of whipped froth which is sometimes served separately or used as an accompaniment to sweet puddings.

Sablé. A kind of short-cake pastry

Sabot au Sang. A stew prepared in olden times.

Sabotière. An apparatus used by the French for making ices.

Saignant. Underdone—a term which is usually applied to meat and game.

Saindoux. Hog's lard—used for frying and for modelling purposes.

Saisir (Faire). To seize—to cook meat over a brisk heat to retain juice.

Salade. Salad—raw herbs, edible plants and raw or cooked vegetables seasoned and dressed.

Saladier. Salad dish or bowl.

Salé. Salted.

Saler. To salt, to season with salt.

Saler les viandes. To cure meat.

Salicoque. Prawn.

Salière. Salt cellar.

Salmi, Salmis. A brown ragout—a term also incorrectly used for *réchauffée* of cooked game.

Salpicon. A mince of poultry or game with mushroom—used for *bouchées*, rissoles, etc.

Salzgurken. (*Ger.*) Small salted cucumbers—a German pickle which is served with roast or boiled meats.

Sandre. Pike, perch, wall-eyed perch.

Sangler. To prepare the ice-mix ready for freezing.

Sapaceau. An egg punch.

Sapote. Sapota (Sapodilla).

Sarrasin. Buckwheat.

Sasser. To sift.

Sauce. A liquid seasoning served with food.

Saucer. To sauce a dish—to cover with sauce.

Saucier. Sauce cook.

Saucière. A sauce-boat.

Sauerbraten. (*Ger.*) Literally 'sour roast'—it is one of the national dishes of Germany.

Saugrene. A French process of cooking—stewing with a little liquid, butter, salt and herbs.

Saumoneau. A very small salmon, samlet.

Saumure. A culinary bath, brine for pickles.

Saumuré. Pickled or marinaded.

Saupiquet. Spiced vinegar sauce.

Sauré. Fried or cured in smoke.

Saurin. A red herring; a freshly cured herring.

Schlesisches Himmelreich. (*Ger.*) A Silesian speciality which consists of sauerkraut and purée of peas.

Schmorbraten. (*Ger.*) A German dish of braised rump steak garnished with mushrooms, gherkins and vegetables.

Schnitzel. (*Ger.*) A term used to denote a thin slice of meat, chiefly veal.

Schwarzbrot. (*Ger.*) Rye bread.

Scorsonère. Scorzonera, a root resembling salsify but black in colour.

Sec, Sèche. Dry.

Séché. Dried.

Sécheur. A drying apparatus.

Seigle. Rye.
Pain de —. Rye bread.

Sel. Salt.

Selin. Mountain parsley.

Semoule. Semolina.

Senelle or **Cenelle.** Hard fruit of the white thorn.

Serviette. Table napkin.

Singer. To dust with flour.

Sirop. Syrup.

Siroper. To mask with or steep in syrup.

Socle. Base, pedestal, or ornamental stand made of rice, fat or sugar.

Sommelier. Wine steward or waiter.

Soufflé. A light baked or steamed pudding.

Souper. Supper.

Soupière. Soup tureen.

Spatule. Spatula.

Succulent. Juicy.

Sucre. Sugar.

Suédoise (à la). The literal meaning of this term is 'Swedish', being applied to a mode of preparing dishes of fruit according to the highest arts of confectionery.

Suif. Mutton suet; tallow.

Suisse (à la). Swiss style.

Sultanes. Sultanas, small seedless raisins.

Suprême. Best,—most delicate.

Surard. Elderberry vinegar.

Sureau. Elderberry.
Grains de —. Elderberries.
Vin de —. Elderberry wine.

Tailler la soupe. A culinary expression which means thin slices or crusts of bread that are placed in a soup tureen—and known as '*tailles*'.

Talmouse. A kind of pastry, sweet or savoury, made in the shape of parson's caps.

Tambour. A fine sugar sieve—also the name of a small dessert biscuit.

Tamis. Tammy; fine sieve.

Tamisé. Rubbed through a tammy cloth or tammy sieve.

Tanche. Tench.

Tartare. A cold sauce made of yolks of egg, oil, mustard, vinegar, capers, gherkins, etc., served with fried fish and cold meats—also a salad dressing.

Tartelette or **Tourtelette.** Tartlet, small thin paste crust shapes (oval or round) filled with sweet or savoury mixtures of fruit.

Tartine. A slice of bread—a sandwich.

Tartre. Tartar—tartaric acid.

Tassajo. South American name for dried meat or powdered meat.

Tasse. Cup.
  En —. Served in cups.

Terrapène. Terrapin—the small American turtle.

Tête de Moine. A cheese made in the Jura—literally 'Monk's Head'.

Tétragone, Tétragonie. Tetragonia, New Zealand Spinach.

Tétras. French grouse; prairie chicken.

Thon. Tunny-fish—a sea fish of the mackerel family which is usually preserved in oil.
  — *Mariné.* Pickled tunny-fish.

Timbale. A name applied to thimble-shaped moulds.
  Moule à —. Timbale moulds.

Tiré. Pulled, as *sucre tiré*—pulled sugar.

Tomber à glace. To reduce liquid until it has the appearance of thick syrup or glaze.

Tôt-fait. Flapjack; a pancake.

Toulouse (à la). A rich white stew of chicken or veal with mushrooms, truffles, etc., used to fill vol-au-vent, etc.

Tourné. Shaped, cut, soured, curdled.

Tourner. To stir a sauce; also to pare and to cut roots.

Tourte. Tart.

Tourtelette. See **Tartelettes.**

Tourtière. Tart mould; pie dish; baking dish.

Toute bonne. Name of a kind of bartlett pear.

Traiteur. Caterer.

Tranche. Slice of meat or fish, melon, bread, or cakes.
  en —. In slices.

Tremper la soupe. To pour the soup over thin crusts or slices of bread placed in the soup tureen.

Tronçon. Small slice.
  — *de saumon.* Middle cut of salmon.

Truitelle. Small trout.

Truite Saumonée. Salmon trout.

Turquet. Maize.

Valence. Valencia, a section of Spain famous for its vineyards—also for its oranges.

Vandreuil. An excellent fish which is found in the sea off the coast of Provence.

Vanille. Vanilla. Fruit of a fragrant plant; one of the most delicate flavourings known—used for sweet dishes.

Vanneau. Lapwing; peewit.

Vanner. To stir a sauce very quickly so as to work it lightly into a smooth paste—this word literally means ' *to winnow*'.

Velouté or **Veloutée.** Velvet-like. Smooth; a rich white sauce made from chicken stock, cream, etc. Also a term applied to cream soup.

Verduresse. Green vegetables; salad herbs; pot herbs; a common street cry in Paris.

Verjus. Verjuice.

Vermicelle. (*Ital. Vermicelli.*) Very fine strings of paste made from the dough of wheat flour; used in soups and puddings, etc.

Vert Pré. Applied to dishes with green garnishing. The name of a green herb sauce.

Viande. Meat; viands.

— **de Carême.** Lenten food.

— **faisandée, hasardée.** Meat kept till it is high.

Villerot. Several French dishes are named after this famous French family.

Vin. Wine.

Vin au blanc—done in white wine.

— **Aigre.** Used for pickling, in sauces and for salads.

Vinaigre. Vinegar.

— **de framboises.** Raspberry vinegar.

Vinaigrer. To season with vinegar.

Violette. Violet; a dark blue flower of a delicate perfume—used crystallized.

Vitelotte. Peach-blow potato—or red kidney potato.

Volière (à la). Poultry or game—cooked and dished with their plumage.

Vopallière. Small chicken fillets—larded, braised and served with truffle sauce; also a name applied to other dishes.

Vraie tortue. Real turtle.

Wurst. (*Ger.*) A term used to signify fresh or smoked sausage.

Zampone. (*Ital.*) Stuffed and salted pigs' feet.

Zéphire. Name of a small oval-shaped forcemeat dumpling; a kind of quenelle, poached and served in a rich white sauce. Anything shaped in a zephire mould.

Zingel. (*Ger.*) A fish of the perch family which is found in the Danube.

INDEX

S

Made and printed by Taylor Garnett Evans & Co. Ltd., Watford, Hertfordshire